Communities and Forests

Where People Meet the Land

Communities and Forests

Where People Meet the Land

edited by

Robert G. Lee and Donald R. Field

Oregon State University Press
Corvallis

The paper in this book meets the guidelines for permanence and durability of the Committee on Production Guidelines for Book Longevity of the Council on Library Resources and the minimum requirements of the American National Standard for Permanence of Paper for Printed Library Materials Z39.48-1984.

Library of Congress Cataloging-in-Publication Data
Communities and forests : where people meet the land / edited by Robert G. Lee and Donald R. Field.— 1st ed.
    p. cm.
 Includes bibliographical references and index.
 ISBN 0-87071-058-3 (pbk. : alk. paper)
 1. Community forests—United States—Management. 2. Forest management—United States—Citizen participation. 3. Community forests—Management. 4. Forest management—Citizen participation. I. Lee, Robert G. II. Field, Donald R.
 SD565.C63 2005
 333.75'0973—dc22

                                 2004026513

Oregon State University Press
500 Kerr Administration
Corvallis OR 97331
541-737-3166 • fax 541-737-3170
http://oregonstate.edu/dept/press

To William R. Burch, Jr.
Mentor, Colleague, and Friend

Contents

Foreword

Hal Salwasser
Dean, College of Forestry, Oregon State University

Peple have interacted with forests for as long as people have existed. This book documents the changing nature of some of these interactions between people and forests in North America. It provides a fresh look at how sociologists view change in the roles of professional foresters, government agencies, and communities in forest management. The concluding chapter suggests that forestry as a science-based and rational profession is a product of modernity and that a postmodern paradigm of community forestry is emerging as an alternative worldview. The cases illustrated in the book's various chapters certainly show that alternatives to traditional, science-based, wood-focused forestry are emerging. What role they will play across the entire forest landscape—a new dominant paradigm, niche paradigms to fit particular situations, or attractive dead ends—is not yet clear.

There is no question that forests and forestry worldwide are in a high state of flux. Since the Earth Summit in Rio de Janeiro in 1992, many if not most nations have participated in developing criteria and indicators for what is being called sustainable forest management or sustainable forestry. In parallel fashion, non-governmental institutions are crafting their own standards or protocols for certifying "sustainable forestry." These include the well-known examples of the Sustainable Forestry Initiative in the USA, the Forest Stewardship Council around the world, and the Pan European Forest Council. For the most part, these certification schemes continue to emphasize traditional approaches to forestry, albeit for a wider array of benefits beyond wood products.

Among the major global forces shaping forestry in the early twenty-first century is the continual growing demand for wood and the dramatic shift to plantation forests to provide the supply. Increasing attention to the roles of forests in global carbon dynamics and their importance in biodiversity conservation are also high on the list of issues. Forests are not as frequently recognized for their role as human habitats. This is certainly not lost on those people who still live in a subsistence relationship with forests, though they may not think of the forest as their habitat in the same way a biologist views habitat. But this people-habitat linkage is being rediscovered by those whose well-being is affected by forests, even though they live elsewhere or are recently re-inhabiting the forest. This book has much to say about these people whose sense of community now incorporates forests.

The context for this book can be described as four major directions that forestry is taking in recent decades and will likely pursue for some time to come. Think of forestry as a wheel with four spokes, each of which delimits a quadrant. Each quadrant represents a spectrum of approaches to forestry that, while varying to some degree, aim for a similar set of outcomes. In one quadrant we have forestry that aims to provide people with a dependable, quality supply of wood and wood products. This quadrant is highly industrialized in countries with private forest ownership and highly centralized in nations where government owns most of the forest. A neighboring quadrant represents forests where producing a wide suite of benefits—recreation uses, social values, special forest products such as mushrooms and berries, and ecological services including water, air, and maintenance of biodiversity—is the goal of forestry. This used to be called multiple use forestry. Next to it lays the quadrant that represents forests where protecting and perpetuating natural forest values are the main focus. And, finally we have the quadrant that represents urban, community, and urbanizing forests. The hub is people and communities; all forests that are managed are ultimately managed for values that these people define.

In developing nations and places within developed countries where people still live within forests, as in villages, towns, and cities with high tree cover, the descriptions of community forestry in this book are very appropriate as a look to where things are headed. Sustaining both the forest and the people requires the active participation of people in decision making and management. In places where large industry or large government controls the forest it is not so clear how communities and people participate. The purposes for both industrial forest plantations and large nature reserves distant from human communities do not lend themselves well to the community perspectives described here. Even for U.S. federal forests in the Pacific Northwest, statutorily mandated to be multiple use forests, people and communities have been relegated to "issues to receive mitigation" after scientists have figured out how the forests should be managed for biological and "natural" values by agencies of government. This new form of scientific forestry is as harsh on people and communities as are the narrowly focused management schemes described in this book as traditional forestry.

Leaving aside the questions about whether industrial or governmental wood production or nature reserve forests have room to accommodate new models of community forestry, there is still a large area within the wheel where people, communities, and forests have opportunities to improve reciprocal relationships. Those forests managed for multiple benefits, if they occur in places with mixed ownerships and clear mandates for achieving a diverse array of outcomes, have great potential for moving toward more community-based approaches.

Why make these distinctions? Because it would be a mistake to think that all forests regardless of who owns them should be amenable to similar management approaches and similar forms of governance. If the industrial plantation forests succeed, the world may be able to source 80% or more of its wood needs from 10% or less of the global forest area, certainly less than 20%. That could free the 40% that is currently accessible by vehicles to be managed by various governance processes for multiple benefits and the 50% that is currently not readily accessible to remain in largely natural states. The environmental, economic, and social implications for such a future will play out very differently depending on regional forest productivity, access to markets, access to technology, forms of ownership and tenure.

There will not be one "science" that informs the future for forestry just as there has not been one science for the past half century. As these chapters ably show, nor will there be one set of values or goals that all communities will aspire to just as there has not been for the past half century. What there will be is a dynamic interaction of people, science, forests, markets, and technologies, all constantly shaping and reshaping the evolution of forestry place by place. This future should be informed by the sciences but shaped by the values which landowners, managers, and communities aspire to sustain.

CHAPTER 1

Introduction: From Scientific Forestry to Community Forestry

Robert G. Lee and Donald R. Field

T he postmodern world is imposing unprecedented change on the forestry profession. Forestry is not the only profession to be affected. The increasing acceptance of nonstandard medicine, including homeopathy, naturopathy, and religious ritual, are accompanying the recognition that the patient and the family are partners in the healing processes. The practice of law has been taken out of the hands of the traditional social elites by the empowerment of those who were previously marginalized, especially women and ethnic minorities. Religion, especially the Catholic Church as an institution, is undergoing rapid democratization in response to an unprecedented crisis of legitimacy that began well before the recent revelations of widespread sexual abuse that have scandalized so many priests and bishops. Traditional social hierarchies are collapsing, and the authority they once held is being dispersed. These changes have led some observers to predict the disappearance of one or more of these professions. Forestry appears to head the list of professions whose demise is, to some, a foregone conclusion.

William Burch (n.d., 1), who was the first sociologist to join a faculty of forestry, has recently lamented that the " . . . post-industrial world finds the forestry profession in decline or being absorbed into vague programs such as bioscience, global environmental policy, environmental science and so forth." He questions the wisdom of dismissing forestry and absorbing it into something as ". . . non-threatening and totally vague as a programme of the 'environment.' Environment, of course, being that which surrounds something or everything, means that it is about everything, and therefore is really about nothing." Burch instead distinguishes forestry as an essential "management science" encompassing not just the commercial value of trees, but the multiple goods, services, and benefits derived from the management of the entire forest system—what some people term "ecosystem-based management." If forestry is a management science embracing the whole forest system, the management and use of a forest only makes practical sense in the context of the lives of people, including people who live near forests, people who care about forests, people who harbor local and indigenous knowledge about forests, and people who produce useful products from forests. We believe Burch is correct in his assessment that forestry is undergoing a transformation from relatively autonomous governance by scientifically trained professionals to far more open and flexible governance by a variety of human communities that draw on a diversity of scientific expertise. The locus of control for this management science is shifting from large and centralized public and private organizations to networks of interacting communities.

The collection of essays in this volume testifies to the nature and extent to which forestry institutions are adapting to social and natural diversity, particularly expressions of such diversity at the level of local communities. Most of the essays focus on the role of communities as mediating institutions—social moorings that stand between the individual and the abstract institutions of the state and multinational corporations. Communities, as a mediating form of social organization, are decentralized, small-scale institutions capable of addressing multiple purposes and adjusting to change (Lee 1990). They embody practical knowledge and mutuality, and are rich in social capital.

A growing emphasis on community-level forestry programs signals a shift in paradigms. What has been known as "forestry" is in decline and is being replaced by a wide variety of initiatives seeking new understandings and widely shared control of forest lands. A summary of this paradigm shift will provide a useful context for interpreting the essays in this book. This will be followed by a sociological discussion of community and a summary of the contributions of each of the essays to an understanding of how a new paradigm of "community forestry" is replacing the tradition of scientifically governed forestry.

Decline of Science-Based Forestry

Forestry, as we have known it, was a creation of the nation state (Peluso 1992; Scott 1995). Scientifically based, centralized control over forests accompanied the transition from feudal to modern industrial societies. Scientific forestry began in Europe, especially in Germany, and spread to European colonies and nations emulating modernity (societies based on rationality and science). European forestry institutions imposed a rational, uniform, and simplistic order on the complexities of localized ecological systems (Scott 1998). In one of the earliest examples of such imposed order, Schama (1995) describes how the Norman Conquest brought simple objectives and centralized control to the local, multi-purpose management of British forests. Simplification was imposed on the complexity of forests and their uses to render them legible and subject them to manipulation by monarchical or state bureaucracies. All forestry knowledge and practices of that time were designed to render forests legible and controllable.

With the rise of industrial society, silviculture and sustained-yield wood production were the heart and soul of forestry practices. They were the principal technological devices by which scientifically trained foresters ordered forests in ways they thought would best benefit human society. The welfare of human communities and all social and economic functions of forests were seen as inevitable by-products of regimented, scientifically based forest management. Explicit attention was not given to community life, since it was assumed that it would automatically be taken care of by meticulous engineering of sustained wood production (Lee 1990). Similarly, the well-being of all forest life forms was to be assured by orderly silvicultural practices. Disciplined silvicultural engineering of commercial wood production was the key to both the productivity and long-term health of the forest.

James C. Scott (1998) used the managed German forest as a parable for modern, scientifically ordered societies. He stated:

> If the natural world, however shaped by human use, is too unwieldy in its "raw" form for administrative manipulation, so too are the actual social patterns of human interaction with nature bureaucratically indigestible in their raw form. No administrative system is capable of representing *any* exiting social community except through a heroic and greatly schematized process of abstraction and simplification. State agents have no interest—nor should they—in describing an entire social reality, any more than the scientific forester has in interest in describing the ecology of a forest in detail. Their abstractions and simplifications are disciplined by a small number of objectives, and until the nineteenth century,

the most prominent of these were typically taxation,
political control, and conscription. (p. 22-23, original
emphasis)

During the last one hundred years, curricula and research programs
in forestry schools throughout the world have prepared foresters to
scientifically order forests (Hays 1959; Kaufman 1959). Foresters were
trained as decision makers who were to use rational and scientific
methods as tools for imposing order or, more recently, who utilized
biological science to protect the natural order of the forest by imposing
order on human society. The "toolkit" with which most professional
foresters were equipped was assembled for agents of the state or
corporation. Economic optimization models for scheduling forest
harvests and simulation models for conserving endangered species both
illustrate how decision-making power has been vested in agents for
large institutions. Foresters were poorly prepared to work with a
diversity of communities to decide on the magnitude and distribution
of multiple benefits. They were also unprepared to engage in
collaborative decision making by utilizing the local and indigenous
knowledge of community members.

More recently, Scott (1998) argued that necessary resilience of social
and natural diversity could be achieved by substituting localized
practical knowledge and a sense of common humanity for the
imperatives of hierarchical coordination and control. Lee (1990) states
that fostering and protecting social and natural diversity would go
hand-in-hand with small-scale, decentralized, institutions capable of
addressing multiple purposes and responding to unforeseen changes.
This institutional transformation is currently underway. A new paradigm
for managing forests is forming. State-controlled forestry is in decline
and community control of woodlands is on the rise. However, what
are communities, and how should they be studied?

Community as an Object of Study

Community is an elusive construct. Sociologists have identified three
dimensions of community (Hillery 1955; Wilkinson 1991). One
dimension is community as *locality—a human settlement with a fixed
and bounded local territory.* This is the definition used by most
economists who analyze local areas where people reside and work.

However, it has limited sociological meaning, since it includes no consideration of relationships among people or patterns of social interaction. While it suggests there is a relationship between geographic location and social life, it does not elaborate on that relationship.

Another dimension is community as a *local social system involving interrelationships among people living in the same geographic area.* Attention is focused on the pattern of social relationships, but not on the content or qualities of these relationships. This definition goes beyond geographic location to attend to networks of interaction and interpersonal knowledge. It is not important whether there is harmony or conflict, loneliness or sharing; all that matters is that people interact in some predictable ways.

A third dimension is *a localized society as a "community field"* (Kaufman 1959; Wilkinson 1991). The term "community field" represents the patterns of interaction through which residents express their common interests. There may be more than one community field, indicating multiple interest-based associations. Wilkinson focused on territorially located fields when defining rural community. However, shared interests may or may not be limited to people who live in a particular place, creating nonterritorial communities based on shared interests (Society of American Foresters 1987).

Identity is also an important dimension of community, and is closely linked to community fields. Like a community field, a shared sense of identity does not require a geographic basis for social interaction. Members of such a community may be widely dispersed, as in the "environmental community," "forestry community," or "loggers' world." Moreover, people need not ever have met or interacted in order to belong to such a community. Some sociologists refer to community morale when talking about community as a sense of shared identity. Communities of "interest" or "affiliation" represent these types of relationships.

Sociologist K. T. Erikson (1986, 9-10) touched upon territory and identity when he described community in terms of people who:

> . . . spend most of their lives in close contact with one
> another, sharing a common sphere of experience which
> makes them feel that they belong to a special "kind" and
> live in a special "place." In the formal language of
> sociology, this means that communities are boundary

maintaining: each has a specific territory in the world as a
whole, not only in the sense that it occupies a defined
region of geographical space but also in the sense that it
takes over a particular niche in what might be called
cultural space and develops its own "ethos" or "way"
within that compass. Both these dimensions of group
space, the geographical and the cultural, set the
community apart as a special place and provide an
important point of reference for its members.

Erikson (1986) also emphasized the central importance of social
norms and networks of interactions for maintaining community
boundaries—both geographical and cultural: "Members of a
community inform one another about the placement of their
boundaries by participating in the confrontations, which occur when
persons who venture out to the edges of the group are met by policing
agents, whose special business is to guard the cultural integrity of the
community." Everything from criminal trials and excommunication
hearings to gossip and shunning demonstrates ". . . where the line is
drawn between behavior that belongs in the special universe of the
group and behavior that does not." (p. 11)

These four dimensions (locality, local society, community field, and
identity), although separated for purposes of analysis, are generally
condensed into one global sense of community—especially when
talking about rural settlements. People have often romanticized isolated
rural settlements and assumed that locality, a local social system, and a
sense of communion are unified in a rural community. The fact that
these three dimensions may rarely coincide completely creates
heterogeneity in the social life of both rural and urban settlements.
Much of the above-mentioned variation in contemporary forest-based
communities could be captured by such social analysis. The persistence
of a sense of identity as a "timber town" in an exurban or
tourism-dependent community is just one example of how social
relationships and community identity may fall out of phase. The
residents of communities based on shared interest, like many
environmental protection associations, seldom live in a particular place.
Occupational communities, as discussed by Carroll, Lee, and McLain
in Chapter 9, are constituted by shared identification with work, such
as logging, brush picking, and mushroom picking.

Coincidence of all dimensions of community is illustrated by some of the classic sociological studies of resource-producing communities. Harold Kaufman's (1939) master's thesis titled "Social Factors in the Reforestation of the Missouri Ozarks" deserves credit as one of the first quantitative and systematic studies of values and attitudes toward forestry among residents of small rural communities. He discussed the problems of deforestation in the Ozarks and the barriers to reforestation. The barriers, according to Kaufman, resided in the culture and a conflict between old forest folkways (such as wood-burning practices and livestock grazing) and forest conservation practices. His discussion of assimilation of reforestation practices documents the importance of social relationships and human attitudes as key determinants for new forestry practices to arise within a community. He suggested that changes in forestry practices will be best promoted by an understanding of the human process of adoption and diffusion of new knowledge among residents of communities.

Landis (1938) in his book *Three Iron Mining Towns* provided what is perhaps the earliest comprehensive examination of the process of resource extraction in relation to community social structure and change. Landis's work traces the discovery, exploration, establishment, and development of iron-ore production in the Mesabi Range, Minnesota. At each phase, Landis discusses the kind of human population present and the community institutions formed—economy, government, education, religion, and family. He further documents change in such institutions during different periods of ore production, and suggests that changes in the structure of community are directly related to each stage of resource extraction.

The Kaufmans' 1946 case study of Troy and Libby, Montana, "Toward the Stabilization and Enrichment of a Forest Community" (reprinted in an abridged form in this volume), also touches on the four dimensions of community. Their report, like Landis's study of mining, is particularly useful in pointing out how rural communities have generally depended far more on the policies and practices of large organizations such as government agencies or private companies than on land-based resources. This resource dependency relationship is an obstacle to the emergence of the new paradigm of "community forestry," as illustrated in Chapter 8 by Bliss and Bailey's discussion of how the pulp and paper industry has contributed to the persistence of rural poverty in Alabama.

Embedding Forests in Community

Forest sustainability is a pervasive theme in contemporary discourse about forest policy. Sustainability is most often framed in the industrial-era forestry paradigm, and expressed in terms of science-based plans (which can be interpreted within the old forestry paradigm as plans by which the state orders nature or society). Decisions about how to sustain forests are aggregated from generally disparate and vague knowledge of social, economic, and biological sustainability, with objective decision-rules designed for each of these three dimensions of sustainability.

Lee and Field introduce Section I with a note reflecting on the significance of historical contributions to understanding how changing social relationships have influenced the perception of forests and practice of forestry. We have reprinted Firey's essay, "Conditions for the Realization of Values Remote in Time," to illustrate why forest sustainability cannot be successfully addressed without placing it in the context of community. Firey drew insights in this article from his (1960) book, *Man, Mind, and Land: A Theory of Resource Use*, which contains Firey's use of a deductive approach to test hypotheses explaining how resource conservation, use, and development are possible. Firey uses formal theory to argue a point that is at least intuitively familiar to researchers using case studies to study community forestry. For current resource practices to result in realizable future benefits, people must understand the importance of sacrifice in the present, trust others to engage in deferential behavior, and believe that conservation practices are the right thing to do. These conditions are generally assured by local social systems in which people share knowledge and concern for a geographic territory, interact regularly, share moral and ethical principles, and believe such community life will persist into the future. For this reason, Firey concludes that future-referring values—a commitment to the future—are only as secure as the social system in which they are embedded.

Field, Luloff, and Krannick review accumulated literature to build on the work of Firey and other pioneering sociologists to describe how the applied researchers have used sociological concepts and methods to address contemporary natural resources issues. Community studies have been a primary theme for sociologists studying agriculture, mining, and forest production. An appreciation for this legacy of community studies is essential for anyone seeking to understand how communities are emerging as the locus of control guiding the use and management of forests.

Langston's essay demonstrates how federal land and water management agencies failed in their mission to secure desired future conditions in eastern Oregon forests and wetlands. She applies a historical approach to the study of forest communities to illustrate how people and forests interact over time. Abstracted from local knowledge and experience and burdened by the old paradigm of centralized control and reliance on accumulating scientific knowledge, federal agencies were caught in the unenviable position of continually reacting to the unanticipated consequences of their decisions rather than seeking to make steady progress toward desired conditions. Langston's historical description provides yet another example of what Scott (1998) refers to as the disaster of relying on making simplification and exercising control. Local communities located in regions originally endowed with abundant natural resources have been affected far more by the reactive decisions of federal agents than by declining resource availability.

As a natural resource historian, Hays highlights the significance of changing public perceptions as well as the transition from centralized control of Great Lake forests by professional elites to shared control by a variety of professions and communities. Clendenning has updated an earlier version of this essay by including information on recent growth in the diversity of influences in human choices about natural resources in the Great Lakes region. Foremost in these transitions is the shift in emphasis from commodity production to amenity protection, urban to rural migration, and recreational use accompanying growth of post-modernism in advanced industrial society. The increasing role of community governance of forests has accompanied growing concern with the environmental quality of forests in a consumption-oriented society.

The chapter authored by the Kaufmans is an abridged version of their 1946 report on Troy and Libby, Montana, prepared for the "Montana Study" sponsored by the U.S. Forest Service. Originally written as a research report, this work was one of the first systematic sociological studies of a forest-based community. An exchange of letters between the Assistant Regional Forester and the Director of the Montana Study is included to illustrate the U.S. Forest Service's ambivalence toward involving these rural communities in governance of a national forest during an era in which exercise of centralized authority was taken for granted (H. Kaufman 1966). The Kaufmans anticipated future community interests in forests that would not reach the Forest Service's policy agenda for fifty years.

The second section of this volume examines sociological conceptions of community from a variety of perspectives to illustrate successes and failures in the integration of communities and forests. Lee and Field provide an endnote to Section II pointing out commonalities and continuities in the complexity of issues discussed in these essays. They extend community theory in a discussion of the community forestry movement. Key principles of community are drawn from Firey, Wilkinson, and others to synthesize contributions of the previous six chapters.

London, Starrs, and Fortmann examine how a California mountain community struggled over twenty-five years to influence the allocation and use of resources on a surrounding national forest. This sociological case study is particularly valuable, since it involved repeated observations to track changes in the way a community interacted with surrounding forests over almost a quarter century. The study makes two important contributions: it provides a needed longitudinal perspective on forest community studies and it shows how local residents grouped and re-grouped around contentious issues. What constituted "the community" for one issue was often a different social network of people from that for the next issue. Examination of local issues over time illustrates the hazards of reifying "community" as a fixed "thing," rather than as dynamic social and political processes involving real people who interact in different ways at various points in time.

Another perspective on forest-dependent communities is provided by Bliss and Bailey in their sociological case study of the failure of the pulp and paper industry to stimulate economic and social revitalization of communities in Alabama's Black Belt. This study uses archival records to reconstruct changes in the community over time. The authors illustrate how the promise of rural community development was not realized by locating pulp mills in rural communities suffering from long-standing poverty. Tax incentives used to attract these industries reduced local tax receipts to the point where schooling was inadequate to prepare socially marginalized African Americans for transitions into modern industrial employment. Bliss and Bailey's contribution raises questions about whether large-scale forest industries actually contribute to the building of local social, human, and economic capital. This work is useful for pointing out that highly centralized and capital-intensive industries, like centralized government, may pose obstacles in the way of a greater role for community governance of forests and their uses.

Four chapters examine alternatives to the conventional definition of community as "locality." They illustrate the value of a self-conscious sociological approach to treating community as a flexible mental construct with multiple possible referents. In Chapter 9, Carroll, Lee, and McLain examine the sociological concept of "occupational community" by focusing on three sorts of forest workers: loggers, brush pickers, and mushroom gatherers. Each group is united by a shared identification with their work, attachments to work rather than to place, social relationships with those who share their line of work, and an ambivalent, if not distrustful, relationship with the U.S. Forest Service as the land management agency upon which most have depended for resource-gathering or production opportunities. Each of these three forest-worker occupations is largely self-organizing and, as a result, finds itself in conflict with any land management agency relying on centralized control and uniform rules to regulate the use of the forest.

In Chapter 10, Bull and Schwab describe how Canada is attempting to involve diverse communities in decisions about forest use and management through "model forest" and "community forest" programs. Their evaluation suggests policy-relevant definitions of community are embodied in each of these programs. They identify how the "community forest" program uses a number of institutional vehicles in an attempt to involve local communities in decision making about the use and management of surrounding forests. These programs are just one expression of how the Canadian government has joined the international sustainable development movement and is experimenting with a paradigm shift that would allocate shared control over forests to various sorts of communities.

Unlike Canada, the United States government has been ambivalent toward the sustainable development movement. This has motivated government agencies to use indirect approaches to promote experimentation with community forestry initiatives. The National Community Forestry Center is a government-sponsored program to promote and facilitate community forestry initiatives by nongovernmental organizations. In Chapter 11, Krishnaswamy describes how this program has adopted many of the principles of community forestry learned in less-industrialized nations, and has put these principles to work to better integrate communities with the governance of forested land, especially public lands. This discussion describes a community forestry movement that is now well under way in the United States, arising from voluntary cooperation of citizens who share a concern with the use and management of forests.

Nonindustrial private forests have long been a concern to the community of professional foresters. Findley, Luloff, and Jones examine sociological survey research to reject four myths foresters have held about the owners of small private forest lands, that they are (1) connected to the land, (2) anti-environmentalists, (3) timber-oriented, and (4) adamant defenders of private property rights. The authors reveal social and demographic complexity rather than homogeneity, and raise questions about how the "forestry community" has stereotyped these landowners in an attempt to impose the simplified views of industrial wood production. Their work demonstrates how the thinking of the forestry profession has perpetuated the nineteenth-century Germanic paradigm of simplified production and failed to understand the social complexity of modern land ownership.

The third, and final, section of this volume examines the integration of urban communities with urban forests. Field and Lee introduce this section by discussing how social changes have shrunk the historic distance between urban issues and forest management and use. Demographic shifts, particularly urban-rural migration, have brought residential use to remote forested regions, and growing awareness of how treed landscapes contribute to human well-being has shaped reforms in urban planning and management.

Although implicit, Firey's theory of resource development is illustrated by McDonough and Vachta's sociological case study of how a local, low-income community in Detroit, Michigan, was empowered by a community forestry initiative. User rights and management responsibility for vacant city lots in Detroit were transferred from the city to local groups of volunteers. McDonough and Vachta recount the processes by which these groups were formed and surmounted the challenges of gaining control over unused land. Principles common to community forestry in general are illustrated by the methods with which local people assumed control, developed pride in their accomplishments, and improved the quality of their lives by participating in shared planning of forest, park, and gardening projects.

Grove, Burch, and Pickett take an ecological approach to studying the interaction of people and urban forests in Baltimore, Maryland. They use principles drawn from landscape ecology to assess the importance of vegetated spaces to urban landscapes, and describe programs instituted in the city of Baltimore that created or perpetuated tree-covered spaces at regional, watershed, district, and neighborhood scales. They use a systems approach to embed human communities in urban ecosystems, using urban landscape ecology to represent the integration of humans and ecological processes. They draw on the community forestry tradition originating in less-industrialized nations to address communities as vehicles for constructing, perpetuating, and managing urban vegetation.

The migration of urban or suburban residents to either forests surrounding cities or remote locations dominated by forest vegetation has created a complex challenge for integrating modern residential communities and forests. Egan and Luloff review existing social surveys and sociological case studies to describe how migrants move to the urban fringe to capture quality of life and environmental services unavailable in more developed settings. They also describe how such residential development creates new problems of incompatible land uses and environmental impacts for people who own and use these forests for purposes other than a residential environment. Solutions to problems of using and managing forests affected by exurbanites are especially complex, and necessitate novel approaches to developing community forestry programs that need to be suited to a diverse population with conflicting objectives.

The concluding chapter in this volume summarizes major themes by examining how communities (as variously defined) mediate the relationship of people and forests. Field and Lee reflect on what has been learned and anticipate emerging patterns of community organization and identification that appear to be reshaping the valuation, use, and management of forests. They suggest ways in which sociologists can continue to identify emerging issues and translate these issues into problems for scientific study. They draw from the work of Firey, especially his (1960) book *Man, Mind, and Land: A Theory of Resource Use*, to illuminate common themes. Foremost among possible issues is the separation of production and consumption in advanced-industrial society, coupled with the migration to forested regions of relatively wealthy beneficiaries of this information-based society. These societal and demographic shifts are already creating new challenges for resource producers. The editors point out how a new paradigm of community forestry is emerging to encompass this reconfiguration of forested landscapes.

References

Burch, William R., Jr. n.d. "Challenges and Possible Futures for the Forestry Profession in a Global, Post Industrial Social Economy—Lessons from Britain." Yale University, School of Forestry and Environmental Studies.

Erickson, K. T. 1986. *Wayward Puritans: A Study in the Sociology of Deviance.* New York: McMillan.

Firey, Walter. 1960. *Man, Mind, and Land: A Theory of Resource Use.* Glencoe, Illinois: The Free Press.

Hays, S. P. 1969. *Conservation and the Gospel of Efficiency: The Progressive Movement 1890-1920.* New York: Antheum.

Hillery, G. A. 1955. "Definition of a Community: Areas of Agreement." *Rural Sociology* 20 (Jan.):11-23.

Kaufman, H. F. 1959. "Toward an Interactional Conception of Community." *Social Forces* 38(1):8-17.

Kaufman, H. F. 1939. "Social Factors in the Reforestation of the Missouri Ozarks." M.A. Thesis, University of Missouri, Columbia.

Kaufman, H. 1960. *The Forest Ranger.* Baltimore, Maryland: The John Hopkins University Press.

Landis, P. 1938. *Three Iron Mining Towns: A Study in Cultural Change.* [n.p.]

Lee, Robert G. 1990. "Institutional Stability: A Requisite for Sustainable Forestry." In the Starker Lectures 1990—Sustainable Forestry: Perspectives on the Pacific Northwest. Oregon State University: Corvallis.

Peluso, Nancy. 1992. *Rich Forests, Poor People: Resource Control and Resistance in Java.* Berkeley: University of California Press.

Schama, S. 1995. *Landscape and Memory.* New York: Alfred A. Knopf.

Scott, J. C. 1998. *Seeing Like a State: How Certain Schemes to Improve the Human Condition Have Failed.* New Haven: Yale University Press. Society of American Foresters. 1987. Report of the Community Stability Task Force. Bethesda, Maryland.

Wilkinson, K.P. 1991. *The Rural Community in America.* New York, Westport, Connecticut, and London: Greenwood Press.

Sociological Foundations for Studying Community and Forests
Continuities in the Sociology of Natural Resources

Donald R. Field and Robert G. Lee

This book is essentially a report on the interplay of people, human behavior, community, and forests. It places forests and forestry within the context of human community. The introductory chapter lays the groundwork for understanding the dynamic relations of people and forests, including the professionals who manage the forests, members of the public who live near and within the forests, users of forest products, and those who otherwise are concerned about the conditions and the future of the forests. Community is fundamental to the relationship of people to forests. This first section emphasizes the inherent ties between community and the social basis of natural resources, the social construction of natural resources, and nature embedded in society. Each of the authors places importance on the dynamic nature of societal change and the resulting reconfiguration of relations of people and the land. The section is also a reminder of the historical connection between humans and resources as the foundation for future directions in those relations.

In the first essay, Firey provides us with a perspective on how society casts the future. He argues a point that is least intuitively familiar to people working in community forestry: for current resource practices to result in realizable future benefits, people must understand the importance of sacrificing in the present, trust others to also engage in deferential behavior, and believe that conservation practices are the right thing to do. These conditions are generally assured by local social systems, in which people share knowledge and concern for a geographic territory, interact regularly, share moral and ethical principles, and believe such community life will persist into the future. For this reason Firey concludes that future-referring values are only as secure as the social system in which they are embedded.

All social systems are subject to change. Firey guides our attention to the stability of institutions as an indicator of stability or instability for a given course of resources management. In the past twenty years, indecision within professional land management agencies has placed into question the role forests play within society and how public lands should be managed. Institutional governance has been inconsistent, reflected first in multiple use management, next in new forestry, and currently ecosystem management. Such constant change suggests a search for a new paradigm to guide our understanding of forests and forest management.

Langston builds on Firey's description of community, local knowledge, and institutionalization of resource management with her historical account of land and water management in eastern Oregon. She points out that federal agencies failed to secure desired future conditions for eastern Oregon forests and wetlands. Langston's description illustrates how agencies fail to accomplish their goals by relying on simplification and centralized control, shielding themselves within professional boundaries rather than being inclusive in embracing community interests and knowledge in decision making. As she notes, conflicts among different user groups often lead to improved resource management. Langston is a proponent of adaptive management as a futuristic form of public land management that responds to changing knowledge in a changing world.

Hayes and Clendenning echo Langston and Firey with their case study on the historical significance of changing definitions of the land and future institutional governance of resources in the upper Midwest. Their story reflects a transition in resource management from centralized control and the exclusivity of professional forest management to combined professional and community management of resources. Foremost in the transition is the shift in perceptions about resources away from an emphasis on commodity production and toward amenity values and protection of the forests. This region is a reflection of the postmodern era of industrial society wherein people are migrating to rural regions characterized by the scenic and aesthetic qualities of mountains, lakes, and forests.

While Firey, Langston, and Hayes and Clendenning provide sketches of the conceptual link between community and the institutionalization of natural resources, Field and colleagues review the contributions of rural sociologists to concept and framework building about people and the land over the past fifty years. Community studies have been the primary theme for sociologists studying agriculture, mining, and forests. Classic studies of the social organization of people on the land and the dynamic nature of change in social relations that are formed offer insights into the present and future directions of forest regions in this country.

The editors acknowledge the leadership of Harold Kaufman in the sociological study of forests and forestry by including Harold and Lois Kaufman's study of the search for forest and community stability in Libby and Troy, Montana, in this section. The Kaufmans studied the dynamic relationship of forest-dependent communities with a federal agency responsible for the management of forests and responsible for the flow of fiber to local businesses. In their study of Libby and Troy, the Kaufmans noted that community stability is inherently fluid, depending upon the links between community and agency and resource availability.

Each of the articles in this section pays particular attention to social change in space and time. The articles illustrate the relationship of a social and cultural system linked to a natural resource system. A change in one sector in the system often ignites a response from another sector in the system. The chapters build a conceptual case for the dynamic nature and shifting balance of community and natural resource relationships.

The pace of social change associated with natural resources, especially forests, has accelerated in the past twenty years. We have witnessed renewed human population migration to rural forested areas, the growth of seasonal homes in amenity-rich rural regions with lakes, mountains, and forests, private settlements in and around public lands, and the emergence of new uses for forest resources beyond timber production. These social changes have ushered in an era in which public-land managers have had to engage a new and diverse clientele and build relations with local communities to protect and manage the lands within their trust. Indeed, forests are taking on new meanings in the twenty-first century. Forests, after all, are a human construct reflecting the cultures of the society creating them. The chapters to follow provide excellent examples of the interplay of community and forests.

CHAPTER 2
Conditions for the Realization of Values Remote in Time

Walter Firey

Over much of the world today people are being exhorted to work for the future. In some countries, in the name of austerity, economic development, or national preparedness, people are being urged to limit present gratifications for the sake of their children and their grandchildren. In other countries they are more broadly admonished to consider the consequences of their present activities upon the welfare of future generations. In either case there is the assumption that "posterity" and "the future" are in some sense real—that these concepts can be given some present meaning. There is the further belief that the behavior of contemporary generations makes a difference for later generations. Finally, there is the implication that present behavior can be controlled to the end of realizing certain values in the future.

These assumptions raise a number of obvious philosophical problems: the meaning of such concepts as past, present, and future; the finiteness, directionality, and predetermination of time; and the continuous, as distinct from the epochal, nature of time. These are problems which, being removed from any kind of observational test, can hardly ever be resolved, though they are none the worse for the asking.

Here we are going to be concerned with a more manageable range of problems. We shall, first of all, be interested in the cultural variability of concepts concerning the future. Second, given a class of values whose realization is located in the future, we shall be interested in the formal conditions under which such values become implemented into behavior. Third, given a class of values concerning the future, which have been implemented into behavior, we shall inquire into the permanence or impermanence of such values.

What, for instance, are the necessary and sufficient conditions under which the conservation of natural resources can be more than a passing hortatory appeal—or a norm that is from time to time enforced by police power? What is the prospect, given the known general properties of all social orders, that groups in control of radioactive materials will so manage and dispose of these materials, now and in the future, as to forestall genetic damage to the human species? What is the likelihood that the capital plant which has grown up in some lands through forced-draft industrialization will outlast the power groups that have directed the sacrificial effort?

Cultural Variability of Concepts Concerning the Future

At the outset it should be clear that any bearing which future events have on present activities can only be through the concepts and ideas which people have concerning those events.[1] Such concepts and ideas may be most diverse. Even a single individual has a plurality of subjective futures, each pertaining to a different aspect of his life, and varying over time with changes in his age, his job, and many other circumstances. So too, different individuals have different subjective futures, the unlikeness of which lies in the concepts and ideas, which those individuals have concerning prospective events. A youth and an octogenarian have putatively different "objective" futures, but the significance of this fact for the present behavior of those individuals lies only in their own and others' differing states of mind (Frank 1939; Hulett 1944; Brim and Forer 1956).

By the same token social groups and whole societies may differ in the concepts they have of future events (Sorokin 1937 [volume 2, chapter 10]; Polak 1955 [see volume 2 chapters 6-13]). Consequently their present activities, so far as predicated on ideas concerning those events, may be expected to differ. Various social classes, religious groups, and nations, through their respective cultures, exhibit a striking variety of future-referring ideas. To a politically conservative individual, for instance, the future is likely to appear as an undifferentiated blank; to a liberal-humanitarian it is seen as a continuous development and improvement over present circumstances; to the chiliast it is a category devoid of meaning. To the contemporary European or American, future events are regarded as being contingent in at least some measure upon present behavior; to the Hindu they are seen as more or less predetermined; to the Chinese they are seen as being continuous with the past(Mannheim 1936, 200-203, 220; Sorokin 1937 [volume 2, 353-60]; Smith 1952).[2]

Nor are these various orientations to the future by any means static. Within one and the same culture there can be pronounced changes over time in the conceptions, which are held of future events. The extent of these changes in the history of Western civilization is striking. Where the medieval mind tended to blur past, present, and future, and tended to consider mundane events *sub specie aeternitatis,* the modern European and American is given to fine gradations of time and to compulsive preoccupation with proximate futures (Sorokin 1937[volume 2, 233-35]; Polak 1955 [chapters 10 and 13]).

"The future," then, can be taken as something more than an ontologically given category which, with the passing of time, gets filled with objective events. Rather, it is, in at least some respects, a phenomenal structure, which human agents, according to the dictates of their particular culture, impose upon events *ex ante.* It is a selective arrangement of events which are viewed in prospect by human agents and which can very widely between societies, groups, and even individuals (Volkelt 1925, 4-5, 9; Barre 1950, 68).

Such variability in concepts concerning the future would suggest that contemporary future-referring values, such as the conservation of natural resources, long-range capital expansion, and even the protection of human genetic endowments, must be placed in a comparative perspective. These values, it would appear, are predicated on a rather unique conception of the future, one that is not characteristic of all cultures. In a sense, it is a variant of the European liberal-humanitarian tradition, with its belief in progress, reason, and human perfectibility. Consider, for instance, the assumptions concerning the realizability of future-referring values, which are expressed by one eminent zoologist: "Through the unprecedented human faculty of long-range foresight, jointly serviced and exercised by us, we can . . . increasingly avoid the missteps of blind nature, circumvent its cruelties, reform our own natures, and enhance our own values." (Muller 1958)

This is a proposition to which general assent could only be found in cultures which, like that of contemporary Europe and America, are committed to a progressive linear conception of human history. Where cyclical or regressive conceptions of history prevail, or where the very awareness of history is attenuated, such a proposition could have little appeal.[3] It is, in truth, a culture-bound expression which only makes sense in the context of a "modern humanism" (Muller 1958) with its unique conception of a controllable remote future.

The Implementation of Future-Referring Values into Behavior

Let us turn now to a consideration of the whole class of values whose realization lies at a remote future time and inquire into the conditions for their implementation into actual behavior. At the outset, it should be clear that there are many kinds of activities, which, by their very nature, require some kind of orientation on the part of human agents to a remote future. Thus the cultivation of certain perennial tree crops, such as the olive, cocoa, and pecan, presupposes many years of care before the cultivator will reap any marketable crop at all. Sustained yield management of forests in several European countries has involved reproduction cycles of more than a century (Zimmerman 1951 [chapter 22]). Amortization of capital investments in some mining and plantation enterprises often transcends the span of a single generation. Maintenance of soil fertility in peasant cultures, such as those of Europe and China, has imposed costs upon generations who have never realized any compensation for their trouble.

From these instances, it is apparent that there are social orders, which somehow motivate their human agents to work for objectives that lie well beyond the life span of those human agents themselves. The question now presents itself: is this sacrificial effort by one generation for the welfare of another generation the function of explicit future-referring values? Or is it rather an epiphenomenal manifestation of certain structural properties of the social orders in question?

This question may be profitably examined in the context of American culture, where the conservation of natural resources has become a generalized philosophy of resource use—a value having all the supposed force of a "moral imperative" (Hardin 1952, 94-100, 248-49). In this social order, where conservation, like virtue, is a value that no one will question, there are some anomalous relationships, which obtain between resource values and resource behavior. Effective resource decisions seem to be dictated by considerations quite remote from those of a moral character. Thus, in a farm-management study of 108 farms representative of the north-central cash grain area of Iowa, it was found that the typical farmer tended to use productive resources in a way that would maximize his profits. Specifically, these farmers used resources in such quantities that the returns deriving from an additional unit of a given resource tended to equal the cost of that additional unit—quite in keeping with the prediction of marginalist economic theory (Heady 1954).

The anomalous relationship between resource values and resource decisions is even more dearly indicated in an attitude study of 1,500 New York farmers who represented all the agricultural counties of the state. According to this study, 78.4 per cent of the respondents said that every farm should have a conservation plan, thus indicating some kind of commitment to conservation as a value; yet only 38.9 per cent of these farmers reported that they had a conservation plan (Moe 1952). Another study found that most of the farmers interviewed in a heavily eroded area of western Iowa genuinely believed in conservation and thought that additional erosion-control measures were needed. Yet no more than one-fifth of the farmers in this area were participating members in their soil-conservation districts, and the application of erosion-control practices by participating members lagged far behind the programs recommended by extension and Soil Conservation Service technicians (Frey 1952). This anomalous relationship between resource values and resource behavior is, of course, related to the difference which exists between society and the individual in respect to their time spans. The individual has a higher "time preference" than society; his economic horizon is more limited; indeed his very life span is shorter. Society and the individual consequently have rather different phenomenal futures.[4]

By what process, then, do some societies succeed in imposing their time spans onto their individual members so that the latter willingly seek the *salus rei publicae* rather than the *salus individualis*? The studies just noted would seem to cast doubt upon the efficacy of future-referring values as sufficient motivating factors for conservation behavior. Yet conservation behavior is a demonstrable fact in many social orders. Somehow conservation values do, under certain conditions, get so incorporated into the structure of interpersonal relationships in a social order that they are realized in actual behavior (Wetten 1949). What are the sufficient conditions for securing commitment to a future-referring value whose realization lies beyond the time span of the individual? What structuring of values must be built into a social order that individuals, in their self-interested use of natural resources, will "automatically" serve the end of conservation?

At least two factors suggest themselves as relevant in this connection: sanctions and sentiments (Parsons 1954, 149, 247). Conformity to values, it may be suggested, requires more than their internalization into the consciences of human agents (Sorokin 1947, 329-330; Parsons 1951, 27-28). It requires an articulation of those values with social relationships in such a way that individuals find it socially expedient and psychologically satisfying to conform to them. Values, which are not thus articulated with social relationships, can have only an ideological status; they will not figure in overt behavior. Many future-referring values have just such an ideological status. In contemporary America, for instance, conservation values have something of this character.

In a content analysis of farmers' verbal statements concerning the conservation of irrigation water in west Texas the present writer found that many of these statements implied an advocacy of water conservation but expressed an objection to any and all regulations on individuals' use of irrigation water. Likewise, a number of other verbal statements which implied the advocacy of water conservation and which further showed a recognition of the likelihood of some form of regulation nevertheless objected to such regulation of individual use of irrigation water. But *no* instances could be found of verbal statements which advocated water conservation, recognized the likelihood of some form of regulation, and further asserted that regulations were for the well-being of the community, yet objected to regulation of the use of irrigation water (Firey 1957). In other words, the combination of a belief in conservation (the value) with a recognition of the likelihood of regulation (the sanction) and with a feeling that the resulting behavior would be for the general welfare (the sentiment) seemed to correlate with an advocacy of regulation.

This finding can perhaps be generalized to a provisional hypothesis that a sufficient condition for individuals' acknowledgment that they ought to accede, in their actual behavior, to future-referring values is a conviction on the part of those individuals, not only that those values have a moral character, but also that they, as individuals, will probably have to conform anyway and, further, that the well-being of the in-group will thereby be furthered. This manifold property by which values become articulated with sanctions and sentiments may be designated as "institutionalization." The foregoing hypothesis, then, may be put more briefly as: a sufficient condition for the realization of values remote in time is that they be institutionalized.

Thus stated, the proposition is not at all a new one. Writing on the cultivation and conservation of perennial tree crops, for instance, a resource economist (Zimmerman 1951, p. 376) has noted that: "All perennial culture, but particularly the planting of trees, rests on the stability of social institutions. No one would be foolish enough to spend a decade or more . . . to build up an olive grove, which can bear fruit for a century unless he feels reasonably sure of a reward for himself and his descendants."

This proposition applies equally well to other future-referring values—those pertaining to the control of radiation hazards, to long-range capital development, to population control, and the like. The realization of such values is contingent upon their becoming institutionalized—upon their becoming so articulated with social relationships that individuals feel (1) that they have to conform to such values anyway, because of the operation of moral and legal sanctions, and (2) that such conformity is for the well-being of the group, to which appropriate private sentiments attach. Indeed, from the standpoint of personal motivation there is a real affinity between self-sacrificing dedication to a remote future and *suicide altruiste*. Both are to be explained in terms of values that have been articulated with social relationships.

The problem, then, of the formal conditions for realizing values remote in time turns out to be a problem of the conditions under which values become institutionalized. The essential process here seems to be a complex feedback mechanism, operating in every viable social order, whereby the minimum terms for survival of the social order get communicated, at least subliminally, to the individual human agents in that social order. These minimum terms for survival of the social order, as transmuted in the perceptions of individual human agents, come then to serve as upper bounds to individual propensities toward maximizing private advantage relative to group advantage. Not all values, therefore, can be institutionalized. Those which, in the eyes of strategically situated individuals, do not appear to serve the ends of social survival, on whatever terms happen to be valued in that social order, are unlikely to become institutionalized. Values that have already been institutionalized but which are no longer perceived as serving the ends of social survival tend to lose their controlling influence over behavior.

This explanation of the sufficient conditions for behavior oriented to a remote future may be illustrated by the following case. In this example, a population, which had previously been engaged in soil-conserving practices, is now gradually discontinuing those practices as the conditions for social survival change. The population in question occupies a mountainous area in the northern Cameroons, whence they took refuge several generations ago from slave-raiders operating in the lowlands. Establishing defensive settlements along the hilltops, these people evolved over the course of time a number of soil-building practices that are not characteristic of peoples in most of West Africa. Their rocky land was terraced, wastes and organic matter were used to build up the soil's fertility, crops were systematically rotated and provision was made for a fallow period. Then, with the advent of French rule and the end of slave raiding, a process of disintegration set in. People began to leave their inhospitable highland area, with the austere discipline its cultivation requires. They descended to the plains where they are reverting to the profligate system of shifting cultivation so ubiquitous in this part of the world (Buchanan and Pugh 1955, 109-11).

Conservation behavior, then, arises where there is a felt need for it. When the felt need disappears, the behavior goes with it. This would seem to be true of future-oriented behavior generally. Of course the tie between "need" and "behavior" is devious. There could be no greater fallacy than to consider it a purely cognitive one in which the individual members of a social order directly apprehended some sort of "reality principle" and then compliantly adapted their behavior to the minimum terms for social survival. "Survival" itself is a culturally variable concept, which derives its specific content from the values, which a particular people has concerning living levels, health, collective identity, etc. Nevertheless there is always some sort of tie between need and behavior, and it is one that is sometimes overlooked in hortatory appeals on behalf of posterity. The following proposition, for instance, suggests a certain lack of realism concerning the conditions for institutionalizing conservation values (Mantell 1955, p. 19): "Daher haben wir die Verpflichtung, neue Waldbestände in ständiger Verjüngung heranzuziehen, auch wenn wir ihre künftigen Verwendungsformen nicht wissen."

The fact of the matter is that future-referring values can only be institutionalized under special circumstances that may be fairly well predicted by one who knows the relevant facts in a given situation (Parsons 1951, 26ff., 167ff.). Future-referring values become realized in the behavior of human agents only when they are reinforced by social sanctions and sentiments so that individuals are adequately motivated to conform to them. Such articulation of future-referring values with social relationships rests on a people's perception of the relevance of those values to a desired mode of survival.

The Permanence or Impermanence of Future-Referring Values

With this idea in mind, we may turn now to the last of the three problems with which we are concerned here: the durability of future-referring values, which have been institutionalized. We have seen that unless values are institutionalized they are not likely to figure in overt behavior. To be institutionalized they must have become so articulated with social relationships that the individual finds it both expedient and satisfying to conform to them. This means that the effectiveness of values—their realizability in human behavior—is contingent on their being sustained by a going social order. What does this imply for their durability?

The inescapable fact, of course, is that every social order has a finite life span. Depending on its organization, resilience, demographic size, and a number of other factors, every social order is mortal (Sorokin 1947 [chapters 34 and 47]). This means that future-referring values, as well as values of any other kind, have no assured survival beyond the life span of the society which sustains them. Their possible re-institutionalization in another or a succeeding social order must be wholly problematic.

A classic example of the abrupt end to some once-effective conservation practices may be seen in the displacement of Roman-

Byzantine agriculture from North Africa by conquering Arab herdsmen. For centuries the Romans, and later their Byzantine successors, had operated an irrigated commercial agricultural economy in North Africa. There they invested in water wells, windbreaks, aqueducts, and other projects, which entailed behavior that was oriented to the future. Arab conquests in the seventh century led to a disintegration of the entire system. Protective tamarisk trees were allowed to die, wells went untended and were buried by sand, and a shifting pastoral economy became ecologically dominant. The invading Arabs had had their origins in the desert areas of Arabia and brought with them an aversion to trees and to water-lift wells. They also brought with them goats and sheep, both notoriously destructive of grass cover. The combined effect of these importations was an extension of desert land, accelerated water runoff, and aggravated soil erosion throughout North Africa. Arab land use completely displaced Roman-Byzantine land use (Murphey 1951).

Not all social orders end so dramatically, of course, but their mortality is just as real. Consequently, future-referring values which become institutionalized in one or another social order must have their eventual denouement. The very circumstance, which makes them realizable in overt behavior—their articulation with a set of social relationships—is the one, which ultimately accounts for their impermanence. Frequently, to be sure, such values will reappear in altogether different places. It is a moot point, however, whether such instances represent genuine continuities or are simply cases of independent invention. Conservation, for example, is a value that has been variously expressed in Hesiod, the Old Testament, Columella, the Paulinis, du Pont de Nemours, and elsewhere. Yet, it is improbable that present-day values of conservation, as institutionalized in western Europe, have any historical continuity with these earlier versions. Rather they would seem to have originated *de novo* in response to adaptive requirements that are peculiar to modern times.[5]

Future-referring values, then, are time- and space-bound; they are tied to particular social orders whose eventual demise they are destined to share. What kind of telesis, then, can we impute to human beings? What is the range of the "telescopic faculty" that has often been attributed to man? In this connection it is not out of place to invoke a distinction that has been proposed between micro-time and macro-time.[6] In micro-time there is a stability of the structural parameters within which purposive behavior takes place; macro-time transcends changes in the social structure. In reference to our present problem, micro-time may be identified with the time span of a given social order; macro-time may be identified with the period, which transcends the time span of a given social order.

The hypothesis may be advanced, then, that man is only able to plan for future, which lie within micro-time, and even then only under certain formal conditions. Beyond that time span, in macro-time, the structural parameters of behavior so change that behavior becomes unpredictable from the vantage point of any particular present. This hypothesis, of course, is only a corollary of our two previous observations that (1) future-referring values only figure in behavior when they have been institutionalized in a social order, and (2) all social systems have finite life spans. If, now, we further recall that future-referring values are themselves most diverse as between societies, historical periods, social classes, and religious groups, our confidence that any particular value may become an abiding possession of *homo sapiens*, for now and evermore, can hardly be great.

These considerations have an obvious, if indirect, bearing upon the "objective" future of a people or, for that matter, of mankind as a whole. We may agree with the observation of one noted philosopher (Peirce 1934, p. 312) that ". . . future facts are the only facts that we can, in a measure, control." The measure, however, is not a generous one. Man's control over his objective future must necessarily be exercised in terms of his various subjective futures. Since the latter are so variable, the controls to which they give rise can hardly be constant. Time may have its arrow, but telesis does not. There is no historical warrant for believing that man can ever have sustained purpose with reference to a remote future. To be sure, planning endeavors which operate within micro-time may, while institutionalized, be quite effective for their day. But endeavors which would transcend the life span of particular social orders can have little prospect of realization. Certainly "the next million years" of "post-historic man"[7] lie quite beyond the range of stable human control. So far as the conservation of natural resources, the control of radiation hazards, or the prolonged maintenance of capital plant are concerned, these must be considered culture-bound endeavors. New social orders, succeeding those of today, may very well evolve concepts concerning the future which will render these issues nonproblematic—that is, phenomenally nonproblematic.

Notes

1 It is not intended here to hypostatize events that have not yet occurred. The status of "future events" can admittedly be only a conceptual one, residing "in people's minds." But it is no less true that these "events," conceptual though they be, can and do serve as referents for still other concepts and ideas.

2 On the functional basis for cultural variability in conceptions of time see Sorokin and Merton (1937) and Sorokin (1943) Chapter 4.

3 On these culturally varying conceptions of history see Sorokin (1937) Volume 2, Chapter 10.

4 On the relationship between individual and group cultures see Sorokin (1947) Chapter 18.

5 On the existential origins of the American conservation movement see McConnell (1954).

6 Proposed first by Claude Lévi-Strauss (1953) pp. 524-553; developed further in Nadel (1957), p. 136.

7 Typical of recent literature which addresses itself to the problem of man's destiny are Darwin (1953), Seidenberg (1950), Haldane (1943), Huxley (1941), and Muller (1935).

References

Barre, Raymond. 1950. *La période dans l'analyse économique.* Paris: S.E.D.E.S.

Brim, Orville G., Jr., and Raymond Forer. 1956. "A Note on the Relation of Values and Social Structure to Life Planning," *Sociometry*, XIV (March):54-60.

Buchanan, K. M., and J. C. Pugh 1955. *Land and People of Nigeria.* London: University of London Press.

Darwin, Charles Galton. 1953. *The Next Million Years.* Garden City, N.Y.: Doubleday.

Firey, Walter. 1957. "Patterns of Choice and the Conservation of Resources," *Rural Sociology*, XXII (June):113-22.

Frank, Lawrence K. 1939. "Time Perspectives," *Journal of Social Philosophy*, IV (July):293-312.

Frey, John C. 1952. Some Obstacles to Soil Erosion Control in Western Iowa. Iowa Research Bulletin 391. Ames: Iowa Agricultural Experiment Station, October 1952.

Haldane, J. B. S. 1943. *Possible Worlds.* New York: Harper.

Hardin, Charles M. 1952. *The Politics of Agriculture.* New York: The Free Press of Glencoe.

Heady, Earl O. 1954. Resources Productivity and Returns on 160 Acre Farms in North-Central Iowa. Iowa Research Bulletin 412. Ames: Iowa Agricultural Experiment Station, July.

Hulett, J. E., Jr. 1944. "The Person's Time Perspective and the Social Role," *Social Forces*, XXIII (December):155-59.

Huxley, Julian S. 1941. *Man Stands Alone.* New York: Harper.

Lévi-Strauss, Claude. 1953. "Social Structure," In A. L. Kroeber (ed.), *Anthropology Today.* Chicago: University of Chicago Press.

Mannheim, Karl. 1936. *Ideology and Utopia*. New York: Harcourt, Brace & World.

Mantel, Kurt. 1955. "Bedeutung und Aufgaben der Forstgeschichte," *Zeitschrift für Agrargeschichte und Agrarsoziologie*, III (April):19-30.

McConnell, Grant. 1954."The Conservation Movement-Past and Present," *The Western Political Quarterly*, VII (September):463-78.

Moe, Edward O. 1952. New York Farmers' Opinion on Agricultural Policies and Programs. Cornell Extension Bulletin 864. Ithaca, N.Y.: Cornell Agricultural Experiment Station, November.

Muller, H. J. 1958. "Human Values in Relation to Evolution," *Science*, CXXVII (March):625-29.

Muller, Hermann J. 1935. *Out of the Night: A Biologist's View of the Future*. New York: Vanguard.

Murphey, Rhoads. 1951. "The Decline of North Africa Since the Roman Occupation: Climatic or Human?" *Annals of the Association of American Geographers*, XLI (June):116-32.

Nadel, S. F. 1957. *The Theory of Social Structure*. New York: The Free Press of Glencoe.

Parsons, Talcott. 1951. *The Social System*. New York: The Free Press of Glencoe.

Parsons, Talcott. 1954. *Essays in Sociological Theory*, rev. ed. New York: The Free Press of Glencoe.

Peirce, Charles Sanders. 1934. *Collected Papers*, Volume 5. Charles Hartshorne and Paul Weiss, eds. Cambridge, Mass.: Harvard University Press.

Polak, Fred L. 1955. De Toekomst is Verleden Tijd. Utrecht: W. de Haan.

Seidenberg, Roderick. 1950. *Posthistoric Man*. Chapel Hill: University of North Carolina Press.

Smith, Marian W. 1952. "Different Cultural Concepts of Past, Present and Future," *Psychiatry*, XV (November):395-400.

Sorokin, Pitirim A. 1937. *Social and Cultural Dynamics*. New York: American Book Co.

Sorokin, Pitirim A. 1943. *Sociocultural Causality, Space, Time*. Durham, N.C.: Duke University.

Sorokin, Pitirim A. 1947. *Society, Culture and Personality*. New York: Harper.

Sorokin, Pitirim A., and Robert K. Merton. 1937. "Social Time: a Mathematical and Functional Analysis," *American Journal of Sociology*, XLII (March):615-29.

Volkelt, Johannes. 1925. *Phänomenologie und Metaphysik der Zeit*. München: C. H. Beck.

Wetten, Nathan L. 1949. "Sociology and the Conservation of Renewable Natural Resources," Proceedings of the Inter-American Conference on Conservation of Renewable Natural Resources, Denver, 1948. Department of State Publication 3382) (Washington, D.C.: Government Printing Office.

Zimmermann, Erich W. 1951. *World Resources and Industries*, rev. ed. New York: Harper.

CHAPTER 3
Rural Sociology and Natural Resources:
Building on Firey

Donald R. Field, A. E. Luloff, and Richard S. Krannich

Introduction

In the previous chapter, Walter Firey highlights some of the major contributions of sociology to the study of natural resources. Our intent is not to duplicate the intellectual story Firey tells, but rather to add some information about personalities who contributed to environmental sociology and natural resources sociology. Like Firey, we conclude there is a sociological creativity, continuity, and longevity in the attention by sociologists to natural resources and the environment. We build on Firey to show that the research conducted by natural resource sociologists is theoretically relevant within sociology and rural sociology; methodologically innovative in integrating social and biophysical measures illustrating interdisciplinary ingenuity; and policy-relevant with a practical problem-solving orientation.

We proceed in the following manner: we first expand upon the scholarship undertaken during the same periods reported by Firey; we then extend the timeline. Firey ends his discussion in the 1960s; we report on research completed through 2000. We focus on natural resource sociology's origins, orientation, and problem-solving tradition represented by the work of rural sociologists from the beginning of the last century to the end of the millennium. In so doing, we contrast such work with the emergent field of environmental sociology that was gaining momentum as Firey was completing his review of the contributions of sociology to natural resources.

Origins: Community and the Countryside

Two threads of research activity place natural resource sociology at the heart of American rural sociology. First, early rural scholars (perhaps because of their appointments in colleges of agriculture at the nation's land grant institutions) focused considerable attention on documenting a new form of community unique to rural America, namely the *dispersed farmstead settlement pattern*. This community formation, in contrast to the traditional New England village, Mormon village, or line village settlements, consisted of a trade-center community and its associated farm hinterland population.

The focal point of research on the trade-center community was an explicit concern with land use patterns and the social organization of rural life in space and time. This body of research and its emphasis on the roles of land and spatial factors represent an important foundation for what eventually emerged as the field of natural resource sociology. Several early rural sociologists, including C. J. Galpin (1915), Carl Zimmerman (1930), C. E. Lively (1932), and T. Lynn Smith (1953), relied upon geographical parameters to describe this new form of community and the relationships of farm families to the community center. Additional studies, which documented the time required to leave the farm gate and travel to town for supplies and return home, helped to define the boundaries of the trade-center community (Wilson 1912). Subsequent analyses began to add characteristics of the farming system, such as acres in production, crop mix, land cover, soil quality, as well as technological changes in farming, to the land use equation. For example, Chittick (1955) examined the role of resource conditions, such as soil type and rainfall patterns, as factors influencing population distributions and patterns of social organization in rural South Dakota.

By the late 1930s and early 1940s, these concerns were fully integrated into the national Bureau of Economic Analysis's work on farm communities. The Bureau's Rural Life Study Series, which focused on a set of comparative analyses of six rural communities thought to represent points along a continuum from high community stability to great instability, is perhaps the best way of describing concerns over land use patterns and the social organization of rural life in space and time. This work, when coupled with the synthesizing efforts of Sorokin and Zimmerman, first published in the *Principles of Rural–Urban Sociology* (1929) and later in Sorokin, Zimmerman, and Galpin's *Systematic Sourcebook of Rural Sociology* (1930), helped to frame the orientation for a rural sociological discipline. According to these authors, the critical elements for study were *people, social organization of community*, and *land*.

The second line of research that can be identified as an early point of departure for the field of natural resource sociology developed in response to the impact of the relative isolation associated with farm life. Specific concerns about rural family well-being and poverty emerged out of the activities of the Rural Country Life Commission of the 1930s. Rural sociologists, including John Kolb (1933), mapped the patterns of social relations among farm and rural families. By using such maps, Kolb established that the nature and extent of social relations among neighbors were shaped by spatial locations of residences. This work was among the earliest to document that hills and valleys (topographical relief) and road systems impeded or facilitated the development of sociability, an important criterion in family well-being. Kolb's work echoed that of Sorokin, Zimmerman and Galpin (1930), who noted that it was the relations between social and nonsocial phenomena (geographical and biological environment) that distinguished the rural sociological research approach.

The association between land and resource conditions and patterns of social well-being and social organization was a focal point of research among a number of early rural sociologists. For example, Benton (1918) examined relationships between depletion of soil fertility and the social organization of farm communities. Similarly, Schickele et al. (1935) examined the effects of soil erosion on the declining stability of community institutions such as schools and churches. Buie (1944) linked soil erosion levels to levels of participation in rural churches, while Hypes (1944) "equated soil erosion with human erosion" (Field and Burch 1988, 18).

Clearly, concern with natural resources helped shape the analytical strategies of rural sociologists from the outset. Moreover, this concern continues to provide a framework for those who approach the understanding of rural life through the eyes of small town/social area analysis (Fuguitt and Field 1972; Fuguitt and Kasarda 1981), rural communities (Wilkinson 1991), and social landscape analysis (Field et al. 2000; Radeloff et al. 2000a, 2000b). Natural resource sociologists have made use of sophisticated spatial analytical tools, including geographic information systems (Luloff and Befort 1989; Bradshaw and Muller 1998), to inform studies on the relationships between natural resources and rural society. Analyses of forest- and mining-dependent communities (for recent examples, see Freudenburg, Frickel and Gramling 1995; Freudenburg, Wilson, and O'Leary 1998) have helped to further define the conceptual foundation and measures of natural resource sociology in rural sociology. The linkage between the emergence of the Rural Sociological Society in 1937 and focused attention on natural resource issues is a central aspect of the history of the discipline. This led in the early 1960s to the development of a formally organized interest group within the Rural Sociological Society, the Natural Resources Research Group. Not coincidentally, these professional traditions contributed to the central role many rural sociologists have played in the subsequent development of environmental sociology.

Environmental sociology, which emerged as a distinct subfield much later than natural resource sociology, has its core connections in general sociology, philosophy, and the humanities. Yet the legitimacy to study the environment within a sociological framework was slow to emerge. Writing in the late 1960s, Sam Klausner (1971) assessed sociologists' attention to the environment. He scanned annual papers presented at the American Sociological Association over a period of ten years, and noted two groups of papers presented concerning the environment. The first included papers by Merton, Broom, and Cottrell that were presented in 1959; the second included papers by Larzarfield, Sewell, and Wilensky in 1967. Klausner concluded that these efforts did not move the sociological community to embrace the environment. Further, he stated, "neither collection of papers demonstrates an interest in transposing physical environmental variables into sociological coordinates" (Klausner 1971, 2).

Almost all commentators on the origins of environmental sociology link its birth to the late 1960s, a period of great social and political unrest in the U.S. and many other countries. Moreover, the commentators usually point to key events, including the Santa Barbara oil spill and growing concerns about pesticide contamination spurred by the publication of Rachel Carson's *Silent Spring*, as the precursors to shifts in public awareness of environmental quality and concerted action by people concerned about environmental issues.

American political activism of this period was an essential element in the emergence of modern environmentalism. Individuals who had participated in a variety of social movements—including anti-war, Black and Gay power, and women's rights—now fixed their attention on the environment. Because they had gained much experience through involvement in other large-scale movements, the start-up time (necessary for central tasks including organizational development, fundraising activities, gaining legitimacy, goal setting, and implementation strategies) for environmental actions was greatly reduced, and the environmental movement was well established by the time of the passage of the National Environmental Policy Act in 1969 and the first Earth Day in 1970.

These events and changes stimulated much of the early work by environmental sociologists, many of whom focused their efforts on attempts to document and understand the changing values and attitudes of people toward environmental problems. The social movement literature played an important role in documenting the environmental movement. Essentially, two major areas of study emerged at this time: (1) large-scale survey research designed to measure environmental attitudes and concerns; and (2) attempts at establishing a theoretical perspective on the societal origins of environmental problems and their implications for future social change. A number of sociologists, including American researchers Denton Morrison, Allan Schnaiberg, Riley Dunlap, William Catton, Craig Humphrey, and Fred Buttel, played important roles in institutionalizing this area of study, especially in graduate programs in sociology. These and other environmental sociologists focused their work on the growing concerns related to problems of environmental degradation, particularly as it reflected human uses and abuses of the environment. By focusing on these concerns, the early environmental sociologists were able to incorporate a wide assortment of related work into their studies, including concerns about the impacts of modern technology, threats of over- and underpopulation, problems of environmental abuse associated with the production systems and political economies of advanced industrial societies, and the potential for conflicts associated with resource scarcity and environmental deterioration. By focusing on such issues, sociologists were able to capture much of the attention that surrounded growing public concerns about environmental crises. As a result, environmental sociology emerged and flourished, beginning in the 1970s.

Conceptual Orientations and Theoretical Perspective

Rural community studies and human ecology reflect the intellectual emphases of natural resource sociology. Social and biophysical variables come together in studies of agricultural, forestry, fisheries, and/or mining resource-dependent communities and their hinterlands. Thus, the examination of human behavior on the land, along rivers, in the mines, and on the seas has been a regular line of social science research, especially in rural sociology. In such studies, attention is often placed on understanding how environmental/natural resource endowments condition social organization and how social well-being is linked to and affected by resource conditions and use patterns.

The research by natural resource sociologists draws from several basic theoretical orientations and traditions. The early emphasis on spatial factors, such as proximity to population centers and topographic features of the landscape, clearly reflects the influences of the theoretical tenets of sociological human ecology (including social area analysis), as well as related work in the fields of geography and regional economics. Much of the work focusing on patterns of community change associated with expansions and contractions of resource-based industries (e.g., research on various resource-dependent communities) draws upon several core theoretical traditions in sociology, including theories focused on the social implications of modernization and urbanism.

Given the emphasis in natural resource sociology on the linkages of localized resource conditions with patterns of community organization and change, it is hardly surprising that community theory has played a significant role in informing the work of many natural resource sociologists.

In an early exemplar of this tradition, Paul Landis (1938) described the formation and development of community institutional structures in association with the discovery and mining of iron ore in the Mesabi Range of Minnesota. He noted the expansion and contraction in community affairs and services as ore production increased or decreased.

W. A. Anderson (1953) described the demise of hops farming in New York State as the acidification of soils increased with successive annual plantings. Dairy farming then replaced hops production as the dominant agricultural activity in upstate New York. Anderson then described the sociological implications of this change not only for the rural farm population, but for the structure and institutions of local communities, including government, banking, services, trade, and voluntary organizations. As a result of the transformation, new trade service communities arose and linkages to the natural resource base evolved as well.

Harold and Louise Kaufman's (1946) study of forest-dependent communities around Libby, Montana, documented the associations among forests and timber and the public agencies charged with their management. In this pioneering study, the United States Forest Service was shown to have a direct influence on the economic structure of the rural community. The political role and influence of the forest industry on the host community was evident in its control of the timber supply, and the inequitable allocation of wood supplies among local mills.

Walter Goldschmidt's mid-1940s study of the impacts of different agricultural models on local community structure also contributes to our understanding of the relationship between natural resources and the human populations dependent upon them (Goldschmidt 1978). Goldschmidt's analysis led him to conclude that farm structure, and by implication class structure, was the principal determinant of rural community well-being. In subsequent years numerous studies have continued to assess the "Goldschmidt hypothesis" in a broad range of rural areas characterized by differing resource conditions and diverse patterns of agricultural organization (e.g., Fujimoto 1978; Green 1985; Harris and Gilbert 1982; Gilles and Dalecki 1988; Lobao 1990; Swanson 1990; Barnes and Blevins 1992).

More recent research representative of the focal themes that characterize natural resource sociology includes a broad range of studies focusing on the ways in which resource development and use patterns affect patterns of social change and social well-being in rural communities and rural regions. For example, since the 1970s there have been numerous studies of the effects of large-scale energy-resource development on patterns of community growth and decline and associated shifts in various dimensions of social well-being (e.g., Freudenburg 1981, 1986; Wilkinson et al. 1982; England and Albrecht 1984; Wilkinson et al. 1984; Gold 1985; Greider and Krannich 1985; Krannich, Greider, and Little 1985; Brown, Geertsen, and Krannich 1989; Krannich, Berry, and Greider 1989; Gramling and Freudenburg 1990; Freudenburg and Jones 1991; Freudenburg and Gramling 1994; Smith, Krannich, and Hunter, 2001). Also, a number of more recent studies have focused on timber-dependent communities and the social implications of changing timber-resource and timber-industry conditions and management practices on both timber workers and timber-dependent communities (for example, Lee, Carroll, and Warren 1991; Brown 1995; Carroll 1995; Freudenburg, Wilson, and O'Leary 1998; Carroll et al. 2000; Joshi et al. 2000; Kusel et al. 2000; Weeks 1990). In a similar vein are a variety of studies focusing on the effects of changing resource conditions and management practices on fishing communities and fishers (see Haedrich and Hamilton 2000; Hamilton and Duncan 2000). Common to these and similar bodies of research in the field of natural resource sociology is a focus on linkages between specific resource conditions and their implications for social organization, community change, and social well-being.

These themes are further represented by the emergence of social impact assessment in the 1960s. Much of this work has explicitly adopted a community systems approach such as that outlined in Roland Warren's (1978) adaptation of social systems theory to understanding community structure, function, and change (see Branch et al. 1984; Little and Krannich 1989). Studies of the linkages between resource conditions and use patterns and various aspects of community adaptability, capacity, and well-being also have drawn on theoretical perspectives on community and well-being derived from Senn (1984) and Wilkinson (1991). For example, Kusel's (1996) discussion of the implications of resource conditions and management issues for community capacity in the Sierra Nevada ecosystem, and Krannich and Zollinger's (1997) discussion of the ways in which various resource dependency contexts may affect the prospects for community action, development, and well-being reflect the application of such a perspective. Applications of the theoretical notion of "social capital" to understanding community capacity and adaptability in the context of changing resource conditions further illustrate the application of sociological theory to the community-based research focus that is so widespread in natural resource sociology (see in particular Flora's [1998] presidential address to the Rural Sociological Society, which also lists other citations to this body of work; also Kusel 1996; Bridger and Luloff 2001).

The conceptual orientation and analytical focus of environmental sociology has rotated from the individual to the nation-state. Some of this work draws, at least implicitly, on theoretical orientations about the linkages between values, attitudes, behavioral intentions, and behaviors (e.g., Fishbein and Ajzen 1975; also see Albrecht and Thompson 1988). Further, social movement theory has underpinned much of the work focusing on the evolution and trajectory of the environmental movement in general (see Albrecht 1975; Downs 1972), as well as studies examining more focused social movement processes pertaining to environmental issues, such as the environmental justice movement (Bullard 1990;; Cable and Cable 1995) and anti-technology movements focusing on issues such as nuclear and toxic contamination issues (Szaz 1994).

This is not to imply that environmental sociologists are of a similar mind in pursuing their research goals. Several distinct approaches and concerns can be identified in this literature. Perhaps the most familiar is the concern of many with describing the emergence of modern environmentalism, measuring environmental concern, and identifying correlations between environmentalism and a range of attitudes, values, beliefs, and sociodemographic characteristics. The work of Dunlap and his colleagues as well as many other environmental sociologists is strongly associated with this literature (for example, see Dunlap and Dillman 1976; Tremblay and Dunlap 1978; Lowe, Pinhey, and Grimes 1980; VanLiere and Dunlap 1980Lowe and Pinhey 1982; Morrison and Dunlap 1986; Mohai and Twight 1987; Dunlap 1992; Dunlap and Beus 1992; Dunlap and Mertig 1992; Jones and Dunlap 1992; Mohai 1992; Kanagy, Humphrey, and Firebaugh 1994). A related literature has focused on elaboration of broad-scale changes in social and cultural orientations toward the environment and their implications for support for environmental protection; examples include theoretical discussions of the distinctions between a "human exemptionalism paradigm" (HEP) and a "new environmental paradigm" (NEP) (see Catton and Dunlap 1980; Milbrath 1984; Kempton, Bister and Harley 1995), and related efforts to develop a variety of scales to measure such distinctions (Dunlap and VanLiere 1978; VanLiere and Dunlap 1981; Albrecht et al. 1982).

A considerable body of work in the realm of environmental sociology has drawn upon various theoretical perspectives focusing on the role of the state and on associated patterns of political–economic organization as factors influencing environmental abuse and degradation and response to resource scarcity at a global level. A key example is Schnaiberg's seminal (1980) work, which in part reflects an application of a neo-Marxist perspective regarding the role of advanced industrial capitalism in contributing to a "treadmill" of over-production, resource exhaustion, pollution, and environmental collapse. Additional work by Schnaiberg and Gould (1994) figures prominently in this vein of environmental sociology, as does earlier work by Anderson (1976) and Heilbroner (1975). Related to this focus are studies of ecological deterioration and scarcity as consequences of the processes of societal growth and development (e.g., Morrison 1976; Catton 1980). More contemporary theoretical perspectives that share a strong emphasis on the role of the state include ecological modernization theories (see Mol 1997).

Other theoretical orientations that have emerged more recently in environmental sociology include postmodernist perspectives focusing on environmental discourse (see Weinberg 1994; Brulle 1996) and the subjective nature of environmental meanings (see Hannigan 1995). In a different vein, Murphy (1994) has applied a Weberian perspective on rationality to examine linkages between nature and patterns of social organization and change.

While the theoretical perspectives that inform environmental sociology are both numerous and broad ranging, they share a relatively macro orientation, frequently focusing on the nation–state or on global processes of political and economic organization. Much of the work in the field is representative of what might be thought of as "grand" theory rather than the middle-range theory that tends to inform work in natural resource sociology. This is reflected in a tendency to deal with the environment in relatively general and nonspecific terms, rather than with precise biophysical conditions in specific spatial contexts with consequences for specific populations or communities.

In contrast to the orientation of natural resource sociology, that of environmental sociology has generally not involved a focus on place-specific or resource-specific conditions or on the status of communities and populations that are associated with particular resources and landscapes. Instead, environmental sociology has most often been oriented toward an understanding of how large-scale social/cultural systems and conditions influence, impact, or respond to various dimensions of environmental quality such as air and water quality and global warming. Environmental sociologists have often addressed these concerns through their studies of broad-based social responses to environmental events or in theoretically oriented analyses of the social, cultural, and political antecedents of environmental problems and crises. As with the other dimensions considered here, it seems that natural resource sociologists and environmental sociologists have initially pursued distinct pathways with respect to both their conceptual orientations and the specific theoretical perspectives that provide the foundations for work in the two subfields.

Problem-solving Tradition

Environmental sociology draws its strength from its theoretical emphasis rather than from its application. While good theory leads to sound principles of application, others have more often answered the call to problem solving. It is through policy analysis and the political process that application has appeared most often in the context of environmental sociology.

We concur with Buttel's (1996) assertion that natural resource sociology, on the other hand, has been characterized by a strong emphasis on application of social science knowledge to solving resource and environmental management problems. Natural resource social science originated with concern for the conditions of rural living and quality of life for rural families. Many natural resource social scientists have been associated with the land grant colleges and universities where much of this research has been conducted. The philosophy of land grant colleges (often referred to as the "people's universities") has nurtured the applied style of research and honed the tools of application. This focus continues today as natural resource social scientists seek to solve resource problems such as soil erosion, reduction of chemical fertilizers applied in agriculture and forest management, mitigation of nonpoint pollution, and documenting of sustainability in resource systems. As social scientists have joined colleges of natural resources and departments of forestry, fisheries and wildlife, and parks and recreation, both within and outside the land grant system, the science of application and the natural resource subject matter have broadened, and the applied tradition has been nurtured (Machlis and Field 1992).

Examples of this applied focus include the development of social impact assessment as both a field of applied scholarly work and a component of the environmental impact assessment process incorporated into decision-making processes used by federal as well as state resource management agencies (see Branch et al. 1984; Interorganizational Committee on Guidelines and Principles for Social Impact Assessment 1994; Taylor, Bryan, and Goodrich 1995; Burdge 1998). More recently, natural resource sociologists and social scientists have played key roles in the development and application of ecosystem management principles by federal natural resource management agencies in the U.S. (for a summary, see Endter-Wada et al. 1998; also Yaffee et al. 1996). Examples of such applications include the federal government's Forest Ecosystem Management Assessment Team (FEMAT) process that developed guidelines for resource management in the spotted owl region of the Pacific Northwest in the early 1990s, as well as several subsequent federal agency ecosystem management efforts such as the Interior Columbia Basin Ecosystem Management Project (ICBEMP) and the Sierra Nevada Ecosystem Project.

Another significant application of natural resource sociology and social science to efforts to resolve natural resource problems has involved the general area of public participation in resource management decision making. Natural resource social scientists have contributed conceptually to the development of strategies and procedures for public involvement, and have evaluated the effectiveness of various approaches to public involvement (see Heberlein 1976; Blahna and Yonts-Shepard 1989; Burdge and Robertson 1990). More recently, natural resource social scientists have contributed to the development of new strategies for public involvement based on principles of community-based collaboration and co-management strategies (Crowfoot and Wondolleck 1990; Daniels and Walker 1995; Walker and Daniels 1996), as well as analyses of the nature and implications of community-based participation in resource management issues and concerns (Weber 2000).

Application of science to problem solving is both an art and science. Drawing upon educational principles and behavioral studies in rural sociology and contemporary natural resource social science, scholars of this applied tradition continue to examine the results of their research and consider the implications for problem solving. Application of science takes many forms. It is an interactive process by which the scientist and client together seek strategies to resolve problems. Clients include farmers, land management professionals, park rangers, wildlife management specialists, local community leaders, extension agents, local citizen groups, and a plethora of other groups and constituencies.

While university-based social scientists continue to play an important role in such interactions, both federal and state resource management agencies have increasingly established social science units or "human dimensions" sections to address the social aspects of resource management, with many of those hired to fill such positions trained in rural sociology or forest social sciences.

Future Directions

Based on the above discussion, it is clear that there are some substantial and long-standing areas of divergence between natural resource sociology and environmental sociology. Our goal in pointing out these distinctions is to advance the discussion of how the fields have developed and where they may be headed. We do not wish to suggest that there are significant tensions between the two fields. Rather, we believe that they have developed and continue to exist as distinct but complementary fields of inquiry, with only limited areas of overlap.

But it is important to note that there are some areas of convergence, and areas where additional synthesis and convergence may hold substantial promise. For example, research focused on issues of environmental equity and justice tends to draw upon some elements central to environmental sociology (e.g., social movement processes) as well as elements that are more closely associated with natural resource sociology (e.g., a focus on the well-being of specific populations in specific community contexts). Similarly, research focusing on the social implications of hazardous industries and toxic exposure incorporates a focus on concerns about environmental quality and environmental attitudes and perceptions that typically have been associated with environmental sociology, but also frequently includes a focus on assessing social impacts and collective response at the community level. Also, while social constructionist orientations have been applied most frequently by environmental sociologists, natural resource social scientists as well as resource management agencies have increasingly adopted such conceptual and theoretical frameworks in attempting to understand such phenomena as place meanings and attachments and their implications for natural resource management (see Brandenburg and Carroll 1995; Williams and Stewart 1998; Eisenhauer, Krannich, and Blahna 2000).

There would seem to be substantial potential for synthesis of additional areas of inquiry. In particular, it would seem useful to bring together into one conceptual and analytic frame both the focus on specific spatial or landscape-based contexts that is characteristic of natural resource sociology, and the focus on larger-scale linkages to national and/or global economies and sociopolitical systems that has characterized much of environmental sociology. While the challenges of working across highly divergent analytic scales with very different units of analysis are by no means insignificant, such an approach would seem crucial in order to provide a more comprehensive understanding of how localized resource use and management patterns are in many ways manifestations of broader social, economic, and political processes, and how those linkages in turn affect the patterns of change and levels of well-being experienced by specific communities and resource users.

References

Albrecht, S. L. 1975. "The Environment as a Social Problem." Pp. 566–605 in A. L. Mauss (ed.), *Social Problems as Social Movements*. Philadelphia: J. P. Lippincott.

Albrecht, S. L., and J. G. Thompson. 1988. "The Place of Attitudes and Perceptions in Social Impact Assessment." *Society and Natural Resources* 1(1):69–80.

Albrecht, D., G. Bultena, E. Hoiberg, and P. Nowak 1982. "The New Environmental Paradigm Scale." *Journal of Environmental Education* 13(3):39–43.

Anderson, C. H. 1976. *The Sociology of Survival: Social Problems of Growth*. Homewood, IL: Dorsey.

Anderson, W. A. 1953. *Social Change in a Central New York Rural Community*. Ithaca, NY: Cornell University Agricultural Experiment Station Bulletin No. 907.

Barnes, D., and A. Blevins. 1992. "Farm Structure and the Economic Well-being of Nonmetropolitan Counties." *Rural Sociology* 57(3):333–46.

Benton, A. H. 1918. *Farm Tenancy and Leases*. St. Paul: University of Minnesota Agricultural Experiment Station Bulletin No. 150.

Blahna, D., and S. Yonts-Shepard. 1989. "Public Involvement in Resource Planning: Toward Bridging the Gap Between Policy and Implementation." *Society and Natural Resources* 2:209–27.

Bradshaw, T. K., and B. Muller. 1998. "Impacts of Rapid Urban Growth on Farmland Conversion: Application of New Regional Land Use Policy Models and Geographical Information Systems." *Rural Sociology* 63(1):1–25.

Branch, K., D. A. Hooper, J. G. Thompson, and J. Creighton. 1984. *Guide to Social Assessment: A Framework for Assessing Social Change*. Boulder, CO: Westview Press.

Brandenburg, A. M., and M. S. Carroll. 1995. "Your Place or Mine? The Effect of Place Creation on Environmental Values and Landscape Meaning." *Society and Natural Resources* 8:381–98.

Bridger, J. C., and A. E. Luloff. 2001. "Building the Sustainable Community: Is Social Capital the Answer?" *Sociological Inquiry* 71(4):458-472.

Brown, B. A. 1995. *In Timber Country: Working People's Stories of Environmental Conflict and Urban Flight.* Philadelphia, PA: Temple University Press.

Brown, R., R. Geertsen, and R. S. Krannich. 1989. "Community Satisfaction and Social Integration in a Boom Town: A Longitudinal Analysis." *Rural Sociology* 54(4):568–86.

Brulle, R. 1996. "Environmental Discourse and Social Movement Organization: A Historical and Rhetorical Perspective on the Development of U.S. Environmental Organizations." *Sociological Inquiry* 66(1):58–83.

Buie, T. S. 1944. "The Land and the Rural Church." *Rural Sociology* 9(3):251–57.

Bullard, R. 1990. *Dumping in Dixie: Race, Class, and Environmental Quality.* Boulder, CO: Westview Press.

Burdge, R. J. 1998. *A Conceptual Approach to Social Impact Assessment.* Middleton, WI: Social Ecology Press.

Burdge, R. J., and R. Robertson. 1990. "Social Impact Assessment and the Public Involvement Process." *Environmental Impact Assessment Review* 10:81–90.

Buttel, F. 1996. "Environment and Natural Resource Sociology: Theoretical Issues and Opportunities for Synthesis." *Rural Sociology* 61(1):56–76.

Cable, S., and C. Cable. 1995. *Environmental Problems: Grassroots Solutions.* New York: St. Martin's Press.

Carroll, M. S. 1995. *Community and the Northwestern Logger: Continuities and Changes in the Era of the Spotted Owl.* Boulder, CO: Westview Press.

Carroll, M. S., K. A. Blatner, F. J. Alt, E. G. Schuster, and A. J. Findley. 2000. "Adaptation Strategies of Displaced Idaho Woods Workers: Results of a Longitudinal Panel Study." *Society and Natural Resources* 13(2):95–113.

Catton, W. 1980. *Overshoot.* Urbana: University of Illinois Press.

Catton, W. R., Jr., and R. E. Dunlap. 1980. "A New Ecological Paradigm for Post-exuberant Sociology." *American Behavioral Scientist* 24:15–47.

Chittick, D. 1955. *Growth and Decline of South Dakota Trade Centers 1901–1951.* Brookings: South Dakota State University Agricultural Experiment Station Bulletin No. 448.

Crowfoot, J., and J. Wondolleck. 1990. *Environmental Disputes: Community Involvement in Conflict Resolution.* Washington, DC: Island Press.

Daniels, S. E., and G. B.Walker. 1995. "Managing Local Environmental Conflict Amidst National Controversy." *International Journal of Conflict Management* 6(3):290–311.

Downs, A. 1972. "Up and Down With Ecology – The 'Issue Attention Cycle'." *Public Interest* 28(Summer):38–50.

Dunlap, R. E. 1992. "Trends In Public Opinion Toward Environmental Issues: 1965–1990." Pp. 89–116 in R. E. Dunlap and A. G. Mertig (eds.), *American Environmentalism: The U.S. Environmental Movement, 1970–1990.* New York: Taylor and Francis.

Dunlap, R. E., and C. E. Beus. 1992. "Understanding Public Concerns About Pesticides: An Empirical Examination." *The Journal of Consumer Affairs* 26(2):418–38.

Dunlap, R. E., and D. A. Dillman. 1976. "Decline in Public Support for Environmental Protection: Evidence from a 1970–1974 Panel Study." *Rural Sociology* 41(3):323–44.

Dunlap, R. E., and A. G. Mertig. 1992. *American Environmentalism: The U.S. Environmental Movement, 1970–1990.* New York: Taylor and Francis.

Dunlap. R. E., and K. VanLiere. 1978. "The 'New Environmental Paradigm': A Proposed Measuring Instrument and Preliminary Results." *Journal of Environmental Education* 9:10–19.

Eisenhauer, B. W., R. S. Krannich, and D. J. Blahna. 2000. "Attachments to Special Places on Public Lands: An Analysis of Activities, Reason for Attachments, and Community Connections." *Society and Natural Resources* 13:421–41.

Endter-Wada, J., D. Blahna, R. S. Krannich, and M. Brunson. 1998. "A Framework for Understanding Social Science Contributions to Ecosystem Management." *Ecological Applications* 8(3):891–904.

England, L., and S. L. Albrecht. 1984. "Boomtowns and Social Disruptions." *Rural Sociology* 49(2):230–46.

Field, D. R., and W. R. Burch, Jr., 1988. *Rural Sociology and the Environment.* Westport, CT: Greenwood Press.

Field, Donald R., Roger Hammer, Tracy Kuczenski, Paul Voss, and Alice Hagen. 2000. "Applied Demography and Natural Resource Management: A Perspective on Social Change Along the Upper Mississippi Flyway." In *Conference Proceedings, Human Dimensions of Natural Resource Management.* University of Minnesota, St Paul.

Fishbein, M., and I. Ajzen. 1975. *Belief, Attitude, Intention and Behavior.* Reading, MA: Addison-Wesley.

Flora, J. 1998. "Social Capital and Communities of Place." *Rural Sociology* 63(4):481–506.

Freudenberg, W. R. 1981. "Women and Men in an Energy Boomtown: Adjustment, Alienation, and Adaptation." *Rural Sociology* 46(2):220–44.

Freudenberg, W. R. 1986. "The Density of Acquaintanceship: An Overlooked Variable in Community Research?" *American Journal of Sociology* 92(July):323–38.

Freudenberg, W. R., and R. Gramling. 1994. "Middle-range Theory and Cutting-edge Sociology: A Call for Cumulation." *Environment, Technology, and Society* 76(1):3–7.

Freudenberg, W. R., and R. Jones. 1991. "Criminal Behavior and Rapid Community Growth: Examining the Evidence." *Rural Sociology* 56(4):619–45.

Freudenberg, W. R., S. Frickel, and R. Gramling. 1995. "Beyond the Nature/ Society Divide: Learning to Think About a Mountain." *Sociological Forum* 10:361–92.

Freudenberg, W. R., L. J. Wilson, and D. J. O'Leary. 1998. "Forty Years of Spotted Owls? A Longitudinal Analysis of Logging Industry Job Losses." *Sociological Perspectives* 41(1):1–26.

Fuguitt, Glenn V., and Donald R. Field. 1972. "Some Population Characteristics of villages Differentiated by Size, Location and Growth." *Demography* 9:295–308

Fuguitt, Glenn V., and John Kasarda. 1981. "Community Structure in Response to Population Growth and Decline: A Study in Ecological Organization." *American Sociological Review* 46:600–15.

Fujimoto, I. 1978. "The Communities in the San Joaquin Valley." Pp. 1374–96 in U.S. Congress, Senate, *Priorities in Agricultural Research of the US Department of Agriculture – Appendix.* Washington, DC: Subcommittee on the Judiciary, 95th Congress, 2nd Session, Part 2.

Galpin, C. J. 1915. *The Social Anatomy of an Agricultural Community.* Madison: University of Wisconsin Agricultural Experiment Station Bulletin No. 34.

Gilles, J. L., and M. Dalecki. 1988. "Rural Well-being and Agricultural Change in Two Farming Regions." *Rural Sociology* 53(1):40–55.

Gold, R. L. 1985. *Ranching, Mining, and the Human Impact of Natural Resource Development.* New Brunswick, NJ: Transaction Books.

Goldschmidt, W. 1978. *As You Sow: Three Studies in the Social Consequences of Agribusiness.* Montclair, NJ: Allanheld, Osburn.

Gramling, R., and W. R. Freudenberg. 1990. "A Closer Look at 'Local Control': Communities, Commodities, and the Collapse of the Coast." *Rural Sociology* 55(4):541–58.

Green, G. 1985. "Large-scale Farming and the Quality of Life in Rural Communities: Further Specification of the Goldschmidt Hypothesis." *Rural Sociology* 50(2):262–74.

Greider, T., and R. S. Krannich. 1985. "Neighboring Patterns, Social Support, and Rapid Growth: A Comparative Analysis from Three Western Communities." *Sociological Perspectives* 28(1):51–70.

Haedrich, R. L., and L. C. Hamilton. 2000. "The Fall and the Future of Newfoundland's Cod Fishery." *Society and Natural Resources* 13(4):359–72.

Hamilton, L. C., and C. M. Duncan. 2000. "Fisheries Dependence and Social Change in the Northern Atlantic." Pp. 95–105 in D. Symes (ed.), *Fisheries Dependent Regions.* Oxford, UK: Fishing New Books.

Hannigan, J. A. 1995. *Environmental Sociology: A Social Constructionist Perspective.* London: Routledge.

Harris, C. K., and J. Gilbert. 1982. "Large-scale Farming and Rural Income and Goldschmidt's Hypothesis." *Rural Sociology* 47(3):449–58.

Heberlein, T. 1976. "Some Observations on Alternative Mechanisms for Public Involvement." *Natural Resources Journal* 16:197–212.

Heilbroner, R. L. 1975. *An Inquiry into the Human Prospect.* New York: W. W. Norton and Co.

Hypes, J. L. 1944. "Crop Response as a Testing Ground for Geo-cultural Regionalism." *Rural Sociology* 14(1):51–58.

Interorganizational Committee on Guidelines and Principles for Social Impact Assessment. 1993. *Guidelines and Principles for Social Impact Assessment.* Belhaven, NC: IAIA.

Jones, R. E., and R. E. Dunlap. 1992. "The Social Bases of Environmental Concern: Have They Changed Over Time?" *Rural Sociology* 57(1):28–47.

Joshi, M. L., J. C. Bliss, C. Bailey, L. J. Teeter, and K. J. Ward. 2000. "Investing in industry, underinvesting in human capital: forest-based rural development in Alabama." *Society and Natural Resources* 13(4):291–320.

Kanagy, C., C. Humphrey, and G. Firebaugh. 1994. "Surging Environmentalism: Changing Public Opinion or Changing Publics?" *Social Science Quarterly* 75(4): 804–19.

Kaufman, H., and L. Kaufman. 1946. *Toward the Stabilization and Enrichment of a Forest Community: The Montana Study.* Missoula: University of Montana Press.

Klausner, Samuel. 1971. *On Man and His Environment.* San Francisco: Jossey-Bass.

Kempton, W., J. Bister, and J. Harley. 1995. *Environmental Values in American Culture.* Cambridge, MA: MIT Press.

Kolb, J. H. 1933. *Trends of County Neighborhoods: 1921–1931.* Madison: University of Wisconsin Agricultural Experiment Station Bulletin No. 120.

Krannich, R. S., H. Berry, and T. Greider. 1989. "Fear of Crime in Rapidly Changing Rural Communities: A Longitudinal Analysis." *Rural Sociology* 54(2):195–212.

Krannich, R. S., T. Greider, and R. Little. 1985. "Rapid Growth and Fear of Crime: A Four Community Comparison." *Rural Sociology* 50(2):193–209.

Krannich, R. S., and B. Zollinger. 1997. "Pursuing Rural Community Development in Resource-dependent Areas: Obstacles and Opportunities." *Research in Community Sociology* 7:201–22.

Kusel, J. 1996. "Well-being in Forest-dependent Communities, Part I: A New Approach." Pp. 361–73 in *Sierra Nevada Ecosystem Project: Final Report to Congress,* Vol. II, *Assessments and Scientific Basis for Management Options.* Davis: University of California, Centers for Water and Wildland Resources.

Kusel, J., S. Kocher, J. London, L. Buttolph, and E. Schuster. 2000. "Effects of Displacement and Outsourcing on Woods Workers and Their Families." *Society and Natural Resources* 13(2):115–34.

Landis, P. H. 1938. *Three Iron Mining Towns: A Study in Cultural Change.* Middleton, WI: Social Ecology Press.

Lee, R. G., M. S. Carroll, and K. K. Warren. 1991. "The Social Impact of Timber Harvest Reduction in Washington State." Pp. 3–19 in P. Sommers and H. Birss (eds.), *Revitalizing the Timber Dependent Regions of Washington.* Seattle: Northwest Policy Center, University of Washington.

Little, R., and R. S. Krannich. 1989. "A Model for Assessing the Social Impacts of Natural Resource Utilization on Resource-dependent communities." *Impact Assessment Bulletin* 6(2):21–35.

Lively, C. E. 1932. *Growth and Decline of Farm Trade Centers in Minnesota 1905–1930*. St. Paul: University of Minnesota Agricultural Experiment Station Bulletin No. 287.

Lobao, L. M. 1990. *Locality and Inequality: Farm and Industry Structure and Socioeconomic Conditions*. Albany: State University of New York Press.

Lowe, G. D., and T. K. Pinhey. 1982. "Rural-Urban Differences in Support for Environmental Protection." *Rural Sociology* 47(1):114–28.

Lowe, G. D., T. K. Pinhey, and M. D. Grimes. 1980. "Public Support for Environmental Protection: New Evidence from National Surveys." *Pacific Sociological Review* 23(4):423–45.

Luloff, A. E., and W. A. Befort. 1989. "Land Use Change and Aerial Photography: Lessons for Applied Sociology." *Rural Sociology* 54(1):92–105.

Machlis, G. E., and Donald R. Field. 1992. *On Interpretation*. Corvallis: Oregon State University Press.

Milbrath, L. W. 1984. *Environmentalists: Vanguard for a New Society*. Albany: State University of New York Press.

Mohai, P. 1992. "Men, Women, and the Environment: An Examination of the Gender Gap in Environmental Concern and Activism." *Society and Natural Resources* 5(1):1–19.

Mohai, P., and B. W. Twight. 1987. "Age and Environmentalism: An Elaboration of the Buttel Model Using National Survey Evidence." *Social Science Quarterly* 68(4):798–815.

Mol, A. 1997. "Ecological Modernization: Industrial Transformations and Environmental Reform." Pp. 138–49 in M. Redclift and G. Woodgate (eds.), *International Handbook of Environmental Sociology*. London: Elgar.

Morrison, D. E. 1976. "Growth, Environment, Equity, and Scarcity." *Social Science Quarterly* 57:292–306.

Morrison, D. E., and R. E. Dunlap. 1986. "Environmentalism and Elitism: A Conceptual and Empirical Analysis." *Environmental Management* 10(5):581–89.

Murphy, R. 1994. *Rationality and Nature: A Sociological Inquiry into a Changing Relationship*. Boulder, CO: Westview Press.

Radeloff, Volker, Alice Hagen, Paul Voss, Donald R. Field, and David Mladenoff. 2000. "Exploring the Spatial Relationship between Census and Land Cover Data." *Society and Natural Resources* 13(6):599-609.

Radeloff, Volker C., Roger B. Hammer, Paul R. Voss, Alice E. Hagen, Donald R. Field and David J. Mladenoff. 2001. Human Demographic Trends and Landscape Level Forest Management in the Northwest Wisconsin Pine Barrens. Forest Science 47(2):229-241

Schickele, R., J. P. Himmel, and R. M. Hurd. 1935. *Economic Phases of Erosion Control in Southern Iowa and Northern Missouri*. Ames: Iowa State College Agricultural Experiment Station Bulletin No. 333.

Schnaiberg, A. 1980. *The Environment: Form Surplus to Scarcity*. New York: Oxford University Press.

Schnaiberg, A., and K. A. Gould. 1994. *Environment and Society*. New York: St. Martin's Press.

Senn, A. 1984. *Resources, Values and Development*. Cambridge: Harvard University Press.

Smith, T. L. 1953. *The Sociology of Rural Life*. New York: Harper and Brothers.

Smith, M. D., R. S. Krannich, and L. Hunter. "Growth, Decline, Stability and Disruption: A Longitudinal Analysis of Social Well-being in Four Western Communities." *Rural Sociology* 66(3):425-450.

Sorokin, P. A., and C. C. Zimmerman. 1929. *Principles of Rural–Urban Sociology*. New York: Henry Holt and Company.

Sorokin, P. A., C. C. Zimmerman, and C. J. Galpin. 1930. *Systematic Sourcebook of Rural Sociology*. Minneapolis: University of Minnesota Press.

Swanson, L. E. 1990. "Rethinking Assumptions About Farm and Community." Pp. 19–33 in A. E. Luloff, and L. E. Swanson (eds.), *American Rural Communities*. Boulder, CO: Westview Press.

Szaz, A. 1994. *EcoPopulism: Toxic Waste and the Movement for Environmental Justice*. Minneapolis: University of Minnesota Press.

Taylor, C. N., C. H. Bryan, and C. G. Goodrich. 1995. *Social Assessment: Theory, Process and Techniques*. Christchurch, New Zealand: Caxton Press.

Tremblay, K. R., Jr., and R. E. Dunlap. 1978. "Rural–Urban Residence and Concern with Environmental Quality: A Replication and Extension." *Rural Sociology* 43(3):474–91.

VanLiere, K. D., and R. E. Dunlap. 1980. "The Social Bases of Environmental Concern: A Review of Hypotheses, Explanations and Empirical Evidence." *Public Opinion Quarterly* 44:181–97.

VanLiere, K. D., and R. E. Dunlap. 1981. "Environmental Concern: Does It Make a Difference How It's Measured?" *Environment and Behavior* 13(6):651–76.

Walker, G. B., and S. E. Daniels. 1996. "The Clinton Administration, the Northwest Forest Conference, and Managing Conflict: When Talk and Structure Collide." *Society and Natural Resources* 9:77–91.

Warren, R. 1978. *The Community in America*. 3rd Edition. Chicago, IL: Rand McNally.

Weber, E. P. 2000. "A New Vanguard for the Environment: Grass-roots Ecosystem Management as a New Environmental Movement." *Society and Natural Resources* 13(3): 237–60.

Weeks, E. C. 1990. "Mill Closures in the Pacific Northwest: The Consequences of Economic Decline in Rural Industrial Communities." Pp. 125–40 in R. G. Lee, D. R. Field, and W. R. Burch Jr. (eds.), *Community and Forestry: Continuities in the Sociology of Natural Resources*. Boulder, CO: Westview Press.

Weinberg, A. S. 1994. "Environmental Sociology and the Environmental Movement: Towards a Theory of Pragmatic Relationships of Critical Inquiry." *The American Sociologist* 25(1):31–57.

Wilkinson, K. P. 1991 (2000). *The Community in Rural America*. Middleton, WI: Social Ecology Press.

Wilkinson, K. P., J. G. Thompson, R. Reynolds, Jr., and L. Ostresh. 1982. "Local Social Disruption and Western Energy Development: A Critical Review." *Pacific Sociological Review* 25:275–96.

Wilkinson, K. P., R. R. Reynolds, Jr., J. G. Thompson, and L. M. Ostresh. 1984. "Violent Crime in the Western Energy-development Region." *Sociological Perspectives* 27(April):241–56.

Williams, D., and S. Stewart. 1998. "Sense of Place: An Elusive Concept That is Finding a Home in Ecosystem Management." *Journal of Forestry* 2:18–23.

Wilson, W. 1912. *The Evolution of the County Community.* Boston, MA: Pilgrim Press.

Yaffee, S. L., A. F. Phillips, I. C. Frents, P. W. Hardy, S. M. Malecki, and B. E. Thorpe. 1996. *Ecosystem Management in the United States: An Assessment of the Current Experience.* Washington, D.C.: Island Press.

Zimmerman, C. C. 1930. *Farm Trade Centers in Minnesota, 1905–1929.* St. Paul: University of Minnesota Agricultural Experiment Station Bulletin No. 269.

CHAPTER 4
Resource Management as a Democratic Process: Adaptive Management on Federal Lands

Nancy Langston

C onflict has long been a key part of American environmental politics, and many people—both environmentalists and critics of environmentalism—think that is a very bad thing. Yet conflicts among different users of public lands have often improved resource management when they disrupted the hold of narrow orthodoxies on policy. This chapter explores two historical case studies, one in the U.S. Forest Service and one in the U.S. Fish and Wildlife Service.

The first case study examines conflicts over old growth forest management in the Blue Mountains of eastern Oregon. For most of the twentieth century, foresters attempted to use the best ecological research of the day to transform old growth forests into regulated, scientific forests. This attempt to bring order to forests backfired, helping to create a forest health crisis across the West (Langston 1995). The second case study examines conflicts over riparian management at Malheur National Wildlife Refuge in the northern Great Basin, where disputes between ranchers, irrigators, and environmentalists have challenged the ability of federal agencies to manage scarce resources.

These cases describe how federal resource managers tried to reduce ecological complexity in order to maximize output from public lands, hoping to minimize conflicts between different users who wanted access to scarce resources. In both cases, a strong sense of professional community within each agency helped create a sense of purpose and pride that led to remarkable results on the ground in early years. Yet, in both cases, professional boundaries helped give rise to orthodoxies in the management of timber, water, grazing, and fire. Recent efforts at adaptive management, however, have helped to bring a democratic process to resource management, breaking down professional insularity and embedding decision making within broader communities.[1]

---

1. My thanks to Robert G. Lee of the University of Washington for suggesting this approach.

Adaptive management is a messy process of developing a management scheme that incorporates multiple human perspectives while responding to changing scientific understanding of dynamic ecosystems. At its best, adaptive management is a way of paying close attention to what happens when landscapes are managed, then altering practices when old ways no longer produce the desired results. This, in effect, entails applying the scientific method to management. The critical step for management, however, comes after the research: the hard part is using all that information to change how one works with the land. It means a dialogue between people and land; it means people knowing the place where they work. Adaptive management at its best is an iterative process that yields new information about ecological and human systems, and then applies that information to develop policies that can respond to changing knowledge about a changing world.

Case Study One: Conflicts Over Old Growth Forests on National Forests

Community stability and a sustained yield of forest products have played important roles in the policy of the Forest Service since its inception. One of the early Forest Service's central goals was to assure a stable, continued, fair supply of resources for local use. Careful conservation of forests, water, and grasses was thought to assure local communities use of resources without depleting the sources of that potential prosperity. However, things did not go as planned. In the Western forests and grasslands, this dream turned into a nightmare for many communities.

Forest Service planners made their decisions with the best of intentions, not because they wanted to destroy the forests or the mills, but because they wanted to make both sustainable. We need to understand the mistakes they made, not so that we can blame them, but so that we can learn from their errors and their many successes. If we want to reach a fair and sustainable future for forests and the communities that depend on them, we need to understand our shared forest history.

When Euro-Americans first came to the Blue Mountains of eastern Oregon and Washington in the early nineteenth century, they found a land of open forests full of "yellow-bellied" ponderosa pines five feet across. These were forests so promising that people thought they had stumbled into paradise. However, after a century of trying to manage the forests, what had seemed like paradise was irrevocably lost. The great ponderosa pines were gone; in their place were thickets of fir and lodgepole pine. The ponderosa pines had resisted most insect attacks, but the trees that replaced them were favored hosts for defoliating insects such as spruce budworm and Douglas fir tussock moth. As firs invaded the old ponderosa forests, insect epidemics swept the dry Western forests. By 1991, on the five and one-half million acres of Forest Service lands in the Blue Mountains, insects had attacked half the stands, and in some stands, nearly 70 percent of the trees were infested (Gast et al. 1991; Langston 1995).

Even worse in the view of foresters and many local citizens was the threat of catastrophic fires. Although light fires had burned through the open pines every ten years or so, few had become crown fires. However, as firs grew underneath the pines and succumbed to insect damage, more fuel became available to sustain major fires. By the beginning of the 1990s, one catastrophic fire after another swept the inland Western United States.

In 1991, the Forest Service acknowledged that its own past management had helped to create a crisis in forest health, necessitating that those practices be changed (Gast et al. 1991). Two dominant and contrasting hypotheses emerged to explain the origins of the forest health crisis. Many environmentalists claimed that things had gone wrong in the inland West because the Forest Service worked hand in hand with the lumber industry to cut trees as fast as they could, devastating the forests. Excessive harvests, soil compaction, high grading that removed ponderosa pines and left only firs behind, combined with even-aged management—all this had led to a simplified ecosystem that became increasingly susceptible to epidemics.

Many foresters had an opposing point of view. The forests had deteriorated, they argued, because the Forest Service had bowed to the demands of sentimental preservationists and refused to manage intensively enough to save the forests from their natural enemies— fire, insects, and disease. Because ponderosa pine is shade-intolerant, they argued, clearcutting, even-aged harvests, and intensive management would be the only applicable methods to assure that fir stands do not replace pine stands. In their view, the best way to make forests sustainable would be to manage them as intensely as possible (Langston 1995).

These two perspectives on the history of forest health problems led to radically different management prescriptions. Neither of these perspectives, however, encompasses the whole truth. Understanding what early federal foresters did in the Blue Mountains ("the Blues"), and why they did it, is critical for devising restoration strategies.

Old Growth Policies

At the turn of the twentieth century, America was in a furor over land management. Disposal of the vast tracts of Western land was often a corrupt process. The new forest scientists argued that science could offer a way out of the chaos of political corruption. By turning to the rules of science, foresters tried to avoid contentious politics. As scientists who had the interests of America and American forests at heart, they felt they were beyond criticism. They alone could serve the public well, they believed, as efficiency rather than short-term profit was their goal (Hays 1959).

To assure there would be forests for the future, the Forest Service believed it important to remove old growth and encourage the growth of young forest. At the turn of the century, foresters defined old growth forests (also called "over decadent" or "over mature" forests) as those in which annual growth did not exceed annual decay. In contrast, scientific regulated forests were young and still growing quickly, so that they added more volume in a year than they lost to death and decay. The scientifically regulated forests were growing in an orderly fashion, so that each year the exact same number of trees came available for harvest—ideally, for eternity (Parry et al. 1983). Scientific forestry, later known as sustained-yield forestry, required regulated forests, so that the annual net growth could be harvested each year, assuming that in a regulated forest, loggers could harvest the net annual growth forever without depleting the growing stock. The harvest was equal to the interest; the growing stock was equal to capital.

The logic of the new Forest Service was simple: if the United States was running out of timber, the best way to meet future demands was to grow more. Since, according to Forest Service surveys in the early 1900s, more than 70 percent of the Western forests were old growth stands, Western forests were losing as much wood to death and decay as they were gaining from growth. To prevent the threat of a timber famine, old growth forests needed to be liquidated so that regulated, sustained-yield forests could be grown instead. The best way to make available the land for growing, regulated production was by promoting sales of old growth.

In 1911, C. S. Judd, the assistant regional forester for the Northwest region, told exactly this to the incoming freshman class of forestry students at the University of Washington. A timber famine was on its way, unless the Forest Service did something soon. As Judd put it, "The good of the forest . . .demands that the ripe timber on the National Forests and above all, the dead, defective, and diseased timber, be removed." The way to accomplish this was to "enter more actively into the timber sale business" and heavily promote sales. This would get rid of the old growth, freeing up land to "start new crops of timber for a future supply" (Judd 1911, unpaged document). As Frederick Ames, another Blues forester (and later Chief of Silviculture for the Forest Service) said in 1906: "From no point of view can we make any mistake in cutting timber of this class [old growth]. The more sales we make the better" (Ames 1910, unpaged document). The unregulated, old growth forest was something to be altered as quickly as possible for moral, not just economic, reasons, to alleviate what one forester in the Blue Mountains, Thorton Munger (1936, unpaged document), termed "the idleness of the great areas of stagnant virgin forest that are getting no selective cutting treatment whatsoever."

Armed with their conviction that old growth was decadent and wasteful, foresters set out to clean up the forest, to make it as productive as possible. Every sales contract and management plan stipulated that contractors had to remove all snags and dead wood, and all insect-and fungi-damaged trees from the cutting site (e.g., Miles 1911). Foresters believed that disease, dead wood, old growth, and fire all detracted from efficient timber production. They were assuming that the role of the forest was to grow trees as fast as it could, and that any element not directly contributing to that goal was bad. Assumptions such as these made it difficult for them to imagine that insects, waste, disease, and decadence might be essential for forest communities; indeed, that the timber-producing part of the forest might depend on the non-timber-producing part of the forest.

Liquidating Old Growth

For all the foresters' desire to remove old growth, the Forest Service sold minimal timber from the Blue Mountains until after World War 1 (Evans 1912; Clary 1986). Forest Service timber was inaccessible, prices were set so high that few contractors were willing to invest, and the lumber industry still had enough private stock to make sales of federal timber unattractive. After World War I, however, markets for National Forest timber opened up, and the Forest Service started to promote sales of ponderosa pine in the Blue Mountains. This enabled them to seriously begin the campaign to regulate the forests by liquidating old growth.

The Forest Service believed that to ensure local prosperity old growth forests needed to be converted to regulated forests, which could supposedly supply harvests forever. However, they also needed markets for timber, and railroads were needed to get the timber to the markets. The development of railroads, particularly after World War I, was extraordinarily expensive. Financing them required capital, which often meant attracting investments from Midwestern lumber companies. However, these companies would only be interested in spending money on railroads if they were promised sales large and rapid enough to cover their investments.

To encourage regional railroad development in the 1920s, Forest Service planners encouraged construction of mills that had annual milling capacities well above what they could supply on a sustained-yield basis. Two large sales during the 1920s from the Malheur Forest alone, for example, offered over two billion board feet of pine, out of only seven billion board feet of timber in the entire forest. Two mills followed after the Malheur mill—one capable of processing sixty million board feet a year; and another that could process seventy to seventy-five million board feet each year (USDA Forest Service 1922). With mill capacities reaching 135 million board feet per year, it would take only fifteen years—not the sixty years of the cutting cycle—to process the two billion board feet in these sales, and only fifty-two years to process all the ponderosa in the forest.

As the Forest Service tried to find contractors for their timber, they made extensive compromises. The Forest Service initially had a strong policy against high grading—the practice of cutting out only the most valuable ponderosa from a mixed stand and leaving behind the less-valuable firs and other trees to form the basis of the future forest.

However, correspondence between sales planners make it clear that contractors were refusing to cut less valuable trees. The Forest Service did not force the contractors to honor their contracts. Soon contractors began demanding a reduction in stumpage prices, claiming that they should be given a discount on ponderosa if they had to cut any other species at all. Starting in 1922, the Forest Service decided that continuing to insist on cutting firs would mean that no one would buy ponderosa, and so the policy against high grading was dropped (USDA Forest Service 1922).

In 1922 the Forest Service in the Blues also abandoned its ideal of light selective cutting and began allowing contractors to remove 85 to 90 percent of the mature forest in each sale, leaving only 10 to 15 percent as a reserve stand for the next harvest cycle. Loggers were now allowed to skid out the timber with caterpillar tractors, even though before 1922 the Forest Service had discouraged this because it damaged young growth. The Forest Service had originally required that big pines be left in the reserve stand as seed trees. However, in the 1920s, they abandoned this policy, and told contractors to cut all pine over fifteen inches in diameter on a sale area. Although many foresters now argue that light selective cutting and fire exclusion destroyed the ponderosa forests by encouraging fir, these silvicultural compromises of the 1920s also contributed (USDA Forest Service 1922).

Concern about the longer-term effects of intense harvests on local communities began to emerge in working circle plans during the late 1920s, even though foresters did not allow this concern to decrease their recommended harvests. In the Malheur River Working Circle Plan starting in approximately 1927, the planner attempted to calculate the annual yield that would be available for local mills beginning in the 1980s, during the second cutting cycle. He realized, with dismay, that harvests would drop by at least 40 percent in the 1980s if cutting continued at current rates (USDA Forest Service n.d.). The planner, however, thought that, because his calculations of growth rates were just rough estimates, perhaps they would turn out to be low; then there would more timber than expected. He also hoped that "utilization efficiency will greatly increase"—so less waste would mean more wood for future mills (USDA Forest Service n.d., unpaged document).

In the Whitman Forest, letters between sales planners, the forest supervisor, and the regional district forester show that, by 1927, the

Forest Service was worried about the mill capacities they had encouraged. E. A. Sherman, the acting regional forester in Portland, criticized a draft of the management plan for the Baker Working Circle, complaining that the mill at Baker was too large and was using up too much wood, in excess of annual allowable cuts. He wrote that "the present milling capacity at Baker of between 40,000,000 and 50,000,000 feet annually . . . greatly exceeds the possible sustained yield from the Government lands in this working circle . . . . It does not look as if a reduction in the milling capacity at Baker sooner or later could be avoided" (Sherman 1927, unpaged document). The sales planner who had prepared the plan Sherman was criticizing agreed that harvest reductions would certainly arrive by the 1980s. Nevertheless, he argued to Sherman that they should do their best to meet the mills' current demands to avert possible immediate closures, even though such harvests would come at the expense of the next cutting cycle. Sherman reluctantly agreed and high harvests continued (USDA Forest Service 1927).

Throughout the 1920s, foresters set up plans knowing that harvests would drop by at least 40 percent over the long term, leading to probable mill closures in the 1980s (USDA Forest Service n.d.). Mill closing is exactly what happened. Harvests collapsed at the beginning of the 1990s—not only because of environmental restrictions, but also because of decisions made in the 1920s. The planners' original motive, however, was not to gain profits from sales of old growth, but to reshape the forests to fit their dream of scientific efficiency. They initially believed their goals were purely rational and that their motives were untainted by desire for gain. What they failed to recognize was the degree to which their culture—a culture that stressed efficiency—had shaped their scientific definitions of an ideal forest.

In their drive to build local support for establishing forest reserves at the turn of the twentieth century, federal foresters had insisted on two beliefs: that Midwestern timber barons were out to steal resources from local people, and that the foresters were on the side of the locals. The federal foresters were going to save the forests, not for preserves, but for perpetual use and productivity. Inspection reports often intimated that outsiders had plundered the land with their wasteful logging techniques, and only the Forest Service could protect local industry from the depredations of out-of-state capital (Langston 1995).

The official policy in the region was to support and promote locally owned mills. However, internal memos reveal the Forest Service was actually not supporting local mills. As the Umatilla Hilgard Project Report (USDA Forest Service 1927) stated, the intent was to "vigorously discourage sales to small operators." Their "inability or unwillingness to adhere to contract stipulations," coupled with their financial instability, made the Forest Service reluctant to work with them. Primarily, small sales interfered "with efficient logging by the larger and more important operators" (USDA Forest Service 1927, unpaged document).

The emerging federal bureaucracies found it far easier to work with larger corporations. The larger lumber operators owned substantial private lands, and were better able to institute scientific forestry practices. Small mills and small logging operations were less efficient, and efficiency was something the Forest Service promoted. By the 1920s, the Forest Service discouraged small local mills and did their best to encourage big capital from out of state (Langston 1995). The intent was not to destabilize local communities, but to regulate the forests, and larger companies could, it was believed, do this more quickly than small companies.

Complexity and Adaptive Management

When foresters looked at old growth forests, they saw not diverse habitat for predators and prey, but instead a chaotic mess. Their hope was to make the forest less wasteful and more efficient by simplifying. As George Bright, a Wenaha Forest silviculturist, stated in 1913: "In the general riot of the natural forest, many thousands of acres are required to grow the trees that . . . under management, could be grown on far less land." At times, the impatience of many foresters became so great that they longed for the day when they finally had the money and the clout to raze the hills and plant exactly what they liked. As Bright argued, if only foresters could clearcut the old, inefficient forests, they could plant a better nature that would produce ten times the amount of useful timber (Bright 1913, unpaged document). Eventually, clearcutting did take place, but their efforts backfired, leading to increasing problems with fire, insects, disease, and conflicts among resource users.

Human communities depended, and still depend, on the forests. But what few early managers in the Blue Mountains realized is that people depend, not just on timber outputs, but indirectly on the ecological complexity that sustains those outputs.

Traditional resource management led to a series of unexpected effects and unintended consequences. When a manager tried to fix one problem, the solution created a worse problem elsewhere. The best of intentions often brought about the worst of outcomes. Attempts to manage natural systems could introduce an element of instability into the systems managers were hoping to control. For example, fire protection and insect control attempted to control natural disasters by eliminating the problem, thereby engineering it out of existence. Fire managers tried to prevent catastrophic fires by suppressing all small fires. Insect managers tried to control insect damage by killing all insects as soon as they appeared, or by simplifying individual stands so insects could not survive. In spite of their best efforts, attempts at fire and insect control only led to worse devastation. Suppressing fires led to fuel accumulations, slowed the growth of many forests, and made future fires more intense. Changing old growth stands to even-aged stands in order to control insects only eliminated insect predators, and contributed to the catastrophic insect damage now apparent in the Blues. A refusal to tolerate low-intensity fires made moderate fires behave more erratically, just as a refusal to tolerate low-intensity insect damage made future damage worse. Failures of fire and insect control generally led not to a re-evaluation of the enterprise, but to more engineering, more sprays, more fire fighters, and more intensive management to fix the problems management created.

As scientific understanding of forests changes, and as society's values change, forest managers have to negotiate some path that adapts to these changes without sacrificing the basis of the forests' future productivity. In the current debates over forest management, science can offer guidance and information as to outcomes of different alternatives, and identify biophysical constraints that define the range of possible alternatives. However, changing social values and priorities, not science alone, will be the primary determinants of sustainable forest management.

Case Study Two: Riparian Management at Malheur National Wildlife Refuge

During the 1980s and 1990s, conflicts over old growth forests were among the most bitter in resource management. Yet, in the first decade of the twenty-first century, conflicts over riparian management have proven even more intense, as water becomes an increasingly scarce and valuable resource. Conflicts over riparian areas have a long history in America, beginning more than a century ago, when drainage and reclamation efforts across the nation led to a noticeable decline in waterfowl, stimulating a national interest in conservation of these birds and their habitats (Vileisis 1997).

For thousands of years in the high deserts of the northern Great Basin, the Donner und Blitzen River moved across a vast floodplain, using a set of sinuous channels that changed from decade to decade, creating a system of shifting wetlands that supported millions of water birds each year. These riparian communities were not stable: floods, changes in rainfall, and changes in animal activities led to dramatic annual changes in the bottomlands. Some years the marshes were lush and green, and stretched from one end of the valley to another; the basin filled with water. Other years little snow fell on the surrounding mountains; by early summer the lowland streams ran down to a trickle, the riparian meadows turned brown, and the marshes slowly dried. Some years the water was so high that numerous pools and ponds formed in the valley, perfect for brooding waterfowl. Other years few pools formed, and available waterfowl-rearing habitat was minimal. Yet, because this basin was embedded in a much larger network of wetlands stretching from California to Canada along the Pacific Flyway, when droughts struck the basin, shrinking the ponds and pools, migratory birds could find other places to rest and feed.

By the 1930s, several decades of overgrazing, irrigation withdrawals, grain agriculture, dredging and channelization, followed by drought, meant that the former wetlands had become a dust bowl. Attempts to increase crop production by making wet areas drier and dry lands moister had stripped the willows and cottonwoods from the banks, imprisoned the Donner und Blitzen River in a ditch, and dried up the meadows and marshes. People did not fare much better than the land: ranches failed, livestock starved, homesteaders went bust, and a primary occupation in the valley became suing one's neighbor over water rights. Water control seemed an unmitigated disaster (Langston 2003).

Conservationists won a major victory in 1934, when failed cattle and irrigation empires along the Donner und Blitzen River were sold to the federal wildlife refuge system, beginning an expansion of a duck ecosystem at Malheur National Wildlife Refuge. Managers attempted to restore an ecosystem that appeared to have nearly been annihilated. In response to what they saw as a crisis, refuge managers adopted drastic measures to re-flood drained lands, re-route water courses, and essentially manufacture new breeding areas for bird populations that seemed on the verge of extinction. In place of a system of wandering channels, where in some years little of the valley might be wet, and other years floods might sweep over the entire basin, eradicating waterfowl breeding habitat, managers hoped to control the movement of water across the land. Hoping to maximize waterfowl production, managers attempted to dictate which ponds stayed full of water, and which meadows were allowed to dry out.

John Scharff, the manager of Malheur National Wildlife Refuge for three decades, led intensive efforts to restore the basin through irrigation engineering and water control. In 1937 alone, refuge staff and workers from three Civilian Conservation Corps camps built over 150,966 cubic yards of levees and dykes, fenced 95 miles with barbed wire, cleared out 83,938 cubic yards of channels, laid 34,680 cubic yards of riprap, and created 35 separate water control structures. Just a year after Scharff had begun work, he stated in his 1937 fiscal year report: "The creation of lagoons, ponds, dikes and canals in all parts of the refuge has indeed proven an incentive for the waterfowl to utilize practically all meadows and formerly dug fields as nesting areas" (Scharff 1937). Interspersed with these descriptions were photographs of marshes and ponds with captions such as "Man-made Water Areas where Waterfowl Romp," (Scharff 1937, 15). Scharff added underneath the photos, "Much better use was obtained from the available water this year owing to the facilities which have been constructed to properly handle the water upon its arrival," (Scharff 1937, 15). Scharff summarized this report with the statement: "It is gratifying to say the least, to see the increased numbers of birds using the facilities which have been provided by our early development work" (Scharff 1937, 15).

The restored wetlands of Malheur National Wildlife Refuge soon formed the centerpiece of a huge riparian marsh complex in southeast Oregon—one large enough to cover the same size area as

Massachusetts, Connecticut, and Rhode Island. By 1987, Malheur's refuge manager, George Constantino, could report that Malheur Lake was "the most important refuge" along the Pacific Flyway "for water-oriented birds." In the language of wildlife biologists, Malheur "produced" 84 percent of the Great Egrets, 55 percent of Snowy Egrets, and 68 percent of Black-crowned Night Herons, representing "a major production area in the Pacific Flyway," (USDI Fish and Wildlife Service 1987, 2). Malheur had become one of the critical feeding sites along the Pacific Flyway, the migratory route of millions of waterfowl and shorebirds.

However, for all its successes, Malheur National Wildlife Refuge has become an increasingly contested landscape. Irrigation and water control on the refuge and on the surrounding private lands have helped create an environment with much less variability than its condition before 1937, and this variability has proven to be critical for maintaining ecological productivity in wetlands. For example, wetlands that are always flooded cannot recycle nutrients as well as wetlands that are sometimes allowed to dry out. Water-control structures allowed managers to fix a set pattern of breeding habitat in place for ducks, but in the end, this decreased the health of wetlands and aquatic habitat, ultimately hurting ducks as well as aquatic species.

To understand these decisions, we need to remember the desperate conditions of migratory bird populations in the first decades of the twentieth century—and the equally desperate attempts ornithologists and conservationists were making to save those birds. In the early 1930s, severe droughts along the Pacific Flyway desiccated wetlands, habitat that had already been drastically reduced by three decades of drainage and reclamation. By 1934, the continental waterfowl population had dropped to a low of twenty-seven million birds; only one hundred fifty egrets and fourteen whooping cranes remained (Vileisis 1997). Conservationists were convinced that preservation of habitat alone would ultimately be powerless against land speculators, reclamation engineers, and drainage districts bent on creating farmland out of wetland. The bleakness of the situation led conservationists to advocate what were engineering solutions for the restoration of Malheur, borrowing the same techniques that had helped devastate the marshes in the first place.

Although the water-control system at the refuge quickly increased waterfowl habitat, trying to maintain the system led Malheur staff into difficulty. Because the refuge's emphasis was on maximum water bird production, anything that seemed to detract from waterfowl production was eliminated. When coyote and raven populations soared, lowering duck nesting success, refuge staff set out poisoned bait, and then had to contend with increased rodent predation of eggs. When beaver returned to the valley and blocked irrigation ditches, staff trapped them out, even though the irrigation system was trying to replicate what beaver had created in the first place.

By the 1950s and 1960s, control of woody vegetation became another major objective for the refuge. Willows were cut, mowed, and sprayed with herbicide to remove predator habitat, make it easier for tourists to see the wildlife, increase mowing efficiency in the hay meadows, increase the number of acres that could be put into full cattle and duck production, and most importantly, to decrease competition for water. Woody riparian plants are phreatophytes, meaning that they extend their roots into the water table and consume a great deal of water. As one 1967 federal report on the Malheur Lake Basin argued, "Many people believe that the high consumption of limited water supplies by phreatophytes is one of the most serious problems in the West" (USDA Economic Research Service 1967, 87). Phreatophyte removal accelerated with the introduction of new herbicides—the 1955 *Yearbook of Agriculture* recommended that for complete control, one must repeat six sprayings of 2,4-D and 2,4,5-T, which later became notorious as Agent Orange (Meinzer 1927; Fletcher and Elmendorf 1955, 427; Robinson 1959). Water experts of the mid-1950s came to believe that they could create more water and control floods through such phreatophyte eradication programs.

Riparian hardwoods are thirsty plants, but using water does not always mean reducing the supply for everything else. Instead, riparian vegetation can maintain a high water table by absorbing runoff and allowing streams to continue flowing longer. Even while they consume water, riparian plants can increase the available supply to other plants. Riparian zones made the boundaries between water and land more complex, and John Scharff, like many other managers, believed that these complexities interfered with his efficient administration of nature, slowing water flow, keeping silt from clogging the streams. The leaves of these trees shade the streams, reducing water temperatures. Their branches and dead wood fall into the water, creating deep pools of scoured gravel where fish can spawn, trapping debris, and forming dams. Refuge staff used to think all this was bad—the point of a stream was to move water from point A to point B as efficiently as possible. However, the more people tried to simplify streams by channeling them and piping them and cleaning them up, the more the waters dwindled away.

The most spectacular of all programs that Scharff initiated was the carp-control project. Pioneers had introduced carp into the nearby Silvies River during the late nineteenth century, hoping to create a reliable food supply (Duebbert 1969). Few people proved to like the taste of carp, however, and carp populations soon exploded, with a host of unintended effects. Carp made their way from the Silvies River into Malheur Lake, perhaps during the high water year of 1952, when floods flushed carp into the lake (USDI Fish and Wildlife Service 1955). As bottom feeders, carp churned up sediments and destroyed sago pondweed. Because sago pondweed was a critical food source for waterfowl, duck populations plummeted at Malheur. By 1955, sago pondweed was almost depleted from Malheur Lake, and by 1957, carp had made their way forty miles up the Donner und Blitzen River. This unruly bit of nature—an unnatural introduction, but profoundly natural in its unwillingness to abide by human rules—became a profound threat to water-bird management at Malheur.

Scharff responded by initiating a series of poisoning projects whose intensity and scope were made possible by two things: first, by technological advances that had resulted from the World War II; and second, by a world view that had declared war on any aspects of nature that refused to accede to human control. The refuge staff set out to control carp by dumping and spraying the fish poison rotenone throughout the system—an enormous project, for it involved treating the Donner und Blitzen River, the Silvies River, all their tributaries, and the lake itself. Several dry years meant the lake levels had dropped quite low, shrinking the lake surface (USDI Fish and Wildlife Service 1955). With water-control structures along the Donner und Blitzen River and the lake, the staff shrunk the lake even further, making carp control feasible.

In the fall of 1955, the poisoning began. With aerial applications of rotenone, followed by drums of toxicant dumped into the water, and finally with staff wading out into the marsh and hacking the heads off dying fish, the refuge killed one and one-half million carp. But two thousand carp escapedand spawned, and within three years, carp were more numerous than before—now that their competitors, native fish much less resistant to rotenone, had been poisoned (USDI Fish and Wildlife Service 1955; USDI Fish and Wildlife Service 1957). Control projects continued for several decades. Two more extensive aerial sprayings were undertaken during low water years, with equally limited success (USDI Fish and Wildlife Service 1977; USDI Fish and Wildlife Service 1987).

What decades of drainage efforts had failed to do, carp managed quite well: they transformed Malheur Lake from splendid duck habitat to something still magnificent but far less productive for waterfowl; introduced carp had inadvertently created another ecosystem, escaping from the bounds people attempted to place upon them. People were responsible for these hybrid ecosystems, but they had little luck controlling them. Eventually the refuge staff admitted defeat in the war against carp, and focused instead on keeping carp populations from increasing to the point that they displaced everything else in the marsh.

In the years since John Scharff retired, management of Malheur riparian areas has become less clumsy, but no less manipulative. Now, instead of using bulldozers to channelize the river, the staff is trying to figure out ways to use bulldozers to return the river to its old route. Willow are being planted instead of being removed, but herbicides still play a role, removing vegetation that might compete with desired native species. The irrigation and water-control system is growing more elaborate, since without it much of the habitat for rare and endangered birds would be lost. Flood irrigation still waters the meadows, but now it creates hay for bird cover, not just for cattle.

The most profound change in the Donner und Blitzen Valley is that refuge staff is no longer trying to fix a single pattern of ponds and meadows and wetlands in place. Instead, they are trying to manage variability back into the system by alternating which meadows are dry and which are wet. Yet, given the constraints of managing a wildlife refuge with extensive investments in structural improvements, this variability can be allowed only within strict limits. For example, the river is now encouraged to meander a little, but not enough to threaten the constructed canals and brood ponds.

Some critics of Malheur Refuge policy have argued that the water-control system should be dismantled, and natural variability should be allowed to dominate. However, is this possible in a world so dramatically altered by people? Malheur's historical variability existed within an entirely different context. It was once only one of a long string of fertile, vast marshes stretching up and down the Pacific Flyway. If most of the Malheur Lakes Basin happened to be dry one year, the birds could stop elsewhere, because the Pacific Flyway consisted of numerous patches of desert, riparian, and wetland habitats. Now, however, the vast majority of those historical riparian areas and marshes are gone, replaced by agriculture, shopping malls, and highways. If natural variability were returned at Malheur, it might be disastrous for entire populations of ducks, sandhill cranes, and shorebirds.

Refuge managers believe that they cannot allow natural systems to be purely natural. They try to restore some natural variability, but not enough to threaten the water systems that have been painstakingly constructed. There is nothing ideologically pure about current refuge policy: it is not an attempt to return to pristine natural conditions, nor is it an attempt to gain complete control of nature.

Such a policy infuriates some environmentalists, who see little difference between John Scharff's regime and current refuge attempts to limit predators and regulate water. However, this critique does not consider some crucial ideas. Scharff, unlike current managers, aimed for ideological purity: his ethic was one of control and improvement. He rarely seemed to doubt that humans could and should take complete control of nature. Some modern environmentalists have an ethic that is equally ideologically pure: naturalness. A thing is good when it is natural, bad when it is not. Controlling predators or water is unnatural, so therefore it is bad.

In the world in which refuge staff actually has to work, neither ethic is particularly helpful. Refuge staff tries to find a reasonable path between extremes. The refuge managers are trying to act pragmatically, rather than ideologically. They are not trying to restore the refuge to some past set of pristine ecosystems; they are trying to adapt to change, making things work as best they can, while minimizing future complications. They are trying to practice adaptive management in an increasingly complicated world.

Conclusion: Lessons for Adaptive Management

Managers of both old growth forests and riparian landscapes once hoped that they could engineer the natural world to produce stable outputs of marketable resources. However, the natural world proved far too dynamic for this. No matter how many facts managers accumulate and how many theories they test, they will never have the knowledge to manipulate natural systems without causing unanticipated changes. Yet they still have to manipulate the environment, which presents a dilemma: how does one make decisions when one knows one will never be able to fully predict the outcome of those decisions?

Adaptive ecosystem management attempts to use some of the findings of dynamic ecology to manage natural resources, not for maximum commodity production (a traditional industrial forest), or for preservation of current conditions (a traditional reserve), but for the perpetuation of patterns and processes that allow ecosystem functioning. Adaptive ecosystem management rests on several critical principles: primarily, all ecosystems change, often in ways that are difficult for us to predict. Because humans have influenced ecological processes and patterns for thousands of years, it is important to understand human disturbances if we wish to understand current ecosystem functions. Management must therefore pay attention to the changing human framework, as well as to a changing natural framework.

In Malheur Lake Basin and the Blue Mountains, federal managers in the early twentieth century made reasonable decisions, given the limited information with which they had to work. Their goals were to assure a fairer distribution of increasingly scarce resources. They recognized that they knew little about how to manage wetlands, in Malheur's case, or ponderosa pine in the case of the Blue Mountains— yet they also recognized that they needed to do something quickly, in the face of accelerating losses. Their policies were at first experimental, a way of applying the scientific method to land management. Unfortunately, in both cases, policies that began as experiments soon became orthodoxy, and managers found it difficult to monitor ecological signs that things might be going wrong, and even more difficult to change policies once they were in place. The critical lesson from these case studies is not that early managers made mistakes—all managers will inevitably make mistakes, since no one can ever have perfect knowledge of how ecological systems work. Rather, the critical lesson from these case studies is to make note of the difficulties resource managers faced when they needed to monitor and change policies. The challenge for modern managers is to devise processes that assure adaptive management can take place.

Nearly a century ago, Frederick Ames (1910), who first worked for the Forest Service in the Blue Mountains and then became chief of silviculture for the nation, warned his fellow foresters that they needed to practice something akin to what we now call adaptive management. Ames argued that before foresters could begin to manage the Western forests, they needed to recognize several things, including the fact that they did not understand the forests well enough to predict their response to management. Nevertheless, they had to manage; even doing nothing at all was a form of management. Therefore, what they had to do was treat "all of sales as a vast experiment," (Ames 1910, unpaged document). Ames outlined an extremely ambitious plan of monitoring: after each timber sale, they would go in every three years and record the response of the site to whatever experimental treatment they had devised. Over the next one hundred years, they could compare the effects of different kinds of logging, fire exclusion, and grazing on different forest conditions. Ames called for close attention to both the forest and the effects of human actions on the forest. In modern terms, Ames was telling his foresters that they needed to practice adaptive management and recognize that foresters could not always predict the effects of their actions.

This was an excellent idea, but unfortunately, it failed to work. Even when conscientious foresters gathered all the data Ames called for, these reports accumulated dust, first on the top of the supervisor's desk, then in the office's filing cabinets, then in cardboard boxes in the storage attics. No one knew what to do with all this information, and it continued to multiply exponentially while managers tried to discern a solution. When foresters did try to monitor the effects of their logging practices, superiors in the regional offices usually chose not to make recommended changes, often for political reasons. Caution seemed easier than adapting to uncertainties, given the pressures on foresters to make timber available for sale (Ames 1915; Langston 1995).

At its best, adaptive management is a way of paying attention to what happens when we cut trees, burn forests, favor pine, or do anything else. But what is most innovative and promising about adaptive management is the way it tries to meet the challenges outlined in this chapter: how do you manage in a world where you know that your models of the forest are always much simpler than the forest itself? No matter how complex the forest is, one still has to manage it; there is no neutral position possible, no way to say we are simply not going to manage land. All attempts to manage are attempts to tell a story about how the land ought to be, and by definition, all these stories are simpler than the world itself.

As the first foresters in the Blues recognized, everything resource managers do is nothing more, and nothing less, than an experiment. The critical step for management, however, comes after the experiment: the hard part is using all that information to change how you work with the land, and this is where the young Forest Service found itself unable to resist pressures to continue business as usual. Monitoring does not necessarily mean big government programs; what it means is people being responsive to what the land is telling them, and being responsible for acting on that knowledge. It means a dialogue between people and land; it means people knowing the place they log, knowing the place they work.

At Malheur National Wildlife Refuge, refuge managers in the 1930s made reasonable engineering decisions in a desperate situation, but by the 1940s, they proved slow to respond to information that suggested their schemes were leading to trouble. Just as forest managers had found it difficult to change policies, when events at the refuge began to spiral out of control, managers did not question their own basic assumptions, but instead tried to hold the system under increasingly rigid control. As in the Blue Mountains, management techniques at Malheur that began as experiments soon became orthodoxy. In the 1930s, the refuge staff developed a set of powerful techniques that made excellent sense in a particular context, given the challenges waterfowl populations faced at the time. However, as Scharff gained power, those ideas became increasingly rigid.

People found it difficult to challenge the developing orthodoxy until outside events forced managers to take new perspectives seriously. In Malheur's case, these outside threats included floods, litigation by environmentalists, and the threat of an Endangered Species Act listing of redband trout. In the Blue Mountains, forest health problems, fire, and litigation played similar roles. In both cases, conflict forced people, institutions, and states to incorporate new ideas into their worldview.

For generations, foresters and refuge managers had enough power that they did not need to acknowledge viewpoints other than their own. Malheur refuge managers and Forest Service planners were reluctant to question their own ideologies until environmentalists used litigation against them. A set of escalating conflicts—conflicts which began as local issues and then became mediated by national institutions—eventually forced groups in Oregon to embrace a political process in which stakeholders coming from different perspectives had to jostle against each other, argue with each other, and listen to each other, in ways that modified each other's actions and beliefs. Because no one has perfect knowledge of how ecological systems work, this process moved us toward much better solutions than any one group could have found on its own.

What mattered most about litigation was that it forced a variety of stakeholders, with multiple voices, multiple stories, and multiple perspectives to communicate with each other. This led to new ideas and eventually new conditions. Federal resource managers ran into trouble when they were permitted to operate with the authority of state power reinforcing their assumptions. Only when political conflict forced managers to allow other stakeholders to have a voice did federal managers begin to question some of the problematic assumptions that seemed so self-evident when they essentially didn't have to answer to anyone else.

Yet, while state power and narrow scientific expertise can enforce rigid and dangerous orthodoxies, the answer is not to take power away from the scientists or the state, and simply give control back to the locals (Scott 1999). For all the mistakes made by technocratic, scientific experts, their expertise is useful and necessary. What is needed is a democratic process that creates a structure for useful conflict. A democratic process should empower multiple voices, and create a method for negotiating conflict. Democracy is not merely a form of external government, but a set of tools for "undertaking the ongoing reconstruction of social life" (Hickman 1998, xvi). Because the world is constantly changing and public values constantly shifting, the ways of providing for the individual and common good have to be experimentally determined (Parker 1996).

What should the role of state power and federal land managers become in such a democratic process? How can adaptive management help create a process that enables the interplay of diverse voices? Federal managers can structure a process that enables different groups, with different amount of power in a local community, to come to the table and be heard. They can force the powerful to listen to the powerless. They can get issues on the table that have been ignored for centuries. They can disrupt orthodoxy.

Federal resource managers' path is now as indirect as the river's course once was. Legal battles constantly reshape refuge and forest policy, much to the eternal frustration of staff that is trying to get their job done. However, such outside influence is a good thing in the end, however annoying it is from day to day. Without constant criticism and political pressures and court cases, refuge management would be far more efficient—and in the end, far more dangerous.

Both the Forest Service and the Fish and Wildlife Service have long been staffed with professionals dedicated to their agency's missions. Often, professionals within each agency shared a common language and a common professional training with others within their agency. Common goals and scientific training united early managers, giving them a strong sense of professional community, and helping them delineate a strong sense of professional boundaries. Wildlife managers, like foresters, gained legitimacy through their ideals and their reliance on science. When critics objected to federal policies, often managers were unwilling to acknowledge that other perspectives might contain valuable insights, feeling that professional foresters or wildlife managers were the only ones who could know what was best for the resource. Managers developed a sense of insularity that gave rise to orthodoxies in the management of timber, water, grazing, and fire, as Ashley Shiff shows in *Fire and Water: Scientific Heresy in the U. S. Forest Service* (1962), and Herbert Kauffman explores in *The Forest Ranger* (1960). As Robert G. Lee (personal communication) has suggested, when the Forest Service was thrust into a larger democratic community, the agency lost its strong sense of a central mission and its espirit de corps, and it is still struggling with the resultant identity crisis.

When managers work in isolation, they can come to operate with the ideological certainties that drove John Scharff's plans or the plans of the Forest Service in the 1940s. Recent managers have had a far more difficult time getting things done than earlier managers ever did, for they have been bogged down in court cases, tied up in endless negotiations with different stakeholders, distracted by petitions to list native fish, and dragged into fights with hot-tempered neighbors. While these are all enormous concerns, they offer a way for federal agencies to chart a responsive course in a changing political, social, and ecological landscape. For example, Malheur National Wildlife Refuge is now paying attention to native fish, calling into question many decades of single-species management that benefited waterfowl but harmed much else. This change has come about in large part because of the threat that redband trout might have been listed under the Endangered Species Act. Such legal threats have brought about new ideas, new conservation agreements, and new policies.

Dealing with ranchers, environmentalists, county commissioners, district court judges, tribal representatives, fisheries biologists, archeologists and engineers—this makes a manager's life complicated. The attempt to make different stakeholders happy makes for an intelligent, evolving, policy—not a perfect policy, but one that can respond to change, just as a healthy ecosystem responds to changes.

References

Ames, F. 1910. Addresses given at the 1910 joint supervisors' meeting for the Northwest region (Oregon and Washington). Forest Service Research Compilation Files, National Archives, Region VI, Entry 115, Box 136.

Bright, George. 1913. "The relative merits of western larch and Douglas fir in the Blue Mountains, Oregon." Forest Service Research Compilation Files, National Archives, Region VI, Entry 115, Box 135.

Clary, D. 1986. *Timber and the Forest Service*. Lawrence: University Press of Kansas.

Duebbert, Harold F. 1969. "The Ecology of Malheur Lake and Management Implications." Refuge leaflet # 412, USDI Fish and Wildlife Service, Bureau of Sport Fisheries and Wildlife. November 1969.

Evans, R. M. 1912. General Silvical Report Wallowa and Minam Forests. Forest Service Research Compilation Files, National Archives, Region VI, Entry 115, Box 135.

Fletcher, Herbert, and Harold B. Elmendorf. 1955. "Phreatophytes—A Serious Problem in the West," in *Water*. U.S. Department of Agriculture Yearbook of Agriculture. Washington D.C.: Government Printing Office.

Gast, W., et. al. 1991. The Blue Mountain Forest Health Report. USDA Forest Service Report.

Hays, S. 1959. *Conservation and the Gospel of Efficiency; the Progressive Conservation Movement, 1890-1920*. Cambridge, MA: Harvard University Press.

Hickman, Larry, ed. 1998. *Reading Dewey: Interpretations for a Postmodern Generation*. Bloomington: Indiana University Press.

Judd C. S. 1911. Lectures on Timber Sales at the University of Washington, February 1911. Forest Service Research Compilation Files, National Archives, Region VI, Entry 115, Box 136.

Kaufman, Herbert. 1960. *The Forest Ranger: A Study in Administrative Behavior.* Baltimore: published for Resources for the Future by Johns Hopkins University Press.

Langston, Nancy. 1995. *Forest Dreams, Forest Nightmares: The Paradox of Old Growth in the Inland West.* Seattle: University of Washington Press.

Langston, Nancy. 2003. *Troubled Waters: Contested Riparian Boundaries in the Inland West.* Seattle: University of Washington Press (in press, publication January 2003).

Meinzer, O. E. 1927. "Plants as Indicators of Ground Water." U. S. Geological Survey Water Supply Paper 577. Washington D.C.: Government Printing Office.

Miles, H. J. 1911. Silvics: Annual Report for the Malheur National Forest. Forest Service Research Compilation Files, National Archives, Region VI, Entry 115, Box 136.

Munger, T. 1936. Basic considerations in the management of ponderosa pine forests by the maturity selection system. Umatilla National Forest Historical Files, Supervisor's Office, Pendleton, Oregon.

Parker, Kelly A. 1996. "Pragmatism and Environmental Thought." Pp. 21-37 in *Environmental Pragmatism.* Andrew Light and Eric Katz (eds.). London: Routledge.

Parry, T. B., H. J. Vaux, and N. Dennis. 1983. "Changing Conceptions of Sustain-yield Policy on the National Forests." *Journal of Forestry* 81:150-54.

Robinson, T. W. 1959. "Phreatophytes," U. S. Geological Survey Water Supply Paper 1423: 1-84.

Scharff, John. 1937. "Report of Activities Fiscal Year 1937, Malheur Migratory Waterfowl Refuge." Refuge files, Malheur National Wildlife Refuge, Princeton, Oregon.

Schiff, Ashley L. 1962. *Fire and Water: Scientific Heresy in the U. S. Forest Service.* Cambridge, MA: Harvard University Press.

Scott, James C. 1999. *Seeing Like a State: How Certain Schemes to Improve the Human Condition Have Failed.* New Haven, CT: Yale University Press.

Sherman, E. A. 1927. Letter to C. M. Granger, District Forester, and John Kuhns, Whitman Forest Supervisor, March 8, 1927, concerning the Baker Working Circle Plan Wallowa-Whitman National Forest Historical Files, Supervisor's Office, Baker.

USDA Economic Research Service. 1967. "Report on Water and Related Land Resources Malheur Lake Drainage Basin Oregon." Based on a cooperative survey by the State Water Resources Board of Oregon and the USDA.

USDA Forest Service. 1922. Planning Report, Sales, Bear Valley Unit, Malheur National Forest 6/30/22. Malheur National Forest Historical Files, Supervisor's Office, John Day.

USDA Forest Service. 1927. Umatilla Hilgard Project Report. UNF Historical Files, S-Timber Surveys, Supervisor's Office, Pendleton.

USDA Forest Service. No date. Malheur River Working Circle Plan. Malheur National Forest Historical Files, Supervisor's Office, John Day.

USDI Fish and Wildlife Service. 1955. Malheur National Wildlife Refuge. Quarterly Narrative Report Sept. to Dec. 1955 Refuge files, Malheur National Wildlife Refuge, Princeton, 2.

USDI Fish and Wildlife Service. 1957. Bureau of Sport Fisheries and Wildlife. "Carp Control Project at Malheur Lake, Oregon 1955-1956." Refuge files, Malheur National Wildlife Refuge, Princeton, Oregon (1957), 35.

USDI Fish and Wildlife Service. 1977. Malheur National Wildlife Refuge, Annual Narrative 1977 Refuge files, Malheur National Wildlife Refuge, Princeton, Oregon.

USDI Fish and Wildlife Service. 1987. Malheur National Wildlife Refuge, Annual Narrative 1987 Refuge files, Malheur National Wildlife Refuge, Princeton, Oregon.

Vileisis, Ann. 1997. *Discovering the Unknown Landscape: A History of America's Wetlands*. Washington D.C.: Island Press.

CHAPTER 5
Human Values and Forests:
Changes in the Great Lakes Wildlands

Samuel P. Hayes and Greg Clendenning

E nvironmental policies regarding the Great Lakes forest result from human choices. Alternative policies arise from differences in the perception and meaning of forests to different people and the values they place upon forested areas. These differing perceptions and meanings (the social construction of nature) reflect the often conflicting and dynamic symbolic meanings of nature, forests, and landscapes that have evolved over time in the United States (Greider and Garkovich 1994; Freudenburg et al. 1995). Environmental and conservation controversies revolve around disputes over such matters. Because the nature and meaning of a forest to people today is vastly different from what it was a century ago, so must both our knowledge about the forest and our interaction with it be different. Our biggest problems lie not so much in our knowledge about the way in which the forest has evolved but in our understanding of the evolution of the human choices that have been made with respect to the forest environment.

Through this perspective, this chapter analyzes changing human choices about the forested wildlands—that area of sparse but growing population beyond the city and the countryside—in the Great Lakes region between about 1840 and the present. This evolution has had three distinct stages: 1850 to 1910, when wood production predominated; 1910 to 1945, when out-migration took place and real-estate values declined drastically, and when these "lands that nobody wanted" were rescued by public ownership and management; and 1945 to the present, a time that has seen a revival of intense interest in the forest. The revolution in forest-related human values that has taken place since 1945 has been so fundamental that a historical approach must inevitably stress change rather than continuity. Such an approach emphasizes not so much the impact of the forest on people as the impact of people on the forest.

The analysis is organized around three phenomena: changes in the way in which people perceived the Great Lakes forest and their relationship to it; the evolution and development of management perspectives; and the changing role of local communities as the specific context in which choices about the forest are made.

Changing Public Attitudes

The most important long-term change has been the way in which people have valued forested wildlands. How were forests perceived in the nineteenth century, and how are they perceived today? What role did (and do) people wish forests to play in their personal lives, and in the lives of their community, region, and nation? To start, we can make a simple distinction between the image of the forbidding forest of the nineteenth century and the attractive one of the twentieth century: a source of pleasure, relaxation, and inspiration. Although "wilderness" historically had a negative connotation, today it has a markedly positive one (Rudzitis and Johnson 1991; Bengston 1994). A dramatic reversal of values has taken place.

These new values do not represent a desire to return to some primitive, pre-scientific, pre-technological society. On the contrary, they represent an integral part of the standard of living of an advanced industrial society. There is a reciprocal relationship between the desire to enjoy the material commodities of the world of conveniences and the desire to enjoy intangible experiences in the world of amenities. Consumption in the United States has changed over the years from an emphasis on necessities to one on conveniences, and later, to an emphasis on amenities; each earlier stage has been retained firmly as each later one evolved. Modern technology has made it possible to live in or near wildland areas while enjoying most modern conveniences. With advances in communications technology and transportation infrastructure, rural areas are now more accessible and we have witnessed resurgence in rural and wilderness areas, a rural rebound and renaissance (see Frey and Johnson 1998; McGranahan 1999; Johnson and Fuguitt 2000). The countryside has become idealized in contemporary society, taking on a nostalgic notion of what a landscape should look like and how communities and social relations should be. In this "post-productivist" countryside, productive uses of land will continue to decline in importance in comparison to competing land uses for tourism, leisure, housing for commuters, second homes, and other consumptive uses. For many migrating urban residents, a critical element of living in or near wildlands is the preservation of the rural landscape, the rural idyll, Arcadia (Halfacree 1997; Halfacree and Boyle 1998).

We know much about these changing values in the years after World War II because they have been examined in detail. There are studies of those who use wildlands for recreation, most of them undertaken because managers wanted to know who the users are and what they prefer. There are also studies of the values of people who purchase land in wildland areas for homes and recreation, a phenomenon in which professional foresters have long been interested. Why, they have asked, do such owners not wish to produce wood on their properties for commercial sale? In state after state, including states in the Great Lakes area, studies have shown that owners value these lands for the natural setting of forest and microclimate, with its cleaner water and air and less-cluttered landscape (see Bourke and Luloff 1994; Birch 1996; Brunson et al. 1996; Campbell and Kittredge 1996; Bliss et al. 1997). In addition, studies of the general population have shown that the public increasingly values forests for wildland and amenity values rather than for production of timber and pulp. American society values its forests for recreation, habitat for wildlife, scenic vistas, and protection of streams and water (Rudzitis and Johansen 1991; Shindler et al. 1993; Mather 2002; Tarrant and Cordell 2002; Tarrant et al. 2003). Watson (1975) examined real estate advertisements in papers in Philadelphia, Harrisburg, and Pittsburgh for properties in Potter County, Pennsylvania, in the north-central highlands of the state. To attract buyers, such descriptive phrases as "at the end of a forest road," "by a sparkling stream," "lies along the boundary of a state forest," and "in a secluded woodland," were used. To clearcut such areas would destroy the very values for which they were purchased—that is, the environmental quality under the forest canopy, which even some form of selective cutting might markedly degrade.

Sparse evidence for earlier years makes it difficult to chart stages in the evolution of these values and perceptions. The main value of the forest in the nineteenth century lay in its wood and the resulting cleared land, which could be farmed. When timber extraction first began in earnest in the Lake States in the 1850s, timber was essential not only for local development but also to stimulate regional and national development. The timber of the Lake States, used for railways, housing, tools, and machinery, fueled the agricultural development of the rich but timberless Plains States region as well as the growing metropolis of Chicago (Mahaffey 1978; Nesbit and Thompson 1989; Cronon 1991). While extraction dominated the landscape during the second half of the nineteenth century, the birth of the movement towards valuing wildlands for recreation can be traced to the turn of the twentieth century. By the early twentieth century the lakes regions of the cutover had become tourist destinations and in some areas the summer-resort industry played an important economic role in local economies by the early 1920s (Murphy 1931; Gough 1997). Despite these early recreational uses of the forests, permanent habitation provided little conceptual space for the permanent role of the canopied forest, let alone sustained and continuous wood production.

At the turn of the twentieth century agriculture was assumed to be the natural successor to the clearing of the forests, the "plow following the axe." But the dreams of establishing agriculture in the region were not to be realized due to a number of factors including poor soils, a short growing season, the costs and difficulty of clearing the land, and poor transportation infrastructure to deliver agricultural goods to markets (Murphy 1931; Mahaffey 1978; Barlowe 1983; Gough 1997). The collapse of agriculture peaked in the 1920s and 1930s and coincided with the abandonment of vast amounts of land by timber interests, leaving millions of acres of land tax delinquent. In 1927 alone there were 2.5 million acres of tax-delinquent land in the seventeen northern counties of Wisconsin (Carstensen 1958; Mahaffey 1978; Gough 1997). During the 1930s large amounts of land reverted to public ownership at the county, state, and federal levels. Wisconsin alone now has over two million acres of county forests, the vast majority of which lie in the northern third of the state (Orleman 1997). In Wisconsin, public ownership was supplemented by other efforts at developing the north through reforestation, fire fighting and prevention, and rural zoning (Carstensen 1958).

Despite these efforts, the struggle over tax-delinquent and tax-reverted lands between 1900 and 1930 involved intense controversies over the agricultural possibilities of the formerly forested land; the hope that it could sustain a high level of farming and support farm communities died hard. Opposition to forestry efforts was vehement at times from the "north." Many felt that forests prevented development, did not pay taxes, and therefore hurt local governments (Carstensen 1958). In addition, many northerners felt that foresters did nothing but serve the interests of the summer people who vacationed in the area; they accused foresters of wanting to turn the region into ". . . a home for the wild animals and a playground for the idle rich of the great cities . . . " (*News North*, May 24, 1912 as cited in Carstensen 1958, p. 49). In Michigan, where the lands reverted to the state, local communities exerted considerable pressure to put them back on the market so that farming could be tried again (Schmaltz 1972). Out of this agonizing debate slowly emerged the view that the forest provided the only potential for a sustained economy, that stability in the long-run flow of wood production would provide relief from the uncertainties of marginal agriculture.

Over the decades there were vast changes in the significance of these wildlands to the people who experienced them. In the nineteenth century they were a raw material for extraction, as people looked beyond the forest to the agricultural lands they hoped would provide permanent homes. In the decades from 1910 to 1945 these lands were unwanted, retained in public ownership, protected, and regenerated by public agencies because of their rapid decline in value to the private economy. But other meanings and uses were being implanted even in those years, and they emerged in the decades after World War II. The lands that nobody wanted became the lands that many people wanted. The value of wood production fell. Real estate values tell the tale—if land competed both for wood production and for environmental amenities such as a vacation home, the latter brought a far higher price. The shift in market values, as contrasted with private values, from the 1920s to the end of the century is a measure of the depth of the transformation in perceptions that had begun a century and a half previously.

An indication of the shift in forest values has been the high levels of population growth and second-home development experienced throughout the forested regions of the northern Lake States since the mid 1960s. The once cleared, or "cutover," region is now largely reforested due to public and private reforestation efforts and large blocks of public land ownership. The forests and abundance of lakes throughout the region have drawn a rising population of second-homeowners, retirees, and those seeking out smaller communities and a rural lifestyle (see Marcouiller et al. 1996; Hammer et al. 1999). In addition, the parts of the northern forests that are accessible to large metropolitan areas like Minneapolis-St. Paul have drawn another group of migrants—commuters. Critical to this regional revival has been the changing general perception of forests and other natural amenities, from a resource to be extracted and used for development to an amenity that is enjoyed and intrinsically valued for its existence, beauty, and recreational opportunities. This shift in public values has also impacted land management by the forest industry. As land has become more valued for its amenity values many corporations have begun selling off blocks of land for residential development (Fantle 2002; Plum Creek 2003).

Evolution of Management Perspectives

Shifting our focus from the evolution of public values with respect to wildlands to those of the people who manage the forest, it is apparent that human choice is still very much a factor—choices made by business entrepreneurs and corporate managers, and by administrators in private and public forest agencies. Central to such management are the managers themselves, but there are an increasing number of technical and professional experts upon whom managers rely for needed skills— scientists, economists, and planners. Forest managerial systems today bring together these skills under single centers of control.

It was not always this way. In the nineteenth century, when extraction of raw materials was the dominant use of the land, individual entrepreneurs made their mark in the Great Lakes states. There are numerous examples of enterprising people who saw a good thing, invested, built mills, and shipped lumber; some established manufacturing plants to utilize the raw material. During this time the timber industry became vertically integrated in order to control costs, from the mills, to the transport systems, to landownership. Men such as Frederick Weyerhaeuser consolidated timber businesses and developed associations in order to control prices and insure profits (Gates 1943; Maybee 1960; Barlowe 1983; Nesbit and Thompson 1989). The cost of timber was low and the investment small relative to the size of the operation. All this enterprise was short term, for long-term management was a concept of the future. Entrepreneurial control, over both wood production and the communities dependent on it, was not part of a long-term, continuously evolving process. The entrepreneurs did not want the land, only the lumber; they were experts in extraction, not land management. Once the timber was cleared, they either abandoned the land, allowing it to revert to the state as tax-delinquent, or sold it to would-be farmers. Timber companies, joined at times by local and state officials, touted the cleared forest lands of the north for their agricultural potential to would-be settlers in the eastern United States and even Europe. Even the dean of the College of Agriculture of the University of Wisconsin, William Henry, promoted the region. His report, *A Handbook for the Homeseeker*, provided glowing accounts of agricultural opportunities and settlement in all of northern Wisconsin. Hard work would lead to boundless prosperity to the industrious settler in the north, claimed the boosters (Carstensen 1958; Mahaffey 1978; Barlowe 1983; Reinhardt 1983; Nesbit and Thompson 1989). Unfortunately, the conditions of the north led to only temporary institutions and little cumulative acquisition of capital and skills. One can speak of the rise and fall of individual entrepreneurs, but, even more important, of the rise and fall of private exploitation as a phase in the long course of Great Lakes forest history.

A few enterprises became the beginnings of more intensive and permanent wood-production management systems. But, unlike iron and copper mining, there was little continuity in wood production. The private wood-production institutions declined and into this vacuum came other, more permanent, public wildlands management. Private entrepreneurs, for the most part, abdicated, and when they returned with greater long-run purpose in the mid-twentieth century they had to return on different terms. These new public forest management systems—county, state, and federal—came first as protectors of a resource that had been depleted in dramatic fashion and then left as orphan land. Unattended, this land became a great fire hazard. Reforestation and protection against fire came to be the major themes of management; slowly and carefully a depleted resource was restored. A breed of caretakers evolved who were distinctive for their time and place, whose training was in the woods, and whose accumulated personal experience gave them an authoritative wisdom about how to protect what they personally knew. They did not exactly welcome the new stage of more technical and complex management that was to come.

After World War II came the era of intensive forest management; both the drive for wood production and the public demand for more forest uses grew rapidly. Management shifted from a protective and custodial approach to greater investments of money and skills to achieve more intensive outputs. Private timber companies preferred a limited set of objectives dominated almost exclusively by wood production, with other uses such as wildlife, recreation, and environmental amenities considered low priorities. Hence they extended their corporate holdings and geared up for continuous and more intensive high-yield fiber growth. The management of public lands involved increasingly varied objectives and uses, which accelerated rapidly over the years from beginnings early in the century, through the expansion of access to the countryside which the automobile stimulated in the 1920s, to the flood of users who came with rising leisure and high-speed highways after World War II. In response, public forest managers adopted a more intensive approach to wildlands resources. These were inventoried and described more precisely; systems of land classification became more intricate, with such elaborations as water-influence and travel-influence zones, natural areas, and wilderness. Specific uses were confined to specific lands.

But one imperative remained primary—to grow trees and harvest wood (Bultena and Hendee 1972). For many years the elementary systems of gathering and classifying information about the forest had been based on that objective. Wildlands were described in terms not of the interaction of species in an ecosystem, but of the standing timber they contained. Despite the growing demands from other types of forest users, the fundamental way in which the forest was thought of, described, and classified remained heavily influenced by a traditional, dominant concern for wood production.

The management system that evolved after World War II was even-age or area management. This approach grew out of the need to develop a simplified method of regulating the flow of products within the forest. Each area was considered as a single unit, one data point, with a volume figure attached to it; it was measured to determine growth, cut as a unit, and regenerated as a unit. The product flow from start to finish was vastly simplified for managers. Area management could be carried out with skills that did not require experience in the woods; it used forest accountants who could quantify the output, computerize the data, and program the resulting manipulations.

Inventory description by aerial photography was developed as a time-saving alternative to on-the-ground measurement.

At the same time, however, the values of the public regarding the meaning and use of forests were changing rapidly. This change in values took place in a realm that was, for the most part, beyond the immediate experience of forest managers; its intensity caught them by surprise. Trained in older ways and accustomed to more traditional objectives and values, public and private managers grew apprehensive as aesthetic and recreational demands on the nations' wildlands increased. Forest managers opposed an expanded national park system, wilderness designations, and wild and scenic rivers, all of which threatened to make inroads into the uses of forestlands for wood production. Frequently, their opposition was ideological, based more on a perceived threat to their values than on an actual decrease in wood production.

The different perspectives of manager and environmental user, one shaped by the efficient manipulation of a resource for wood production and the other by the aesthetic appreciation of wildlands experiences, have continually come into conflict since World War II. One result has been an increase in the variety of skills required for public forest management. No longer do professionals come overwhelmingly from the field of wood production, although these still make up the majority.

There has also been a marked increase in the contribution of scientific and technical information to forest planning and management. For years the transfer of new forest-planning policies into management decisions was often slow, especially if it challenged established policy. From the very start of public involvement in management decisions in the 1950s, one of the most significant citizen strategies was to absorb the ideas in publications of forestry experiment stations, the literature in professional journals, and the research of forestry schools, and to bring them to bear on management decisions. In numerous hearings, information meetings, and environmental impact analyses, forest managers were forced to confront new knowledge. They were faced with a science information transfer vigorously conducted by citizens and facilitated by the new group of professionals in management itself, who were younger, fresh from forestry school, and more eager than their elders to bring the latest in forest science to their tasks. Over time the agency and its personnel have undergone evolutionary change. The U.S. Forest Service is now a much more diverse organization, both professionally and in terms of the educational background of its employees. Paralleling these changes in staffing have been changes in the beliefs and values of Forest Service personnel. While many still believe that the Forest Service currently places its highest priority on traditional commodity production, most personnel, especially newer and younger personnel, see themselves and the public as more supportive of non-commodity values such as recreation, wilderness, and other amenities (Cramer et al. 1993).

Changes in management systems, philosophy, and personnel represent a profound paradigm shift in forest management. The predominant management philosophy for public lands is commonly referred to as "ecosystem management," a management style that focuses more on ecological health and sustainability than on commodity production. The general objective of ecosystem management is to manage for the integrity, vitality, and resilience of the ecosystem. Ecosystem management further recognizes that management must encompass large land areas defined by ecological boundaries rather than legal or political boundaries. This necessitates collaboration and collective decision making among a broad array of social and political stakeholders (Grumbine 1994; Christensen et al. 1996; Cortner and Moote 1999; Yaffee 1999). This represents a profound shift from the philosophy of sustained-yield management, which emphasizes products and outputs, to a management philosophy that emphasizes future states and conditions, biological diversity, and ecological functions and processes.

With this shift, three themes have emerged: a concern for the health of ecosystems; a preference for both landscape-scale and decentralized management; and demands for a new kind of public participation that integrates civic discourse into decision making (Cortner and Moote 1999). Ecosystem management is as much about social and political process and conditions as it is about ecological processes and conditions. It is about changes in the ways in which society views and values forests and natural resources, the ways in which society manages these resources, and the manner in which management choices and decisions are made. It is about coordination, cooperation, and collective decision making because ecosystems and ecoregions are rarely, if ever, owned and managed by a single landowner (Cortner and Moote 1999).

Community Choices

There is a third set of choices we should examine, coming from an altogether different vantage point—the local community. Debate over wildlands policies often involves people far beyond the local community—business corporations whose headquarters and stockholders are established far away, public lands managers located at distant state and national capitals, and wildland users, both actual and vicarious, who most often live in the major metropolitan centers remote from forestlands. But ultimately these debates deal with specific uses of specific lands in specific communities. Located amid the wildlands, these communities have their own perceptions, values, and choices with respect to the forests around them. What have those choices been?

In the raw-material-extraction phase of the history of the Great Lakes forest, these communities were almost wholly an adjunct to the extractive economy. They provided its labor and they serviced it. They came and went as the entrepreneurs and their timber came and went. Lumber and mill towns were spread throughout the North Country, rising and failing with the fortunes of the economic firms on which they depended. A review of this phase of community history finds a sense of fatalism in that era, a realization that the raw material in the woods would not last forever. At the same time, however, there was an intense preoccupation with the current moment of economic success, without much looking ahead. Perhaps a farming economy would follow, but there was no clear plan of action. When the mills collapsed, it was seen as the natural order of things. No one expected permanent communities to endure in the rush to provide the raw material needs of the burgeoning cities to the south.

The years from 1910 to 1945 were equally insecure for communities throughout the North Country. Several attempts were made over time to build communities on the basis of agriculture, and the limited agrarian economy provided short-lived hope during the prosperous farming years before 1920, but poor soils ultimately led to failure. In the nineteenth century, one could become resigned to the fact that timber would disappear as the foundation for sustained community growth, but it was difficult to believe that the soil provided no firmer foundation. When agriculture collapsed with a vengeance in the 1920s, local communities grudgingly opted for permanent county, state, and federal ownership of tax-reverted land.

The cutover lands of the Great Lakes states represented one of the most severe political problem areas of the 1920s and the New Deal—a legacy of the first century of development, from the 1840s to the 1940s, when the forest rarely served as a basis for building sustained communities. The years after World War II were vastly different. The forestlands became an integral part of the new economy of the Great Lakes region. In a few communities, wood production provided an important base; but in many more the main asset of the forest lay in its role as an environment for home, work, and play in the new economy of recreation, leisure, travel, and tourism. One is struck by the degree to which specific forest landmarks such as Hartwick Pines or the jack-pine home of Kirtland's warbler have become distinctive objects of identification for their nearby communities, or the way in which such areas have become vital to agencies that promote travel and tourism. The entire northern third of the state of Wisconsin is an icon of forests and wildlands: "To many residents, northern Wisconsin is more than a place to live; it is a chosen landscape, a place with a distinctive character that inspires affection—clean water, extensive forests, access to land, natural beauty, serenity, abundant fish and wildlife" (Wisconsin Department of Natural Resources 1996). Of equal importance with tourism and recreation is the attractiveness of forest areas to young people seeking a pleasant environment for home and livelihood and older people seeking amenities for retirement. The environmental quality of forest areas, relatively unspoiled and undeveloped, has been a major reason for their recent settlement, and it has given rise to demands that the forest be managed to enhance those amenities rather than to compromise them (Nelson and Dueker 1990; Cromartie 1998; Rudzitis 1999).

Of current concern in many of these areas is the role of local communities in environmental and natural resources management, a role that is now emphasized. Many suggest that community-based solutions result in improved resource management and resource conditions, improved social and economic conditions, and increasingly democratic decision making (Agrawal and Gibson 1999; Cortner and Moote 1999; Wondoleck and Yaffee 2000; Brick et. al. 2001; Swanson 2001). Many examples of community-based, collaborative management solutions have been documented across the country including the Quincy Library Group (QLG) in northern California. The QLG successfully integrated input from timber interests, local environmentalists, local citizens, and representatives of local government to create a management plan for three national forests (Marston 2001). Similarly, the Malpai Borderlands Conservancy exemplifies community-based and collaborative management that transcends boundaries and extends beyond public lands. The Malpai Borderlands Conservance encompasses nearly one million acres of both public and private land in southwest New Mexico and southeast Arizona. This is a successful collaborative management effort between private ranchers, state and federal agencies, and the Nature Conservancy. Similar collaborative efforts have been tried in the Lake States as well. One such effort is in the Pine Barrens region of northwestern Wisconsin where local, state, and national interests have tried to create a "comprehensive interagency landscape-scale management plan" for a 1,500-square-mile region (Borgerding et al. 1995; Northwest Regional Planning Commission 2000).

There are often clear differences of opinion in a community on environmental issues. Several studies have indicated a marked difference within communities between the attitudes of political and economic leaders on the one hand, and the general public on the other. The former are more interested in rising levels of population, jobs, real estate values, and taxes, while the latter are far more concerned with environmental quality. In addition, the population of rural communities experiencing population growth may also be divided over issues related to the environment; new residents often favor environmental protection and preservation while long-term residents favor economic development (see Smith and Krannich 2000 for a review). Community opinion can be further clouded when there are large numbers of seasonal and recreational homeowners; in these areas seasonal residents have been found to be more supportive of environmental conservation than their year-round counterparts (Green et al. 1996).

In the competition between environmental and developmental forces to shape decisions about forested wildlands, there is considerable emphasis on the relative political jurisdiction of community, state, and federal authority. For the most part, local communities seek to protect the quality of their environment by means of local zoning actions to ward off the adverse effects of development. This is supplemented by action against specific large-scale projects, which have usually been initiated from outside the community or the state, such as nuclear or coal-fired electric generating plants, and waste-disposal sites or incinerators. In previous decades such development went forward with little opposition. Now it is seriously questioned, a reflection of the changed value and meaning of forested areas to the general public. Those advocating large-scale development seek to shift the location of decision making upward to the state and federal levels to override this opposition from local communities. Large-scale private enterprise has steadily advocated more federal power and authority in such matters to overcome objections from communities concerned with their own quality of life.

The relationship between local communities and external groups concerned with environmental quality is more mixed. Environmental groups often seek the creation of programs such as federal wilderness and wild and scenic rivers and state protection for wildlands from more intensive development. Often this leads to local opposition when it appears that these programs will create an influx of recreationists who will interfere with local patterns of life and degrade the environment with litter, noise, and crowds, or when such actions reduce local property-tax revenues. Yet the common interest of both groups in maintaining high levels of environmental quality often leads to effective cooperation after initial suspicions are overcome. Environmentalists from outside the community defend local authority in the wildlands, depending in pragmatic fashion upon the degree to which environmental quality objectives can be met.

These relationships are a product of the years after World War II. In earlier times less-complex demands came from local communities as they simply called upon state governments to aid them in their economic distress, to acquire and manage forestlands, and to put an economic floor under their communities. We are now in a period of history when these lands are highly desired, their use is subject to intense competition, and the competitive pressures represent different values. One can find enormous variations among communities in the North Country on this score. Some seek rapid economic development and population growth; others emphasize environmental amenities. Within the same community one can find similar divergent tendencies. The context has changed from an emphasis on relationships between dominant and dependent regions to one on conflict between political forces within the north country itself.

Conclusion

The history of human choices in the Great Lakes forest has gone through several distinct stages, which have been especially dramatic since World War II, as an advanced industrial society has taken shape in the United States. New perceptions regarding the role and meaning of forests have arisen that emphasize forests as an environment for home, work, and play rather than as a source of commodities. While management systems, with strong and deep roots in the earlier commitments of scientific and professional foresters to wood production, have responded to these changing values slowly and often with strong and bitter resistance, they are evolving and adopting more ecosystem-based management programs. At the same time, the forest community has changed markedly, absorbing many of the new environmental values and expressing them in community quality vis-à-vis many adverse influences from both within and without. As rural areas rich in wildlands and amenities continue to grow in population and homes, traditional resource extraction is likely to continue to decline in importance as a forest management goal. With increasing numbers of seasonal homes, retirees, and amenity migrants, the forests of the upper Lake States become increasingly valued for their amenities—as a place to recreate, to relax, and to escape from urban areas. This phenomenon is even more apparent for areas that are proximate to major urban areas such as Minneapolis-St. Paul as more commuters leave the city and relocate to the forest wildlands. The rise of the post-productivist countryside marks the fall of the extractive forest.

These are the current conditions highlighted by historical analysis and upon which future policy must be firmly based. If there is historical guidance to our current task of formulating forest policy, it can be found not in the remote past but in the massive changes in human perceptions of the forest that have taken place during the past forty years.

References

Agrawal, Arun, and Clark C. Gibson. 1999. "Enchantment and Disenchantment: The Role of Community in Natural Resource Conservation." *World Development* 27(4): 629-49.

American Forest Institute. 1977. Research Recap #10. Washington, DC.

Barlowe, Raleigh. 1983. "Changing Land Use and Policies: The Lake States." In *The Great Lakes Forest: An Environmental and Social History*. Susan L. Flader (ed.), Minneapolis: University of Minnesota Press.

Bengston, D. N. 1994. "Changing Forest Values and Ecosystem Management." *Society and Natural Resources* 7: 513-33).

Birch, T. J. 1996. "Private Forest-landowners in the United States – 1994." USDA-Forest Service Resource Bulletin NE-134. Northeastern Forest Experiment Station, Radnor, PA. 183p.

Bliss, John C., Sunil K. Nepal, Robert T. Brooks Jr., and Max D. Larson. 1997. "In the Mainstream: Attitudes of Mid-South Forest Owners." *Southern Journal of Applied Forestry* 21(1): 37-43.

Bordgerding, E.A., G. A. Bartelt, and W. M. Cowen, eds. 1995. "The future of the Pine Barrens in Northwest Wisconsin: a workshop summary." Solon Springs, WI, 21-23 Sept. 1993. Wisconsin Department of Natural Resources, Madison.

Bourke, Lisa, and A. E. Luloff. 1994. "Attitudes toward the Management of Nonindustrial Private Forest Land." *Society and Natural Resources* 7: 445-57.

Brick, Philip. 2001. Of imposters, optimists and kings: finding a political niche for collaborative conservation. In *Across the Great Divide: Explorations in Collaborative Conservation and the American West*. Philip Brick, Donald Snow, and Sarah Van De Weteing (eds), Washington, DC: Island Press.

Brunson, M. W., D. T. Yarrow, S. D. Roberts, D. C. Guynn, Jr., and M. R. Kuhns. 1996. "Nonindustrial Private Forest Owners and Ecosystem Management: Can They Work Together?" *Journal of Forestry* 94(6): 14-21.

Bultena, G. L., and J. C. Hendee. 1972. "Foresters' Views of Interest Group Positions on Forest Policy." *Journal of Forestry* 60:337-42.

Campbell, Susan M., and David B. Kittredge. 1996. "Ecosystem Management on Multiple NIPF Ownerships." *Journal of Forestry* 94(2): 24-29.

Carstensen, Vernon. 1958. Farms or Forests: Evolution of a State Land Policy for Northern Wisconsin, 1850-1932. University of Wisconsin, College of Agriculture, Madison.

Christensen, N. L., Ann M. Bartuska, James H. Brown, Stephen Carpenter, Carla D'Antonio, Robert Francis, Jerry F. Franklin, James A. MacMahon, Reed F. Noss, David J. Parsons, Charles H. Peterson, Monica G. Turner and Robert G. Woodmansee. 1996. "The Report of the Ecological Society of America Committee on the Scientific Basis for Ecosystem Management." *Ecological Applications* 6(3): 665-91.

Cortner, Hanna J., and Margaret A. Moote. 1999. *Politics of Ecosystem Management*. Washington, DC: Island Press.

Cramer, Lori A., James J. Kennedy, Richard S. Krannich, and Thomas M. Quigley. 1993. "Changing Forest Service Values and their Implications for Land Management Decisions Affecting Resource Dependent Communities." *Rural Sociology* 58(3): 475-91.

Cromartie, John B. 1998. "Net Migration in the Great Plains Increasingly Linked to Natural Amenities and Suburbanization." *Rural Development Perspectives* 13(1): 27-34.

Cronon, William C. 1991. *Nature's Metropolis: Chicago and the Great West.* New York: W. W. Norton.

Fantle, Will. 2002. "For Sale! Timber Companies Are Unloading Pristine Northern Wisconsin Forest Land at an Alarming Rate." *Isthmus* (November 15): 13-15.

Freudenburg, William R., Scott Frickell, and Robert Gramling. 1995. "Beyond the Nature/Society Divide: Learning to Think about a Mountain." *Sociological Forum* 10(3): 361-92.

Frey, William H., and Kenneth M. Johnson. 1998. "Concentrated Immigration, Restructuring and the 'Selective' Deconcentration of the United States Population." P. 79-106 in P. Boyle and K. Halfacree (eds), *Migration into Rural Areas: Theories and Issues.* New York: John Wiley and Sons.

Gates, Paul. 1965. *The Wisconsin Pine Lands of Cornell University.* Ithaca, NY: Cornell University Press.

Gough, Robert. 1997. *Farming the Cutover: A Social History of Northern Wisconsin, 1900-1940.* Lawrence: University Press of Kansas.

Green, G.P., D. Marcouiller, S. Deller, D. Erkkila, and N. Sumathi. 1996. "Local Dependency, Land Use Attitudes, and Economic Development: Comparisons between Seasonal and Permanent Residents." *Rural Sociology* 61(3): 227-45.

Greider, Thomas, and Lorraine Garkovich. 1994. "Landscapes: The Social Construction of Nature and the Environment." *Rural Sociology* 59: 1-24.

Grumbine, E. R. 1994. "What Is Ecosystem Management?" *Conservation Biology* 8(1): 27-38.

Halfacree, Keith. 1997. "Contrasting Roles for the Post-productivist Countryside." P. 70-93 in Paul Cloke and J. Little (eds.), *Contested Countryside Cultures.* New York: Routledge.

Halfacree, Keith, and Paul Boyle. 1998. "Migration, Rurality and the Post-productivist countryside." P. 1-20 in P. Boyle and K. Halfacree (eds), *Migration Into Rural Areas: Theories and Issues.* New York: John Wiley and Sons.

Hammer, R. B., Hagen, A. E., and P. R. Voss. 1999. Approximating geographic patterns of residential development during the past half century and forecasting future trends: are Wisconsin's North Woods disappearing? Paper presented at the Annual Meetings of the Southern Demographic Association/International Conference of Applied Demography. San Antonio, Texas. Oct 28.

Johnson, K., and G. Fuguitt. 2000. "Continuity and Change in Rural Migration Patterns, 1950-1995." *Rural Sociology* 65(1): 27-49.

Mahaffey, Charles G. 1978. Changing images of the cutover: a historical geography of resource utilization in the Lake Superior region, 1840-1930. Ph.D. Dissertation, University of Wisconsin-Madison.

Marcouiller, D. W., G. P. Green, S. C. Deller, N. R. Sumathi, and D. L. Erkkila. 1996. Recreational Homes and Regional Development. Madison: University of Wisconsin-Extension Report no. G3651.

Marston, Ed. 2001. "The Quincy Library Group: A Divisive Attempt at Peace. In Philip Brick, Donald Snow, and Sarah Van De Weteing (eds.), *Across the Great Divide: Explorations in Collaborative Conservation and the American West.* Washington, DC: Island Press.

Mather, A. S. 2001. "Forests of Consumption: Postproductivism, Postmaterialism, and the Postindustrial Forest. Environment and Planning C." *Government and Policy* 19:249-68.

McGranahan, D. 1999. Natural Amenities Drive Rural Population Change. Agricultural Economic Report Number 781.

Maybee. R. H. 1960. Michigan's While Pine Era, 1840-1900. Lansing: Michigan Historical Commission.

Milbrath, L. W. 1977. "An Extra Dimension of Representation in Water Quality Planning: A Survey Study of Erie and Niagara Counties, New York, 1976." Buffalo: State University of New York, interim report.

Murphy, Raymond E. 1931. "The Geography of the Northwestern Pine Barrens of Wisconsin." *Transactions of the Wisconsin Academy of Science, Arts and Letters* 26: 96-120.

Nelson, A. C., and K. J. Dueker. 1990. "The Exurbanization of America and its Planning Policy Implications." *Journal of Planning Education and Research* 9(2): 91-100.

Nesbit, Robert C., and William F. Thompson. 1989. *Wisconsin: A History.* Madison: University of Wisconsin Press.

Northwest Regional Planning Commission and Wisconsin Department of Natural Resources. 2000. Northwest Sands Landscape Level Management Plan. Pub-SS-953 2001. Madison: Wisconsin Department of Natural Resources.

Opinion Research Corporation. 1977. The Public's Participation in Outdoor Activities and Attitudes Toward National Wilderness Areas. Princeton, NJ.

Orlemann, Andrew. 1997. County Forest Management and Planning in Wisconsin. Master's Thesis, University of Wisconsin, Madison.

Plum Creek. 2003. Real Estate – Plum Creek Timber: Growing Value from Exceptional Resources. Retrieved August 26, 2003 from: http://www.plumcreek.com/realestate.

Reinhardt, Hazel. 1983. "Social Adjustments to a Changing Environment." In Susan L. Flader (ed.), *The Great Lakes Forest: An Environmental and Social History.* Minneapolis: University of Minnesota Press.

Rudzitis, G. 1999. "Amenities Increasingly Draw People to the Rural West." *Rural Development Perspectives* 14(2): 9-13.

Rudzitis, G. and H. E. Johansen 1991. "How Important is Wilderness? Results from a United States Survey." *Environmental Management* 15(2): 227-33.

Schmaltz, N. J. 1972. "Cutover Land Crusade: The Michigan Forest Conservation Movement, 1899-193 1" Ph.D. dissertation, University of Michigan.

Shindler, Bruce, Peter List, and Brent S. Steel. 1993. "Managing Federal Forests: Public Attitudes in Oregon and Nationwide." *Journal of Forestry* 91(7): 36-42.

Sierra Club. 1980. National News Report, March 7. San Francisco, CA.

Smith, Michael D., and Richard S. Krannich. 2000. " 'Culture Clash' Revisited: Newcomer and Longer-term Residents' Attitudes towards Land Use, Development and Environmental Issues in Rural Communities in the Rocky Mountain West." *Rural Sociology* 65(3): 396-421.

Swanson, Louis E. 2001. "Rural Policy and Direct Local Participation: Democracy, Inclusiveness, Collective Agency, and Locality-based Policy." *Rural Sociology* 66(1): 1-21.

Tarrant, Michael A., and H. Ken Cordell. 2002. "Amenity Values of Public and Private Forests: Examining the Value-attitude Relationship." *Environmental Management* 30(5): 692-703.

Tarrant, Michael A., H. Ken Cordell, and Gary T. Green. 2003. "PVF: A Scale to Measure Public Values of Forests." *Journal of Forestry* 101(6): 24-30.

Watson, M. K. 1975. "Behavior and Environmental Aspects of Recreational Land Sales." Ph.D. dissertation, Pennsylvania State University.

Wisconsin Department of Natural Resources. 1996. Northern Wisconsin's Lakes and Shorelands: A Report Examining a Resource under Pressure.

Wondolleck, J. M., and S. L. Yaffee. 2000. *Making Collaboration Work: Lessons from Innovation in Natural Resource Management.* Washington DC: Island Press.

Yaffee, Steven L. 1999. "Three Faces of Ecosystem Management." *Conservation Biology* 13(4): 713-25.

CHAPTER 6
Toward the Stabilization and Enrichment of a Forest Community

Harold F. Kaufman and Lois C. Kaufman

Editors' Preface

This chapter is a condensed version of a report with the same title prepared for the Montana Study in 1946. The Montana Study was an effort by the University of Montana to better understand rural communities so that their persistence and development could be facilitated. It was directed by Baker Brownell, Professor of Philosophy at Northwestern University on leave at the University of Montana. Brownell hired Harold and Lois Kaufman to study two adjacent timber-dependent communities in Montana: Libby and Troy. The best introduction to their report is an exchange of letters between A. G. Lindh, Assistant Regional Forester in Lincoln County, Montana, and Brownell.

These letters only hint at the sensitive nature of a study that examines the actions of a resource management agency. What the letters do not reveal is the extent to which the report sacrificed independent scholarship to the interests of maintaining a spirit of cooperation with the U.S. Forest Service. Many issues identified in the report could have been examined in greater depth had the study been done under different auspices.

The constraints land management agencies place on research are as much a concern today as they were in the 1940s. Organizational prerogatives and myths are still threatened by facts—especially by facts that limit policy options for expressing the core values of an organization. Primary emphasis on wood production was long the central concern of the U.S. Forest Service, with issues of community stability or development secondary to "getting the wood out." The U.S. Forest Service's orientation toward timber was evident in the lack of subsequent interest in any empirical sociological studies of forest-dependent communities; there was no follow-up to the Kaufmans' study. Moreover, examination of communities was discouraged in many regions—especially on the Tongass National Forest in Southeast Alaska where congressionally mandated acceleration of timber harvesting was later adopted to maintain "community stability."

For these reasons, sociologists studying natural resource systems are as interested in formal land management organizations as they are in communities that depend on lands managed by these agencies. To implement the holistic framework for sociological study identified by Firey in Chapter 2, investigations must look at how communities depend on large formal organizations as much as, or more than, they depend on land-based resources. The Kaufmans only hint at this important implication. Yet it deserves emphasis as an additional theme cutting across the papers in this volume.

Exchange of Letters Between Lindh and Brownell

August 30, 1946

Dear Mr. Brownell:

After many delays, we have finished mimeographing the report by Dr. Harold F. Kaufman and Dr. Lois C. Kaufman, entitled, "Toward the Stabilization and Enrichment of a Forest Community." I am delivering an advance copy of the report to you with this letter.

In looking back over the two years during which we have jointly considered first, the problem of having the study made, the second, the job of getting the report out, it appears that the Forest Service owes you a large debt of gratitude for your leadership and patient counsel. Please accept the sincere appreciation of the Forest Service group which has responsibility for developing the forest management plan for the Lincoln County area.

I have one major criticism of the report by Dr. Kaufman. It is not intended to be a criticism of his work since I think he ably and honestly carried out the plan which was agreed upon. The criticism is this: by implication and by occasional statements throughout the report, it appears that the Forest Service has conducted its planning and the management of its timber in the Lincoln County area without due regard for the people of the several local communities. I believe that I am correct in interpreting the instructions and nationwide policies guiding the work of the Forest Service when I say that the human and community dependency side of timber management planning is receiving and will receive its full share of attention. Actually, in the past, the timber of the national forests of this region was not very much needed in the local and national economy since most of the timber was being harvested from private lands. Under those conditions, the Forest Service was grateful to have a few customers for ripe and overripe timber and the social and economic effect of national forest timber policy was small. Suddenly the timber of the national forests is needed since there is a shortage of timber in private ownership in many parts of the west as well as most of the east and south. With the growth of pressure on the national forests for maximum use of all sorts of timber and with the increased feeling of community dependency on dwindling timber being felt in most parts of the country, the job of planning the timber management and disposal policy on the national forests has become much more important, more difficult, and more fraught with conflicts between social objectives and economic obstacles. Under these new conditions, it may be considered that national forest timber management and disposal planning is in its infancy. It was with a realization of this that the Forest Service welcomed the cooperation of the Montana Study in opening up this opportunity to examine the human side of the timber planning job.

I could go through the report page by page and state the current Forest Service position. Some of this would involve criticism of our own past positions and in some instances it would involve criticism of Dr. Kaufman's conclusions from the existing facts. However, it appears that locally, within the immediate area concerned, more good will come from the study of the problems presented here prior to the publication of the details of the proposed timber management plan for the unit.

Frankly, the forest planners are still engaged in the basic job of shaping the forest management and timber disposal plans and have a number of unsolved major problems. Perhaps study of the Kaufman report by community and group leaders will result in the development of community plans and programs which will help solve some of the forest problems.

I would appreciate it if you would transmit a copy of this letter with a copy of the report to each of those to whom The Montana Study makes its distribution.

Very sincerely yours,

A.G. Lindh
Assistant Regional Forester, Division of Timber Management

August 31, 1946

Dear Mr. Lindh:

I have received your letter of August 30 along with the advance copy of the Kaufman report. I am glad to include a copy of your letter with the reports which we shall send out.

As I look over the final assembly of the report upon which so many of us have worked to a greater or less degree for many months, it seems to me nothing less than thrilling that the results of this pioneer work should shape up so well in the final form. May I congratulate you, particularly, and the Forest Service upon the magnificent cooperation which you have given us and upon your willingness to have us make an objective, critical report, let the chips fall where they may.

I have long known that the Forest Service, ever since its early days under Gifford Pinchot and Theodore Roosevelt, has been one of the most progressive and public-minded agencies in the United States. After my two years of close contact with the Forest Service in Montana during my work with the Montana Study, I am more than ever convinced that the Forest Service is motivated by a high interest in public welfare and in efficient management of timber resources in the United States, for the benefit both of the people of the country as a whole and of the communities located in the forest region. In fact, our project itself, in which you encouraged another and independent agency, the Montana

Study, to make an objective, critical report of the Lincoln County situation, is proof enough that the Forest Service is concerned primarily in the truth and public service.

In the work of this report, our directives to Dr. Kaufman were to record what he saw and heard in Lincoln County and to make his own, individual conclusions and recommendation as a thoughtful, public-minded individual concerned in the sociological and community problems of the region. By the nature of his report, he was limited to the interpretation of local conditions. If he found that the Forest Service policies and practices were believed to be bad by local people, it was his business to report it. Where this was the case, it is evident that either the policies and practices of the Forest Service were not understood or that the local application of them had not expressed the social attitude for which the Forest Service as a whole has long been known.

At best, the situation is a difficult one with the inevitable conflict between managerial efficiency and general public welfare. Even the wisest direction when confronted by concrete problems in the field is bound to make compromises or other types of decision which will not fully carry out these two important objectives. In the long (sic) and at long range I believe that these two objectives, efficiency and public welfare, will be identical but I realize that in the immediate problem it is often extremely difficult to decide to which one priority should be given without ruining the entire project by that decision.

It comes down eventually to a statement in your letter of the 30th, namely, that timber management policy, which must make use of the full national forest resources, is essentially a new problem. The pressure for maximum use of timber from the national forests is new. There are no basic precedents for handling this problem, particularly in relation to social and community adjustments. The Forest Service has had a fine record in this respect in regard to grazing lands, land tenure, recreation, and the like. I am confident that a similar record will be made in this newer field of use of national forest resources.

Meanwhile, it is inevitable that all parties to a sustained-yield program, with the present undeveloped policies and traditions in this field, will be subject to criticism. Some of that criticism probably is justified but I, for one, am confident that the Forest Service is the kind of agency that welcomes criticism and profits by it.

Sincerely,

Baker Brownell
Director, The Montana Study Professor of Philosophy
(on leave) Northwestern University

Introduction

The stabilization and enrichment of life in a forest community are broad social objectives. A pertinent question to ask is why stability is declared the objective of planning in a forest community. What is the meaning and what are the implications of this term? What specific projects and programs might be initiated in the community studied by which this objective might be realized? A discussion of these and related questions is the purpose of this report.

Of desirable community characteristics probably the one most conspicuous by its absence in forest areas has been that of stability. The exploitative timber industry has been a migrant one, having within a century and a half moved from one coast to the other. Consequently, the communities built around this industry have been noted for their instability; they have been either boom towns or ghost towns.

The boom town is characterized by a rapid increase in population, in employment, and in apparent wealth; by shortages of goods and services; and by social maladjustments. Social change rather than being orderly and planned is sporadic and haphazard. In the boom communities which are booming because of rapid liquidation of the forest resource, ghosts foretelling an unhappy future frequently lurk. These are the ghosts of an exhausted resource, of unemployment, of a declining population, and of empty and decaying buildings. With such a future in view, the incentive is lacking for building permanent houses and stores, and stable institutions and organizations. Rather the philosophy, "eat, drink, and be merry for tomorrow we may die," is more appropriate.

The Libby-Troy community is not only in an area in which the traditionally unstable forest industry is the dominant one, but this community is also in a state which during its history has known much instability. The Montana booms and depressions in mining, in livestock raising, and in dry farming are well known. Consequently, the question is pertinent as to whether a stable forest community in Montana can be realized.

Community Stability—What It Is and What It Is Not

The term community stability, as used here, does not imply a static condition, the absence of change, or the necessity of maintaining the status quo. The basic implication is orderly change rather than a fixed condition. Synonyms of stable are lasting, permanent, and durable. But for an institution to be lasting, especially in the modem world, it must gradually change to meet new conditions. For this reason the most stable type of community in the present day would probably be one in which there was orderly change toward given goals; those goals embracing "the good life" in whatever way that might be defined.

Community stability as the term is used here is a broad social objective. It is impossible to know all the principal answers, even for one small community. No blueprint is possible. Furthermore, in a democracy it should be the task of the people in the local community to determine finally their goals and procedures. All that is attempted in this short report is to suggest tentatively some approaches that should be considered and to indicate some problems that require solution if reasonable stability is to be gained in the Libby-Troy community.

As a community is made up of people living and working in a physical environment, there are of necessity several types of approaches to stabilizing the community. A three-fold classification is made here. (1) The land use approach. A rural community's survival is dependent on the conservation and wise use of its natural resources. (2) The industrial and employment approach. For the highest standard of living a community must have, among other things, efficient industries and it must provide adequate services. (3) The social welfare and organizational approach. From this point of view the satisfactions and interests of people and the organizations and institutions necessary for meeting their needs are considered. In order to see the community as a whole, all of the above approaches are needed. This report begins with a short description of the Libby-Troy community, and then considers possibilities for more efficient organization and expansion of industries, trades, and services.

It is significant that some of the major problems and trends in the Libby-Troy community are of nationwide importance. Chief of these are the conservation of natural resources, labor-management relationships, and the centralization of economic control.

The Forest Community

A community is composed of many elements, among them, the people, their material possessions, and the natural resources of the area. Attention is focused here on the relationships of people with each other and on their adjustment to their physical environment—the two-way relationship of people and natural resources.

Place and People

The Libby-Troy community is located in the west and south portions of Lincoln County, Montana. Lincoln County is in the extreme northwest corner of the state, and is bordered on the west by Idaho and on the north by British Columbia. The county has an area of approximately 3,750 square miles; the Libby-Troy community may be regarded as covering from two-thirds to three-fourths of the total area of the county. Ninety-seven percent of the land area in the county is in forest. This makes Lincoln County the first forest county in the state in terms of volume of timber.

In 1940 over 5,000 people lived in the Libby-Troy community; over 1,800 in the county-seat town of Libby and nearly 800 in the town of Troy. Five-sixths of the total population resided either in or relatively near these two centers.

Possibly two-thirds or more of the basic income of the area comes from the forest. The forest furnishes a livelihood for workers in sawmills and wood remanufacturing plants, in logging, and in the Forest Service. Other major sources of employment, but far below the forest in importance, are agriculture, the Great Northern Railroad, and mining. Agriculture in the area is limited because of soil, climate, and topography. Sale of beef cattle is the major source of cash income for farmers.

Indications of both stability and instability are found in the community. Signs of stability are found in the civic organizations, schools, and churches, all with a long history; in the attractive and well-built courthouse and city hall located in Libby; and in some substantial and attractive homes. Indices of instability are the temporary business structures, unkempt streets and sidewalks, and the many rather hastily constructed dwellings. This sense of impermanence is expressed by residents when they say, "You can't expect too much from a sawmill town.

Libby shows greater economic prosperity than Troy, largely because it has the two largest and most stable industries in the community— the Libby Mill and the Zonolite mining operation. The former employs approximately 500 to 600 workers at full capacity and the latter approximately 50 to 60. The population of Libby along with its economic activity has continued to increase over the years. Each decennial census beginning with 1910 shows a definite population increase in Libby and vicinity. On the other hand, Troy reached its zenith of industrial activity in the late 1920s when it was a division point on the railroad, had a medium-sized sawmill, and had some mining. Since then, these sources of employment have either markedly declined or disappeared entirely.

Stabilizing the Community

Although many forces and activities in the area are contributing to a more stable community, many real problems remain to be faced and solved. There is a need for trained leadership with vision, for widespread participation on the part of all groups, and for cooperative action toward common ends. The possible projects and programs that might be considered as promoting community stability are manifold. Attention is focused here, however, on ten strategic areas of the physical, economic, and social life of the community. These are:

(1) Developing a stable timber industry with the greatest possible remanufacturing.

(2) Practicing sustained yield forestry on timber lands and wise use of other natural resources.

(3) Promoting greater public participation in determining forest policy.

(4) Creating a more diversified and balanced economy.

(5) Securing adequate leadership in community affairs.

(6) Providing greater assistance to youth, especially with reference to vocation guidance and training in citizenship.

(7) Strengthening the rural home.

(8) Creating a more community-centered religious emphasis.

(9) Developing a forest-centered tradition.

(10) Organizing for united action of the greater Libby-Troy community.

Community Projects

The chief problems facing agricultural producers in the community are efficient production, better integration of part-time agriculture and outside employment, diversification of crops, and enlargement in the size of farms. As possibilities for profitable expansion in agriculture are decidedly limited, emphasis should be placed on improving the condition of those now farming rather than on increasing the number of farmers. Courses of action include a reconnaissance study that would classify agricultural land and determine profitable types of production and long-term educational and technical assistance programs. Resources available for the study include the State Agricultural College, the Forest Service, county government, and the farm organizations; while soil conservation district technical advisors, home agents, or a local agriculture committee could assist with educational programs and assistance.

Wise recreational planning is necessary for maximum economic returns from the tourist trade and for the greatest satisfaction to local residents. Such planning includes consideration of tourist facilities, roads, advertising, game and fish management, preservation of scenic beauties, and promoting community attractiveness. Civic organizations, like the Libby Chamber of Commerce and the Troy Development Association, might take the lead in working out a recreational program but many other groups, such as the Forest Service, providers of tourist accommodations, and groups interested in game and fish management and regional beautification, would also be involved.

Considerable study concerning the development of water resources in the area is being carried on by various federal agencies, with a possibility of action in the future. Thus, one or more civic organizations should assume responsibility (along with the local newspaper) of keeping the community informed on developments and encouraging public discussion so that when specific action is considered the community will be ready to take an intelligent stand with respect to it.

As part of the larger problem of the use of water resources, the desirability of public ownership of the water and electricity utilities in the community might well be considered.

In order to identify additional employment opportunities in trades, services, and industries and to provide information for planning the vocational program in the schools, a survey should be conducted jointly by the schools and civic organizations.

Farm and labor groups, among others, might well consider the formation of cooperative organizations to supply one or more types of services—e.g. groceries, petroleum products, farm supplies, credit (credit union), and electricity (REA).

Attention should focus on reducing the cost of public services in isolated areas. To this end a state zoning law is needed, but in the absence of such a law, local regulation of settlement in isolated areas can help.

A clean-up, paint-up, and build-up program for town and countryside might be initiated. This would include the removing of debris from vacant lots, demolition of unsafe and rundown buildings, the improvement of streets and sidewalks, and the beautification of homes. Civic organizations should take the leadership in such a campaign.

The building of a new, modern hospital would be an important step in improving health and medical care. There is also a real need in the Libby-Troy area for more extensive health education and more comprehensive medical care. Prepayment plans, an increase in the number of physicians, and the coordination of services in a hospital could play a part in improving the health of the community.

The citizenship training and vocational guidance and training functions of the school should be strengthened. The use of the school as a community center should be encouraged.

The county should cooperate with the Extension Service in bringing a home agent to the county. Leadership is badly needed in the field of homemaking and family life.

Cooperative endeavors of the churches in the area should be encouraged, as should the application of ethical principles and leadership to community problems.

A council representing the major organized groups in the greater Libby-Troy community should be established. The principal function of such a council would be to coordinate various programs and projects of community-wide concern.

The Forest Program

Major features of the forest utilization policy that have been evolving during the last ten years are (1) that the Libby-Troy area be operated as one sustained yield management unit and (2) that the Libby Mill be the major manufacturer of sawlogs and be sustained at a given level. Forest products not utilized by the Libby Mill have been available to other operators but there is no assurance as to the amounts. Planning for raw materials has been done for only one operator. During World War II, sawmills, at least those of any size, were discouraged from coming into the area, although operators were referred to other locations.

The present forest policy was well expressed in the "gentlemen's agreement" made in 1942 between the Forest Service and the Libby Mill. Under this arrangement, the Libby Mill agreed to selective cutting on their own lands and in return, the Forest Service would permit the mill to cut up to fifty-five million feet from the national forest.

An enabling act, Public Law 273, passed by Congress in 1944, makes it possible to give present forest policy legal status. This Act enables timber lands under the jurisdiction of the Secretary of Agriculture or of the Interior to be combined with reasonably large private holdings into one sustained yield management unit. In return for following desirable forestry practices the private cooperator is to be sold public timber without competitive bidding. The primary objective of the cooperative enterprises set up "under the Act is to obtain the community stability and other public benefits which flow from uninterrupted operations under a sustained yield management plan" (U.S. Forest Service, 1944).

Under this agreement, the national forest and the forest land of the Libby Mill in the Troy and Libby working circles would be combined in one management unit. It is to be proposed that of the eighty million feet estimated allowable cut the Libby Mill utilizes seventy million feet. Two-thirds of the latter amount will come from the national forest and one-third from the forests owned by the Libby Mill. National forest timber may be purchased by the Libby Mill at appraised value and without competition.

One function of this survey has been to sample community opinion with respect to the forest policy outlined in part above. Interviews of some length (up to several hours) were conducted with nearly 100 representative persons who had definite interest in forest policy. In addition, questionnaires on the forest program were filled out by nearly 450 individuals. In all, some expression of opinion on forest policy was obtained from probably one-sixth or one-seventh of the adult population. Business people in Libby were on the whole most favorable to the present forest program while the small timber operators (actual and potential) and Troy leaders were most unfavorable.

The public appeared to support overwhelmingly the principle of sustained yield in forest management, was less certain that it would be followed, and was deeply divided as to how national forest timber should be utilized. The chief merits of the present forest program as described by those interviewed were: (1) nearly nine-tenths of the timber in the area to be placed on sustained yield management basis; (2) the stabilizing of an efficient and community-minded operator (3) resulting in an industry which has the advantage of size; and (4) other administrative advantages. Major limitations and disadvantages were: (1) inordinate power in the timber industry to be given the private cooperator (in the agreement under Public Law 273); (2) undue social and political influence resulting from such a monopolistic position; (3) labor is disadvantaged; and (4) the stability of one community created at the expense of others.

It is most significant that arguments favoring present forest policy stress efficiency—industrial and administrative—while unfavorable arguments emphasize discrimination resulting from too much power given one group. Thus, the basic issue is not rapid liquidation of the forest resource versus sustained production but rather concerns the problem of protecting the public interest and distributing equitably the rewards from the forest. The analysis of community opinion suggests the two basic questions raised by this report. First, what type of industry in terms of type of product, size, and number of operators is most likely to survive in the area and to supply continuous and full employment? Second, with a given type of industrial organization, what controls are necessary to insure that the public interest is best served and that the welfare of the whole community is promoted?

Specific suggestions or recommendations as to forest policy include the following. Community stability is accepted as the long-term social goal. This broad aim comprises three elements or objectives with respect to forest policy: (1) the forest objective—the timber lands should be so managed that a continuous supply of forest products is available to the industries dependent upon them, (2) the industrial objective—the maximum of manufacturing possible within the limitations of raw materials, costs of production, and markets should be promoted so as to offer the highest possible employment in the area, (3) the social objective—forest policy (in its non-technical aspects) should be democratically determined so that the best interests of all major groups in the community are served and the rewards from the forest are equitably distributed among those dependent on it. These three objectives must be integrated and no one of them sacrificed to the others if community stability is to be realized. It is suggested that forest programs be evaluated in terms of these objectives.

A more comprehensive plan of forest management and utilization is needed than has been proposed thus far. The need is to plan for the stability of the whole community; this is much broader than assuring one plant of the necessary raw materials. Therefore, it is recommended that no attempt be made to put the proposed cooperative agreement between the Libby Mill and the Forest Service into effect until the industrial and social aspects of the forest program as described herein are worked out in much more detail.

Many assumptions and inferences have been made with respect to the type of industrial organization that would be most desirable in the community. What is needed, however, are specific proposals buttressed with all the available facts. Thus, it is recommended that a study be made of the industrial pattern or patterns most likely to survive in the area and that this information be made available to the public before any decision is made concerning a cooperative unit, a federal unit, or the volume of national forest timber allocated to the Libby Mill. It is assumed, of course, that the Libby Mill is an essential part of any industrial pattern likely to survive in the area.

After this industrial study is completed and if the economic facts indicate that a stable timber industry in Troy should be created, planning to this end should be initiated. In working out a forest program no community should be overlooked in the planning and none should be allowed to decline, unless such a policy has been established to be in the greatest public interest in the long run, both locally and nationally.

If the best interests of all major groups in the community are to be served, the public must have a voice in determining forest policy. This is especially true if competitive bidding is ruled out in the sale of national forest timber. Heretofore, all major decisions have been made, chiefly or entirely, by the Forest Service and the one large operator. Therefore, ways in which the public can participate more extensively in forming forest policy should be studied. A committee with strong Forest Service support should be formed to advise on the public aspect of the management and utilization of the timber area. This committee might consist of representatives from the public, labor, timber operators, owners of timber land, and the Forest Service. Such a committee would not only represent a cross-section of community opinion in determining forest policy but it would also have the important educational function of keeping the public informed on forest programs. The study groups now in session in the community considering forest programs and policies might well take up the question of the composition of this committee, its method of selection, and its various functions.

The Forest Service has the key position in any program of timber management and utilization which has community stabilization as its major social objective. Traditionally, the major function of the Forest Service has been to manage federally owned timber lands. But another and important role (as implied in Public Law 273) has been thrust upon this organization—that of leadership in forming public policies relating to the forest. In carrying out this function the Forest Service at various times must assume the roles of leader, expert, educator, arbiter, and protector of the public interest. Thus, it is recommended that increased attention be paid to the role of the Forest Service in planning for community stability and in related public service functions associated with the management of the forest. This implies study of specific techniques and procedures to use in carrying out this role and the training (both academic and in-service) of personnel who are to perform this function.

Conclusion

The forest situation in south Lincoln County presents real problems, but also great opportunities. The community has a relatively large acreage of forest land which, if managed properly, would provide continuous crops of timber. The public is, however, greatly divided as to how this raw material should be utilized. Thus, this report closes with the same question with which the discussion on forest policy was opened: Can the public, labor, industry, and government plan together for the common welfare? The writers have high hopes that the Libby-Troy community will answer this question in the affirmative. If they do, they will set a precedent which may have nationwide significance. It will demonstrate the success of democratic planning in conserving the forest resource and in the promotion of community well-being.

References

USDA Forest Service. 1944. "Policy and Instructions Governing the Establishment of Sustained Yield Units under the Provisions of Public Law 273." Unpublished mimeograph.

Diversity and Change in Forest-based Communities
Diversity in Interactions between Communities and
Forests

Robert G. Lee and Donald R. Field

C ommunity issues and concerns of today's policy makers and
forest managers vary substantially from what their
counterparts worried about fifteen years ago. Attention has
shifted from community stability as a function of sustained-yield timber
production to broad issues of community forestry. Chapters 7, 8, 9,
and 12 address questions that are basic to understanding forest-based
communities in the context of a variety of policy environments,
questions dealing with both historic and contemporary issues. Chapters
10 and 11 directly address programmatic attempts to implement
community forestry. A basic understanding of the structure and
function of communities provides a common foundation among all
these essays for addressing both today's and tomorrow's problems.

Extended case studies providing a longitudinal perspective on
community allow insights into structure and function unavailable in a
cross-sectional snapshot. Three of the chapters in this section take a
long-term view of community dynamics. London, Starrs, and Fortmann
describe over two decades of change in Quincy, California. Over this
time, community residents grouped and re-grouped around
contentious issues, depending on how their interests were affected by
policy proposals to bring change to the natural resource base supporting
the community. Community was not a fixed item, though the physical
place remained much the same and a large fraction of the residents
remained in place over this period. A focus on "the Quincy community"
as a fixed "thing" obscured the changing relationships between
residents, including the possibility that the sense of community had
also changed. Even the U.S. Forest Service shifted its position from
supporting local economic stability by providing a sustained supply of
wood to opposing community initiatives for co-management of
resources on federal lands. This chapter demonstrates that community

cannot be understood without looking at its dynamic social and political context.

Bliss and Bailey use archival data to examine how fifty years of economic change affected rural towns in which pulp mills were located in the Black Belt of Alabama. They describe how the availability of jobs did not substantially improve the marginal status of rural African Americans in a small town. Their essay raises questions about what large-scale forest industries actually contribute to the building of local social, human, and economic capital. The implication of this story is that highly centralized and capital-intensive industries, like centralized government, may pose obstacles to community forestry initiatives that would provide local people a greater role in community governance.

Extended case studies inform the view of occupational communities presented by Carroll, Lee, and McLain in their discussion of logging, mushroom gathering, and berry picking. These long-established occupations incorporate strong social bonds with fellow workers and identification with the work as a central life interest. This form of community organization contrasts sharply with the segmented adjustments of individuals to economic change found in many occupations. Unlike occupational adaptability that is achieved by education and training for a complex labor market, local knowledge and a personal reputation are keys to success. Members of these occupational communities can suffer more wrenching adjustments if there is change in the institutional conditions that have allowed their communities to prosper. Making permission to access resources contingent upon certification, training, and carefully supervised permitting processes could favor individualized work styles and render redundant the functions of occupational communities.

Finley, Luloff, and Jones present facts to refute the popular mythology foresters have shared about small private forest landowners. Foresters have historically looked at small private forestlands as a source of wood supply, and ignored the multiple functions these lands serve in the lives of their owners. This essay documents the importance of aesthetics, recreational use, wildlife appreciation, and environmental protection to small private forest owners. It points out that these owners are seldom adamant defenders of private property rights, and more often than not see themselves as stewards for resources important to the public as well as themselves. This conclusion shows that small landowners see themselves as part of a larger community that depends on and benefits from these relatively small fragments of forest.

Two essays review recent efforts to implement community forestry initiatives in North America. Recent Canadian initiatives in community forestry are discussed by Bull and Schwab. "Model forest" and "community forest" programs have attempted to provide an expanded role for stakeholders and members of local communities in decisions made by government agencies and licensees. Canada's forest tenure system differs substantially from that of the United States in that most forestlands were retained by the state and long-term rights to harvest and manage forests were allocated to private timber companies. This institutional structure has often led to strained relations between local communities and both the government and private companies. Not unrelated to these arrangements, labor unions have played a far more deliberate role in forest policy making than in the United States. Bull and Schwab summarize how Canada has attempted to move toward shared control over forest policy decision making by various sorts of communities. Experiments with "model forest" and "community forest" programs are efforts to join Canada with the larger international sustainable development movement.

A far more decentralized community forestry initiative in the United States is described by Krishnaswamy. The National Community Forestry Center seeks to promote the institutionalization of community forestry in the United States by facilitating the development of local knowledge and problem-solving capacity. It is inspired by successful community forestry projects in lesser-developed nations, and, as such, works directly with various nongovernmental organizations formed to advance the interests of both local and occupational communities. Attention centers on promoting voluntary cooperation of citizens who share common concerns with the management and use of both public and private forests, including occupational interests dependent upon forests.

CHAPTER 7
Power Plants and Forest Plans: Two Decades of Mobilization in a Mountain Forest Community

Jonathan London, Paul F. Starrs, & Louise Fortmann

Introduction

In the 1980s, residents of Quincy, a rural community with a population of about five thousand, located in northern California, mobilized repeatedly to protect their access to forest resources on the surrounding U.S. Forest Service-controlled Plumas National Forest. This forest constitutes 70 percent of surrounding Plumas County. First, the town protested the imposition of fees for cutting firewood in the forest. A subsequent mobilization in 1983, against a proposed wood-fired power plant, was analyzed in Fortmann and Starrs 1990. This study compared a successful Quincy mobilization to an attempted but dramatically unsuccessful mobilization against the same firm and type of power plant in Westwood, a waning town less than fifty miles from Quincy. Community characteristics and structural attributes explained much of why Quincy was successful. In both of these mobilizations, Quincy residents sought to halt the actions of outside institution: the Forest Service and a southern California-based energy company. The dynamics of these mobilizations were analyzed by Fortmann (1990), who argued that opposition was best understood as a defense of claims to local customary rights to resources on the national forest.

By the 1990s, mobilization in Quincy had taken on a distinct form. Some of the same activists who had been involved in the 1980s movements became founders of the Quincy Library Group (QLG), which would evolve into a nationwide poster child for local management of natural resources—an entity lauded by many other watershed and community forestry groups[1], yet denounced in full-page advertisements in the *New York Times* funded by the Sierra Club. During the same period, the Maidu, local Native Americans, and some non-Maidu supporters had formed the Maidu Cultural and

Development Group (MCDG), which separately contested management access rulings related to the Plumas and Lassen National Forests (London 2001).

This chapter updates the story of local mobilization over Plumas National Forest issues through the past two decades. A review of the original case study (Fortmann and Starrs 1990) is followed by descriptions of the approval of a wood-burning cogeneration facility in Quincy three years later, the "timber wars" of the mid- to late-1980s, and the emergence of the QLG and the MCDG. Our analysis demonstrates the power of a processual, historical, and multi-scale analysis (Massey 1994). While point-in-time analyses may highlight one or more critical incidents, only a cross-temporal approach can capture broader patterns of community change or the expanses of social structures. Analyses of communities that limit examination to the locality similarly obscure the significant ways that communities are shaped by (and in turn, shape) broader social, political, and economic forces (Parsons 1977, Pred 1986). The use of cross-temporal and multi-scale data in this case provides a view into the shifting alliances and oppositions from the local to the national scale. In particular, the data show a community evolving from a defensive to a proactive creative mode, as well as developing an increasingly sophisticated understanding of the complexity of the institutions with which it was dealing. The three periods of mobilization are distinguished here as: (1) conventional local planning processes; (2) local engagement in externally defined planning processes; and (3) local creation of new planning forms.

Conventional Local Planning Processes
Power Plants and Resource Rights[2]

California, with its global economy and thirty-four million residents, is a rapacious consumer of energy, as the energy shortfall "crisis" of early 2001 demonstrated. Increases in the state's population and the demands of energy-intensive high-tech industrial manufacturing have kept utilities searching for energy sources and new energy technologies. This was especially true in the early 1980s, when investment tax credits and state legislation favored alternative-energy development. Much of the legislation was inventive and proactive, but there was a codicil: plants had to be built before the end of 1985 to take advantage of most of the incentives and benefits.

In the 1980s, Ultrapower, a power-manufacturing division of a southern California company, developed plans for a string of wood-fueled power plants, including one in Westwood and another in Quincy, brand-named as Ultrapower plants. The firm argued that its plants offered significant economic, environmental, and energy-independent benefits, including the creation of fifty to seventy-five new local jobs with each project, an increased local tax base, local construction jobs for a typical twenty-million-dollar, eleven-megawatt project, and improved forest management. The primary fuel source would be wood waste remaining after timber harvesting and chipped wood taken in pre-commercial thinning. Yet there was concern in both communities about the effects a commercial power-plant operation would have on firewood supply. Although the Ultrapower advance staff explained to local residents that plants were only proposed where there was sufficient suitable wood, "We always encounter the firewood issue," said one senior company official. Indeed as a Quincy resident and plant opponent put it: "Firewood was the critical issue. A big-city image that Ultrapower projected hurt them. However, the firewood was the big thing. There was also a general distrust of the Forest Service and their policies."

But although Westwood residents were even more dependent on firewood than their Quincy neighbors were, they ultimately favored the Ultrapower plant, which was built and operating by the mid-1980s. Difficult economic straits in Westwood dated from the 1940s, and in the 1970s the forest products firm that had built and run the company town had sold its houses at fire-sale prices and pulled out. When the Ultrapower plant was proposed in Westwood, a brief protest took place, but townspeople acquiesced, accepting what they believed was an inevitable step that also offered job prospects.

However, residents of Quincy, a community geographically much more accessible to California's population centers and filled with immigrants seeking a rural, small-town lifestyle, blocked the plant in a broad groundswell of opposition. The Quincy protest was a multi-issue campaign that brought together diverse local interests. As one opponent summarized the town's feelings, "Not everyone objected to the same thing. Each person might have a different pet peeve, but the net effect was almost universal opposition." The most important and most emotional issue was, though, a much-proclaimed perceived threat to local fuelwood supplies. "Wood is the primary heat for most people here," commented a local Forest Service employee, and wood—obtained largely from the surrounding Plumas National Forest—was already a controversial issue before Ultrapower came to town (Fortmann and Starrs 1990). Residents feared that the effective control they had hitherto exercised over "their" supply of firewood would be severely diminished with the building of a wood-fueled power plant. Presenting a positive image for the plant was a continuing problem for the relatively few proponents in Quincy, as it was for Ultrapower. In addition, an active campaign by some plant opponents portrayed the alternative energy plant as a greedy exploiter of federal and state tax-credit largesse.

In both Quincy and Westwood, protest organizing began with a small group. But in Westwood the effort never went beyond a few letters to the local newspaper (which was printed in Quincy), and a handful of questions in public meetings sponsored by Ultrapower. Efforts against the plant in Quincy began with a few members of Friends of Plumas Wilderness (FOPW) who had prior experience with environmental protest. This core group of some forty Quincy-area residents rapidly enlisted support from hundreds of locals. Core plant opponents realized that the protest could easily be portrayed by plant proponents as "environmentalist," and countered that possibility by refusing to allow opposition to be narrowed to one or two issues and organizing into a broad coalition called the American Valley Biomass Committee (Quincy is located in the American Valley.) They brought in new members, gathered petition signatures, raised several thousand dollars, published and distributed brochures, and ultimately were credited by everyone from county supervisors to Ultrapower company officials with stopping the plant project. Many of the opponents of the plant in Quincy were novices at public protest, yet realized the impact of their actions, as a newfound activist remarked: "There were a number of people, like me, who really got involved against Ultrapower who hadn't been involved in anything like this before. . . . I'd like to think this'll have a lasting effect. People will remember that their energy changed the supervisors' minds." The Biomass Committee leveraged the experience and knowledge of a few people by access to multiple non-environmental organizational networks.

Quincy's political location as the county seat was a critical factor in the conflict: protestors could and did drop in at the courthouse to talk with members of county government, go to county board of supervisors' meetings, and in general make known their presence and views. Opponents and proponents alike could track the process of permit approval for Ultrapower that would prove crucial in the defeat, and all had ready access to information about the case.

From this combination of Quincy residents would emerge the successful protests against the Ultrapower facilities, and an overturning of considerable support for the power plant in the traditional power base of the community—as one case in point, the local newspaper publisher. From this freshening of skills, a community inclination toward self-protection, and an increasing recognition that recently arrived residents could be "O.K.," in the lexicon of the more long-standing residents, would emerge an awareness that political and economic action did not have to be reactive or passive. Instead, the community in Quincy could, in fact, set the pace, the agenda, and even the terms of negotiation over access to resources. And this could come through stepped-up involvement with the Forest Service (as the largest landowner, albeit a public one), and with private logging and milling enterprises.

The ultimate success of the opposition in Quincy can be credited to the fact that migrants from urban areas and long-term residents cooperated; they did not split into factions, but worked together, sharing skills, experience, and first-hand knowledge of local politics and economics. Long-term residents were catalyzed into action by the injection of the newcomers' organizing skills and their own willingness to join with newcomers in declaiming against the acts of other perceived "outside" forces: Ultrapower and the U.S. Forest Service.

Variations on a Theme of Power

In 1985, two years after the Ultrapower struggle, Sierra Pacific Industries (SPI), the owner of the major local timber mill (and the largest private landowner in the state, with mills throughout the Sierra Nevada), proposed a cogeneration plant on the site of its existing mill. Again, the community mobilized, but this time the context, sides, and outcomes were different. In the years after the Ultrapower battle, the Northern Sierra, like much of the Pacific Northwest, had moved to the brink of what would later be known as the "timber wars," in which appeals of timber sales by local and regional environmentalists, falling

Forest Service budgets and harvest levels, and a timber industry reorganization and consolidation would generate significant social tension in such forest communities as Quincy. During the timber wars the definition of "local" shifted within much of the community—"local" could now include out-of-area timber firms, but exclude or marginalize resident environmentalists.

In contrast to the Ultrapower case, the majority of the Plumas County Board of Supervisors supported the new proposed plant. For the majority, plant support was synonymous with support for the "local" timber firm: this issue was considered a matter of community loyalty in the context of the timber wars. In addition, the county planning director made a preemptive determination that the plant would have no negative environmental impact, and would therefore require no site development review. Without a review, no public input or hearings were necessary.

This lack of public input and the perceived "rubber-stamp" approval re-mobilized the coalition that had earlier opposed the Ultrapower plant. Even in the polarized environment of 1986, the American Valley Biomass Committee was reformed and included both local environmentalists and loggers. Among the most vocal opponents of the plant was a local logger who stated in a contemporary newspaper interview, "Why did this project only come to our attention as a back-page article in the newspaper one day after the appeal period ended? Changes in the county building codes . . . have allowed SPI to circumvent the public scrutiny that halted the smaller Ultrapower project." He went on to clarify his complaint as based on democratic principles of public process: "I am not against the SPI sawmill operation or the cogeneration plant, but I am against the county process, which allows its approval with no public hearings. It's a mistake to rubber-stamp a project of this size without public input" (Little 1985). Opponents also questioned assurances from SPI and the county that the plant would not add to air pollution or jeopardize local fuelwood supplies.

Rod Stevens,[3] a local attorney and one of the leaders of FOPW, recounted what he perceived as the alliance between the board of supervisors and the applicant timber firm: "SPI decided that they wanted to put in a cogen facility and it was exempted by the Plumas County Board of Supervisors while I was gone. They had a public meeting . . . and they turned out, they closed the mills . . . and they went over to the high school. There were five hundred or six hundred of them. ...[A] couple of members of the FOPW tried to go in and argue, and they were intimidated and hooted at and threatened and it was all stage-managed in my mind by [the president of the Plumas County Board of Supervisors] and SPI" [cited in London 2001].

SPI's Quincy mill manager countered concerns by contrasting the current proposal with the Ultrapower project: "This is one company owned by one person. We've been here a long time and we're going to be here a lot longer. There's a lot of difference between us and Ultrapower." Another company official described the plant as reducing air and wastewater emissions while simultaneously providing an economic benefit through increased stability. "One reason [the firm] wants to get as efficient a power plant as it can is to remove the company from the ups and downs of the timber industry."

The contrasting characters of the two plants also contributed to the approval of the SPI plant. While the Ultrapower facility was to be a freestanding power plant intended for commercial generation of electricity, the SPI facility was ancillary to the operations of the timber mill. The Ultrapower plant would have burned wood cut directly from the forest; the cogeneration plant would burn scrap from the mill and non-merchantable biomass from timber harvests. This treatment of forest biomass intrigued some local environmentalists who had for some years predicted a wild fire and forest health crisis, were nothing done to thin the forest and reduce fuel levels. Nonetheless, the approval of the SPI cogeneration plant served to heighten the polarization of the local timber wars.

Local Engagement in Externally Defined Planning Processes

Community Conflict over the Plumas National Forest Land Management Plan

The Plumas National Forest, which covers 70% of Plumas County, dominates the regional economic, political, and cultural landscape. All eyes were therefore on the Forest Service when it initiated the development of the Plumas National Forest Land and Resource Management Plan (LMP) in 1986. Under the 1976 National Forest Management Act, all national forests must complete a LMP every ten years to serve as a general plan, laying out resource extraction and protection goals for the entire forest over a ten- to twenty-year period. While LMPs are intended to strike a careful balance between the diverse, often competing, interests of resource extraction and resource protection, the Plumas LMP instead ignited a firestorm of protest from all sides. This protest roiled the county for nearly five years, and set in motion political and social reactions that would continue into the next century.

On August 26, 1988, after nearly eight years of planning, the Plumas LMP was issued. On August 27, the first of what would become fifteen appeals was filed against the plan by the San Francisco office of the New York City-based Natural Resources Council. Appeals appeared destined to push the Forest Service in irreconcilably different directions. The local FOPW called for an annual timber harvest of 220-247 million board feet (MMBF); the Plumas Board of Supervisors called for between 300 and 310 MMBF; and a timber industry coalition called for 330-380 MMBF. The Forest Service's own proposed Allowable Sale Quantity (ASQ) was 265 MMBF.

Comments delivered at public hearings and in written comments and appeals illustrated strong and varying views on the Plan. A top official at SPI declared, "We who live here, work here, pay taxes here, and die here should be able to get the government's ear. We're part of the forest and our lives are at stake" (Little 1986). A resident from nearby Sierra County warned that reductions in harvest levels would turn local communities into "welfare recipients and pot growers." Justifying the county's stance, a Plumas county supervisor predicted, "People in and out of jobs will stay in the county if there is a promise of better times ahead. [The promise of increasing timber sales] contributes to economic and social stability by encouraging the timber industry and timber workers to stay in [Plumas] County" (Little 1989a).

On the other hand, local environmentalists represented by FOPW advocated for the so-called "amenity" alternative, largely based on FOPW's own "Conservationist Alternative." This rejected all clearcutting and proposed the use of single-tree and small-group selection harvest, the expansion of wilderness areas to include an additional 131,000 acres, and the creation of a comprehensive Greater Plumas Wilderness Area. FOPW criticized the plan for its reliance on clearcutting and for timber harvest areas that overlapped visual-quality and wildlife habitat areas. FOPW filed its appeal in 1988, but the Forest

Service did not act on this appeal until 1994, when the agency denied it with no explanation. FOPW members were critical of the refusal of the Forest Service to consider their alternative, despite its extensive scientific justification. Rod Stevens explained the agency's perceived illogical action as based in "politics" as opposed to science. "You can't argue with the evidence in this document. It supports our position. But at the regional level they take their marching orders from Washington, D.C. And in Washington, the decision was made before this thing even started" (Little 1988c). Stevens' analysis of the Forest Service's chain of command presaged the Washington-oriented strategy the QLG would later follow.

The appeals filed by national environmental organizations and their regional representatives similarly criticized the plan's emphasis on clearcutting and its impacts on old growth and wildlife habitat. Because the Plumas National Forest was the second timber-producing forest in California to file a LMP, national environmental organizations were concerned about precedents it might set.

The Forest Service appeared to view conflict as inevitable. Forest Service representatives pointed to the conflict as evidence of the quality of its work—not as an indication of its inadequacy: "You judge your efforts by the quality of your opposition. With all the opposition that's coming up, we must not have done that bad a job" (Little 1988d). The Forest Service's depiction of the conflict as legitimizing its plan becomes more suspect as more details of the opposition are examined. While FOPW called for less harvesting than proposed by the plan, their Conservationist Alternative still included significantly more harvests than were occurring at the time. One FOPW leader commented, "We can treat the entire forest as a high-quality visual area and not do any clearcutting and still come up with 247 million board feet, which is more annual board footage than the Plumas Forest has produced in the last decade."

In addition, while some industry comments supported clearcutting, the main industry groups called for significantly less clearcutting than proposed by the plan. Among the most outspoken activists spearheading the local pro-timber Yellow Ribbon Committee, one even went so far as to circulate an anti-clearcutting petition, explaining that "clearcutting is a Forest Service policy and not one of the loggers." Instead, she declared, "Every logger is against clearcutting, but you know who takes the rap. We care about what goes on in the woods but we don't set the policies. The Forest Service does" (Chico News and Review August 22, 1991). Reacting to similar sentiments in an earlier letter to the editor in the local paper, Rod Stevens described himself as "more encouraged by reading that letter than by anything I have seen or heard in the last ten years in this county." Stevens articulated this common ground between loggers and environmentalists over the issue of clearcutting in an op-ed piece: "What do environmentalists believe we have in common with the Yellow Ribbon Committee? We believe that we are all honest people who want to continue our way of life. We believe that we all love the area in which we live. We believe that we enjoy beautiful views, hunting, fishing and living in a rural area. We believe that we are being misled by the Forest Service and by large timber which controls the Forest Service, into believing we are enemies when we are not" (Little 1989b).

Stevens' piece introduced the notion of the Forest Service as instigator, not victim, of community conflict. This notion is supported by Cathy Stone, a colleague of Stevens in the local environmental activities, who promotes the idea of Forest Service as the prime mover in the escalation of conflict. Stone contends that, in the late 1980s and early 1990s, Forest Service personnel were leaking information about timber sale appeals (including the identity of the appellants, which often included Stone herself) to the local radio stations. She claims that this was an attempt by the Forest Service to divert pressure from the agency by branding local environmentalists as community traitors. After years of conflict with the timber industry, Cathy Stone says that she and other local environmentalists came to the "...realization that we had mis-identified the enemy." According to Stone, it was this realization that catalyzed the formation of the QLG. She became convinced: ". . . that our traditional viewpoint that the Forest Service was in the pocket of the timber industry and the industry was pretty much getting what it wanted was wrong. . . . They thought they were beat. And the other was just this, smell to high heaven aspect, of here are Forest Service employees using Forest Service facilities in order to wage a political campaign to manipulate the politics of the local level with the intention of inflaming one side against the other. And whether they intended it or not, the inflammation was even a call to arms" (cited in London 2001).

An official with the Plumas National Forest contests this reallocation of blame back onto the agency, and instead transferred responsibility back to the timber industry:

So timber wars, I would say a lot of the . . . hyperbole?
. . . anyway a lot of the STUFF about that, a lot of it was
about profit. And then there was the impact on
communities. But a lot of it, the war, the polarization, a
lot of that was created to try to keep profits up. This is
for me personally, this is a personal comment. I have seen
time and time again, industry use, and I think that's
morally corrupt, to use mom and pop relationships in
town to say we are driving communities to the brink of
extinction. And it was to keep their production up. I find
it inexcusable. When we closed mills because of
automation to say publicly, and I know that for a fact, I
can give you numerous examples where mills were closed
because industry did not want to retool them for a
different type of product, or and/or they changed
automation. But they directly said in their news release
that this was a result of reduced volume from national
forests (cited in London 2001).

Another view of the origins of the timber wars origins was provided
by some small-scale mill operators who complained of a conspiracy
between the Forest Service and the large timber firms. They felt the
Forest Service tended to favor contracts with large firms and
clearcutting, and that this was based on administrative convenience.
They derided such practices as sell-outs to big business and devastating
to the local community. In 1991, a small mill operator posted signs on
his log trailers with slogans such as: "Can't find a job? Don't blame
the owl." The sign went on to contend that the: "Local [district]
ranger's apparent priority is to let dead timber rot rather than to make
small salvage sales to local timber operators while continuing to prepare
and sell large green sales for the benefit of big business" (*Chico News
and Review* August 22, 1991).

Whether or not one group was responsible for the timber wars—
environmental extremists, agency provocateurs, or industrial mom-
and-pop propaganda—the common ground envisioned by Rod
Stevens' editorial remained elusive into the early 1990s. For several
years, harassment of local environmentalists, sabotage of logging
equipment, battles over yellow ribbons flying on county trucks, and
timber sale appeals rocked the community.

By the early 1990s, all sides of the conflict seemed battle-weary and open to alternative ways to achieve their goals. Local environmentalists like Stevens and Stone also began to view the appeal/litigation strategy favored by the regional and national groups as a rear-guard battle, able to stop the most egregious attacks on the forest, but unable to establish more permanent positions to ensure sound ongoing forest management. Cathy Stone described her shift in tactics in the early 1990s: "We came to realize that litigation can only do so much in terms of affecting, not just citizen enforcement of the law but also in affecting public forest management and policy. You can lead a horse to water but you can't get him to drink. You can lead the Forest Service to quit logging old growth, but you can't get the Forest Service to properly manage the forests if it doesn't want to" (cited in London 2001). Stone's frustration over the inability of appeals, litigation, and other conflict-based strategies to promote substantive forest protection and health can be seen as a logical conclusion to the era of the timber wars. Community mobilization that set factions against each other may have seemed inevitable during the late 1980s and early 1990s, but timber warriors such as Rod Stevens and Cathy Stone began to seek other methods.

Supporting, not forcing, proper forest management can be seen as the *modus operandi* for new forms of community mobilization that rose to prominence in the early 1990s. Variously termed community forestry, collaborative stewardship, or co-management, these new forms involved: collaborative relations between multiple stakeholders (often including former adversaries); restorative forestry (neither traditional harvests nor preservation); and an integrated vision of healthy communities interrelated with healthy forests (Bernard and Young 1997; Cortner and Moote 1999; Wondolleck and Yaffe 2000, Baker and Kusel 2003). Community forestry or stewardship groups do not merely seek increased use of the forest, but also tend to promote alternative forest management systems that meet multiple objectives (such as fire-risk reduction, habitat protection, and local economic vitality) in a sustainable framework.[4]

In Plumas County, community forestry manifested itself in two innovative forums for managing local national forests: the Maidu Cultural and Development Group (MCDG) and the Quincy Library Group (QLG). The remainder of this chapter describes the rise and development of these two organizations.[5]

Local Creation of New Planning Forms

Formation and Original Initiatives of the Quincy Library Group

When the telephone rang one fall morning in 1992 in Rod Stevens's law offices in downtown Quincy, he and others in FOPW had been involved in what Stevens called "a scorched-earth" policy of filing appeals on Forest Service sales in roadless and other sensitive areas of the Plumas National Forest. This was the only strategy that he and most environmentalists could envision for protecting roadless areas, in the absence of a viable Forest Service policy for protecting old growth and roadless areas.

On the other end of the line, Stevens recognized Plumas County Supervisor Wayne Tolley's voice. For ten years, Stevens and Tolley had marshaled opposing forces in the region's timber wars. Tolley had served as a key supporter of the timber industry in local as well as state and national policy. Following is Stevens' account of the conversation:

> And then all of a sudden there was the phone ringing and it was [County Supervisor Tolley]. And he said, "You know . . . sort of . . . before you hang up, I'd like to tell you that that plan you guys did with the Wilderness Society and the NRDC in 1982 to '86 . . . we should have taken it then." I said, "I told you, you dumb SOB: I mean, you told us to fuck off, so fuck off." And he said, "You know, this town is sick. You and I have made it sick. This is not good." So I said. "It's good for me!" But as we talked, you know . . . it was sick. [The town] was dying! So I started talking to them, and I was wrong. They were going to do something real. So we started the same place we've always been, which was, "'Don't tell us about the rules yet. We want to divide the land."

After this phone call, in meetings that soon followed between Stevens, Tolley, and SPI's Chief Forester, during the fall of 1992, the core of the QLG was forged. In the year that followed, the three cofounders, along with an ensemble of approximately twenty other timber industry, environmentalist, and civic leaders, would develop their QLG Community Stability Proposal (CSP).

The CSP had as its premise the perception of its founders that "present U.S. Forest Service management is inadequate to meet the objectives of any of its members" (Quincy Library Group 1993, 1). In contrast, the QLG developed its proposals to meet the diverse objectives of timber firms, forest communities, and environmentalists. The CSP explains that it was developed "to promote forest health, ecological integrity, adequate timber supply, and local economic stability" (Quincy Library Group 1993, 3). The measures in the proposal are intended to "allow local communities to survive while long-term plans are developed, yet afford adequate environmental protection during the interim period" (Quincy Library Group 1993:3).[6]

Taken as a whole, the QLG's proposal describes the "territory" of the strategic convergence among the protagonists of the local timber wars. The zones are spatial manifestations of the interests and values of the QLG and its individual members. By zoning the land, the QLG created a new spatial order in which forest product harvest and forest protection were to exist "on the same page." More than a management plan, the QLG area map can be understood as a representation of the collaborative social relationships and arrangements that made this management plan possible in the first place.

From 1993 through 1996, the QLG attempted to convince the Forest Service to implement its CSP through administrative avenues ranging from the supervisors of the three national forests in the QLG area, to the regional forester, to the Washington, D.C. office, and even the Clinton Administration. Frustrated by the slow progress, the QLG took its proposal to Capitol Hill seeking congressional support. After much political wrangling, the Herger-Feinstein QLG Forest Recovery Act was signed into law as part of the 1998 Omnibus Appropriations Act.

While the QLG represented unprecedented collaboration among its core members, its development also involved significant conflicts with a variety of entities. Opposition from the various sectors of the environmental movement was based on a territorial politics. For some local and regional environmentalists, QLG's plan represented a potential annexation and subsumption within the QLG area. As the Sierra Nevada Forest Protection Campaign's Jane Tenney put it, "We didn't pass a bill in their backyard, but they did in ours!"[7] To some national-level environmentalists, the legislated pilot proposal represented the withdrawal of these national forests from their political purview. For many environmentalists, the QLG's ability to derive symbolic benefits as a local community-based group, while mobilizing significant national political support, appeared to evict the environmental movement from its homes both in the grassroots and inside the Beltway. The resulting environmental counterattack branded the QLG as both "too local" and "not local enough."

The QLG has also inspired divergent reactions at different levels of the Forest Service. While some Forest Service personnel welcomed it as potentially reinvigorating the agency's mission and operations—a "green light" for innovation—others feared a loss of institutional autonomy from above, with increased congressional intervention, and from below, as the QLG inserted itself into the agency's chain of command.

For some firms and individuals relying on the national forests for their livelihood, the group represented a needed support for maintaining access to the commodities of the forests in an age of tightening environmental regulation. For others, especially smaller logging firms and cattle ranchers, its predominance in forest management was seen as threatening to silence their interests. Finally, within the community forestry movement itself, the QLG's national success and status makes the group both a standard bearer and a potential threat to the viability of a movement that draws critical support from its local roots to survive.

Formation and Initiatives of the Maidu Cultural Development Group

> "Who are we becoming? And what are we losing touch
> with? [The MCDG] is about putting us back in touch
> with our ancestors."
> —Ryan Harlan, MCDG Cofounder, 1998

The Maidu people have inhabited the northern Sierra Nevada for at least one thousand years, perhaps since the last ice age ten thousand years ago (Dixon 1905). Over the past 150 years, successive waves of settlers and government policies have reduced the Mountain Maidu from the sovereigns of the northern Sierra Nevada region to a group without a legally recognized territory.

The Maidu Cultural and Development Group (MCDG) was formed in 1995 by several Maidu community leaders and non-Maidu supporters who sought to increase the role of the Maidu in the forest management and economic development activities in the area. Given that some of these founders had not been on speaking terms for over a decade, the MCDG represented a breakthrough in social organization and conflict resolution for the Maidu. Group members shared the belief that the ecological vitality of the forest and the social vitality of the Maidu community could only be achieved through a revival of the land-based Maidu culture in which natural and social systems were closely linked. The MCDG's Maidu Sense of Place Action Plan (Maidu Cultural and Development Group 1998), articulates this connection between ecological and cultural vitality: "Spiritual strength and material livelihoods come from healthy land. When the land is sick, the spirits go away; communities fall apart." The MCDG's two-pronged effort to link the Maidu community to the land and to a sense of their longstanding history and identity allowed the group to attract a wide coalition of founding members. Some saw the group as a way to attain improved status for the Maidu in their dealings with federal agencies and other government entities. The MCDG offered access to political arenas that the un-recognized and landless Maidu could not formerly attain.[8] For other members, the MCDG offered the potential for a physical or territorial space in which the Maidu could restore a sense of pride through the exercise and redevelopment of their land stewardship expertise.

Because most of the founding Maidu members of the MCDG were not part of any recognized tribal entity, they viewed the group as a vehicle through which to rally support for their vision within the Maidu community and advocate for it with the Forest Service and other agencies. Many members described being motivated to form the organization by the urgency of revitalizing the community before the last generation with direct experience of traditional Maidu lifeways passed away. Non-Maidu members of the MCDG, mostly county and federal agency personnel, saw the MCDG as a venue in which to support the non-recognized Maidu community in ways that would be otherwise impossible.

The MCDG's first project, supported by a rural community assistance grant from the Forest Service, was the "Maidu Sense of Place Map," which indicated the Maidu names for prominent landmarks in Indian Valley. While current place names reflect the history of white settlement and conquest, the Maidu names evoke the mythic origins, as well as the earlier uses and natural characteristics, of these sites. The MCDG has taken further steps to request that these names be included by the Forest Service and by the U.S. Geological Survey on official maps. In the absence of formally recognized land claims, this map can be seen as a way the Maidu may address their legal alienation from the land by re-establishing a kind of symbolic ownership.

In 1998, the MCDG created the Maidu Sense of Place Action Plan, outlining a strategy to use Maidu culture as the basis for integrated economic development in Indian Valley. After the Plumas National Forest rejected their special use permit application for elements of this action plan (a Maidu "living village" educational facility, ethnobotanical nature trails, and vegetation restoration sites) the MCDG repackaged their plans as a proposal to become a national stewardship pilot site. This successful proposal combined land management, cultural education, and economic development objectives as part of an overall program of "Maidu Stewardship." The MCDG's vision of stewardship was a multi-layered approach to simultaneously restoring the ecological health of the land, institutional relationships with the Forest Service, and the sense of pride and cultural vitality within the Maidu community.

In addition to their land management activities, the MCDG have developed two sets of protocols, one guiding the application of traditional Maidu ecological knowledge to the analysis, planning, and implementation of ecosystem management projects, and the other guiding collaboration and communication between the Maidu and the Forest Service. Traditional ecological knowledge teams, including Maidu experts assisted by technical consultants from other Indian groups, will assist in the development of both sets of protocols.

The Maidu Stewardship Area can be understood as what Lefebvre (1991) calls a "counter space." Before the formation of the MCDG, the Maidu relied primarily on a past-based strategy to justify any claims on the land that could be paraphrased as "We were the original inhabitants/ we were displaced/ we deserve compensation." While offering a degree of challenge, this historical claim could be accommodated without too much disruption of the prevailing status quo of forest tenure and power relations. The MCDG's stewardship strategy, in contrast, articulates the Maidu's claim to the landscape as vested in their active occupation and stewarding of the land, therefore visibly impressing themselves on the politics and practices of the present and the future. By working to establish the Maidu Stewardship Area, the MCDG has taken critical steps to assume the role as "organizers" of space, and therefore engaging more directly in the arena of state power. The Maidu Stewardship Area would also allow the Maidu to have increased privacy and heightened control over the staging and management of their ceremonies.

The MCDG sought to rework Maidu identity in the eyes of the dominant society by presenting Maidu culture as an attraction and an asset to the broader community, as opposed to a liability. The MCDG hope that the final product of the Living Village and Stewardship Area, as well as their efficacy in the process of developing and maintaining the area, will help demonstrate their competence, countering the view of many local non-Maidu of the Maidu as degenerate, or simply deprived, Indians. Instead, the Maidu would be seen as knowledgeable stewards of "a pre-contact forest for the 21st century" in the words of one of the MCDG co-founders, Ryan Harlen.

This active engagement with state power has itself produced new political spaces, along with new associated conflicts. For example, the patterns of conflict between (and within) the various levels of the Forest Service and the MCDG can be understood as products of the reconfiguration of space and authority over the national forests. While the Forest Service has always embodied contending forces of centralization and decentralization (Kaufman 1967), the late 1990s brought a series of swings of authority between the core and the periphery of the agency.

On the one hand, the turn toward ecosystem management has allowed the local knowledge and experience of forest-level personnel in devising site-specific management systems. At the same time, initiatives from the regional and national level have concentrated control at the upper levels of the agency. By becoming one of the twenty-one national stewardship pilot sites, the MCDG has inserted itself in the chain of command at a level above that of the local national forest; therefore vesting itself with unprecedented authority. This has disturbed the prevailing power and spatial relations and opened new possibilities for contesting control of the forest. In particular, it has shifted the status of the Maidu in relation to the local national forest leadership from a landless, government-less, largely silent population, to a national pilot site, authorized by the highest levels of the agency. In turn, this new Maidu voice has threatened local forest leadership and provoked bureaucratic resistance in the form of repeated delays and shifting conditions for approval of the MCDG's stewardship plan.

Conclusions

What do the cases of the community-specific opposition against Ultrapower, the approval of the SPI cogeneration plant, and the rise of both the QLG and the MCDG tell us about social mobilization in forest communities?

First, the two-decade scope of this analysis suggests the benefits of a longitudinal methodology. Had the account concluded with the Ultrapower saga, one might have presumed that Quincy maintained a unified opposition to any non-local presence in the forest product sector, and was steadfast in its opposition to any facility that might make use of forest byproducts for energy production. Yet, just a few years later, the locally based SPI plant would go on-line with a very small outcry from the public. While some local/non-local tension was evident in the second instance, it manifested itself in different ways in the timber wars and subsequently in the context of the QLG and the MCDG. The meanings associated with being perceived as "local" or "non-local" shifted over time, as did the entitlements to intervene in the management of area forests. For example, in the SPI cogeneration conflict, the firm, which is headquartered over 150 miles away in the Sacramento Valley, became a local cause célèbre for the county board of supervisors. In contrast, the local Forest Service leadership was considered above the fray during the timber wars, and then beyond the pale in the context of the QLG.

Second, the cases have also demonstrated the utility of a trans-local perspective on rural communities. While appealing (and easier to construct) the notion of the "little town in the big woods" simply does not accommodate the webs of policy, economics, and culture that loop through all communities, no matter how remote. It is worth asking if the early mobilizations in Quincy were pretty much stand-alone and local because their focus was protection of local places and local interests by blocking outside actions. In contrast, the QLG's and MCDG's focus on creating new form for forest management decisions placed them in trans-local arenas. QLG engaged in much broader systems of management and policy reaching to higher levels of the

Forest Service, congress and the executive branch. MCDG adapted models from other Native American groups and strengthened its position through coalition building and becoming part of a larger strategy.

Third, these cases illustrate patterns of conflict and collaboration that are often best explained by examining both the relationships between the claims on the resources, as well as between the claimants. In particular, it is important to distinguish between different modes of forest tenure, including statutory and nonstatutory forms. These cases have represented tenure based on private ownership, administrative jurisdiction, historical/tribal territories, resource use rights, and rights to sit at the table where forest management decisions are made. For example, Ultrapower's claim to clearcut timber to power the regional electric grid was deemed incompatible with local claims for firewood, while SPI's claim to ensure the viability of their local mill was deemed superior to local protesters' claims of due process. The QLG and MCDG were able to forge collaboration between former adversaries as members came to view each other's claims on and visions of the forest resources as compatible. In contrast, both organizations encountered conflicts with the local Forest Service leadership to the extent that their claims to authority over forest management threatened that of the agency.

Finally, these cases suggest that forest communities will continue to be critical localities in which tensions between forest policy, forest product industries, and forest ecology will manifest in diverse forms of social mobilization. Given that earlier accounts of community mobilization in this region (Fortmann and Starrs 1990) could not predict the varieties of conflict and collaboration that took place in the 1990s, it is likely that forest communities will continue to represent important sites of study into the next century.

Notes

1 Community forestry or community-based natural resource management is relatively new in the U.S., but has a long history elsewhere. See Poffenberger 1990; Western and Wright 1994.

2 Much of the following section is adapted from Fortmann and Starrs (1990).

3 All personal names are pseudonyms.

4 During the 1990s regional and national networks developed to support the emergence of community forestry. The events in Quincy were therefore to be understood as part of a regional phenomenon.

5 Much of the following section is adapted from London (2001). All subsequent interview quotes are cited from this source unless otherwise noted.
6 Full text available at www.QLG.org
7 The QLG's Cathy Stone critiqued Tenney's use of "backyard" to describe the QLG Area as representing the same kind of spatial expansion and appropriation of which Tenney accuses the QLG.
8 Federal recognition is the legal status granted by the federal government to certain Indian tribes that qualifies them to engage on a government-to-government basis with Congress and federal agencies (The Advisory Council on California Indian Policy 1997). Only recognized tribes are able to serve as beneficiaries of trust resources (including land), recipients of federal Indian programs and holders of treaty rights. To be recognized, a tribe must demonstrate that it has been a stable cultural, social and political unit over time (Pevar 1992).

References

The Advisory Council on California Indian Policy. 1997. The ACCIP Recognition Report: Equal Justice for California.

Baker, Mark, and Jonathan Kusel, eds. 2003. *Community Forestry in the United States: Learning from the Past, Crafting the Future*. Washington D.C.: Island Press.

Bernard, Ted, and Jora Young. 1997. *The Ecology of Hope: Communities Collaborate For Sustainability*. Montpelier, VT: Capital City Press.

Chico News and Review. August 22, 1991. New Winds in the Woods: Forest Changes Shake up Timber Towns.

Cortner, Hanna J., and Margaret A. Moote. 1999. *The Politics of Ecosystem Management*. Washington, D. C: Island Press.

Dixon Robert. B. 1905. "The Northern Maidu: The Huntington California Expedition." *Bulletin of the American Museum of Natural History* 17:119-346.

Fortmann, Louise. 1990. "Locality and Custom: Non-aboriginal Claims to Customary Usufructuary Rights as a Source of Social Protest." *Journal of Rural Studies* 6(2): 195-208.

Fortmann, Louise P., and Paul F. Starrs. 1990 "Power Plants and Resource Rights." Pp. 179-94 in Robert G. Lee, Donald R. Field, and William Burch, eds. *Community and Forestry: Continuities in Natural Resources Sociology*. Boulder, CO: Westview Press.

Kaufman, Herbert. 1967. *The Forest Ranger: A Study in Administrative Behavior*. Baltimore, MD: Johns Hopkins University Press.

Lefebvre, Henri. 1991. *The Production of Space*. New York: Blackwell. (Originally published 1973.)

Little, Jane Braxton. 1985. S-P Biomass Plant Permit Appealed. *Feather River Bulletin*. December 31, 1985.

Little, Jane Braxton. 1986. Plumas Rallies Behind Maximum Timber Harvest. *Feather River Bulletin*. May 7, 1986.

Little, Jane Braxton. 1988a. Logging Conflicts . *Feather River Bulletin.* August 7, 1988.

Little, Jane Braxton. 1988b. Crosses Denounce Quincy Logging.*Feather River Bulletin.* August 17, 1988.

Little, Jane Braxton. 1988c. Appeal Already of Plumas Plan. *Feather River Bulletin.* September 7, 1988.

Little, Jane Braxton. 1988d. Nobody Likes this Plumas Forest Plan. *Feather River Bulletin.* October 19, 1988.

Little, Jane Braxton. 1989a. Plumas Forest Plan Hit By Appeals. *Feather River Bulletin.* January 11, 1989.

Little, Jane Braxton. 1989b. [Please provide title of article]. *Feather River Bulletin* September 20, 1989.

London, Jonathan. 2001. Placing Conflict and Collaboration in Community Forestry. Unpublished Ph.D. Dissertation. University of California, Berkeley.

Massey, Doreen. 1994. *Space, Place and Gender.* Minneapolis: University of Minnesota Press.

Maidu Cultural and Development Group. 1998. Maidu Cultural and Development Group Sense of Action Plan for the Living Village and Stewardship Area. Unpublished document. March 1998.

Parsons, James J. 1977. "Geography as Exploration and Discovery." *Annals of the Association of American Geographers,* March, 67(1): 1-16.

Pevar, Stephen L. 1992. *The Rights of Indian Tribes: The Basic ACLU Guide to Indian and Tribal Rights, Second Edition.* Carbondale: University of Southern Illinois Press.

Poffenberger, Mark, editor. 1990. *Keepers of the Forest: Land Management Alternatives in Southeast Asia.* West Hartford, CO: Kumarian Press.

Pred, Allan R. 1986. *Place, Practice and Structure: Social and Spatial Transformation in Southern Sweden: 1750-1850.* Cambridge, MA: Polity.

Quincy Library Group. 1993. Community Stability Proposal. Unpublished document.

Western, David, and R. Michael Wright, editors. 1994. *Natural Connections: Perspectives in Community-based Conservation.* Washington, D.C.: Island Press.

Wondolleck, Julia M., and Steven L. Yaffee. 2000. *Making Collaboration Work: Lessons from Innovation in Natural Resource Management.* Washington, D.C: Island Press.

CHAPTER 8
Pulp, Paper, and Poverty: Forest-based Rural Development in Alabama, 1950-2000

John C. Bliss and Conner Bailey

O n a sweltering summer day in 1965, in Wilcox County, Alabama, then-Governor George B. Wallace addressed a small crowd of landowners, local political dignitaries, and industrial leaders. They had gathered to dedicate a brand-new highway bridge spanning the Alabama River, facilitating delivery of pulpwood to the new MacMillan Bloedel mill at Pine Hill. Recruiting the mill to this isolated, poor corner of a poor state was central to the state's forest-based rural-development strategy, and Governor Wallace was proud of the accomplishment. Wallace predicted that, thanks to the area's abundant forest and water resources, combined with the state's aggressive industrial-recruitment policies, "This region is going to bloom like a rose!" (*Wilcox Progressive Era*, July 8, 1965, as quoted by Walkingstick 1996). By the 1990s, the region had been transformed into a world center of pulp and paper production. Yet, in 1998, 34 percent of all Wilcox County residents lived in poverty, suffering the highest poverty rate in Alabama (U.S. Census Bureau 2001).

Governor Wallace's optimism was not without some justification. The Black Belt and Coastal Plain of Alabama had slowly but steadily been transformed over the previous half-century from a landscape of worn-out cotton plantations, failing farms, and idle pastures, into one dominated by pine and hardwood forests. Mother Nature was responsible for most of the transformation, seeding abandoned farm and pasture with pines, gums, and oaks. More recently, landowners had begun to convert their agricultural lands to plantations of loblolly pine, anticipating growing markets for pine pulpwood.

The industrial recruitment policies Wallace promoted were easily justified by the magnitude of need for economic development in this poorest region of Alabama. Evidence of the region's deep poverty was everywhere to be seen: substandard housing, shocking family-health statistics, and persistently high unemployment. To Governor Wallace and many other observers, the region's abundant forest resources appeared to hold the key to economic growth and rural development.

Looking back at Governor Wallace's prediction, it is instructive to evaluate the extent to which the forest, in combination with particular rural-development strategies, has led rural Alabama to "bloom." What role have forests, forestry, and the forest industry played in shaping the current condition of Alabama's rural communities? The Alabama experience provides a case study in the dynamics, limitations, and prospects for sustainable forest-based development in the rural South. Our focus is on the state of Alabama, particularly during the period 1950 to 2000, when the state's forest-based rural-development strategy was conceived and implemented. This chapter is about the relationships between rural communities, the forests that surround them, the forest industry upon which they are dependent, and the social, political, and economic context in which they interact. Rather than focusing on individual communities, we draw attention to the broader economic, ecological, and political context within which timber-dependent rural communities are situated.

Our intention is not to diminish the promise of forest-based development, but rather to critically analyze one region's experience in the hope of deriving useful lessons for application in the South and elsewhere. The synthesis we provide here is derived from a series of related research projects spanning nearly a decade, involving a large number of colleagues to whom we are deeply indebted (see acknowledgements).

We begin with a brief overview of the region's history and present a snapshot of conditions at the end of the twentieth century. We then describe the persistence of race-based social inequality in those parts of Alabama where the forest products industry plays an especially dominant economic role. We focus next on changes in land-ownership patterns that have accompanied the rise of the industry, then on impacts of Alabama's industrial recruitment policies on human capital investment. We close with an assessment of lessons learned, and with a challenge to the view that healthy, productive forests inevitably lead to healthy, prosperous communities. As a corollary, we argue that policies that are good for the forest products sector are not necessarily good for rural communities.

The Rise of the Pulp and Paper Industry

When European settlers first moved into what is now the southeastern United States, they found extensive forests and abundant wildlife. The coastal plains were dominated by longleaf and slash pine forests interspersed with bottomland hardwoods. Further to the north, oak-hickory forests dominated. These forests were a diverse set of ecosystems that had been shaped, largely by fire, to meet the needs of Native Americans who lived in this region (Walker 1991).

The impact of European settlers during the eighteenth and nineteenth centuries transformed the landscape of the South. Moving inland from the coast, early settlers cut timber for building materials and naval stores (ships' masts, timbers, resins), and to clear the land for agriculture. The first great timber boom of the coastal plain occurred along major rivers, the most important route for trade goods until well into the twentieth century (Jackson 1995). In the Piedmont region, forests were cleared primarily to open land for farming (Walker 1991). Poor farming practices on thin soils led to severe soil erosion. Ultimately, farms were abandoned and a natural process of reforestation began. The Depression of the 1930s hastened this process of conversion from farmland to forestland. By the mid-1940s, the extent of forested acres had increased dramatically. The postwar economic boom led to rapid increases in demand for wood products, especially paper. Drawn principally by the region's abundant forest resources, water, and transportation, and its inexpensive labor, the pulp and paper industry began to make major investments throughout the South (Oden 1974).

Southern state governments, desperate for any boost to flagging state economies, entered into bidding wars to attract wood products companies, principally pulp and paper companies (Cobb 1993). Free land, new roads and bridges, cheap labor, corporate-friendly government, and generous tax abatements were offered as enticements. The state of Alabama began using incentives to recruit manufacturing plants to the state as early as 1923 and intensified recruitment efforts after World War II. State legislation enabled local governments to establish industrial-development boards to recruit industry and create jobs.

The pulp and paper industry was headed south; it remained only to select specific sites for building plants and accessing wood supplies. Aggressive recruiting influenced the specific sites where pulp and paper plants were to locate, though there was little doubt that these facilities would be located along major rivers and in proximity to the available wood supply. By 1992, Alabama led the South in pulpwood production (Miller 1994), boasting sixteen pulp and paper mills. Rural Alabama became the "wood basket" of the nation and home to a world-class industry. One industrial complex deep in the heart of Alabama's coastal plain was now the world's largest producer of wood pulp, and the Port of Mobile the nation's second-largest exporter of forest products (Alabama State Docks 2001).

The expansion of the forest products sector in Alabama and other Southern states during the 1960s and 1970s reflects a widespread relocation of U.S. manufacturing plants from the "rust belt" to the "sun belt" (Falk and Lyson 1988). Many manufacturers have continued to move even farther south, to Mexico and other nations where costs of labor and environmental compliance are lower. For the most part, the forest products sector has stayed, becoming deeply rooted in the land, and exerting a profound influence over life in the rural South.

A Forest-based Economy

Today, forests dominate the Southern landscape, permeate regional culture, and are the economic mainstay of many rural communities. Forests cover 68 percent of Alabama's land base (Vissage and Miller 1991). Most of the forest (62 percent) is owned by nonindustrial private forest owners. Forest products companies own 25 percent of the forest. Most of this land is held by pulp and paper companies either outright or in long-term timber leases. Other corporations own an additional 7 percent of the forest, and the state and federal governments own the remaining 6 percent.

The forest products sector is, by some measures, the leading manufacturing sector in the economy of Alabama, accounting in 1999 for $4.3 billion in value added, $10.7 billion in value of shipments, $1.5 billion in payroll, and 41,500 jobs (U.S. Census Bureau 1999). Pulp and paper manufacturing in turn dominates the forest products sector, accounting for 62 percent of the sector's total value of shipments and 56 percent of total payroll. Harvests of pulpwood in 1996 accounted for 49 percent of total harvests in Alabama and 14 percent of total national pulpwood supply (U.S. Forest Service n.d.).

Figure 1. Timber-dependent counties (cross-hatched) and pulp and paper mills (dots) in Alabama 1996 (Howze et al., 2003).

Much of Alabama can be classified as timber dependent. A timber-dependent county is one in which 25 percent or more of manufacturing employment is in forest-based industries. By this measure, twenty-four out of forty-six rural non-metropolitan counties in Alabama (i.e., those non-metro counties with more than half their population living in rural areas) could be considered timber dependent in 2000. Most timber-dependent counties are located in western Alabama, especially in the south-central region (Figure 1).

The growth of Alabama's forest products industry, especially the pulp and paper sector, has created an enormous market for timber grown by the state's many nonindustrial private forest owners. In southern Alabama, where the growing season exceeds 220 days per year, trees grown in intensively managed plantations can be harvested for pulpwood in as few as fifteen years. Moreover, the relatively flat topography facilitates site preparation, plantation management, and harvesting, and numerous mills in the area provide a ready market for pulpwood. Together, these factors have encouraged conversion of millions of acres of former agricultural land to loblolly plantations. As of 1999, over 1.5 million acres of forestland in the southwestern quadrant of the state were in loblolly plantations, an increase of 66 percent since 1990 (Vissage 2000a, 2000b).

During the last two decades of the 20th century, investment in Alabama forestland was an attractive option for corporations and wealthy individuals interested in diversifying their portfolios. Such investments were especially attractive in the wood procurement zones of large pulp and paper mills. As a consequence, small forestland tracts were consolidated into larger landholdings (Bliss et al. 1998), in contrast to the national trend towards forestland fragmentation. This trend in Alabama is likely to continue into the future. It could increase dramatically if research on genetic engineering were to yield the increases in productivity and reductions in costs of production promised by some proponents (Sedjo 1999).

The pulp and paper industry has had substantial positive economic impact on the state of Alabama, providing direct and indirect employment opportunities where formerly few existed (Flick and Teeter 1988). However, in the period 1950-1990, while economic conditions generally improved across the state, rural timber-dependent counties lagged behind both urban and rural counties that were not timber dependent in important socioeconomic indicators, including median family income, households in poverty, educational attainment, and employment (Table 1). Perhaps most revealing, these counties have suffered steady declines in population despite massive investments by the forest products industry.

Why, despite the rapid evolution of the southern pulp and paper industry into global prominence, has the nation's "wood basket" remained among its poorest regions? The answer to this question is multi-dimensional and complex. Problems of persistent poverty predate emergence of the industry and cannot be completely addressed with reference to any one economic sector. But we believe our analysis is relevant to understanding the potential and limitations of forest-based development in Alabama and elsewhere. Our analysis focuses on Alabama's history of racially based social inequity, an increasingly concentrated pattern of land ownership, and systematic under-investment in human capital. Rather than challenging these conditions, development of Alabama's forestry sector accommodated them, ensuring that forest-based development would not dramatically affect the foundational causes of rural poverty.

Table 1. Comparison of socioeconomic indicators among Alabama counties with and without pulp and paper mills (after Joshi et al. 2000).

	1950	1960	1970	1980	1990	2000
Median Family Income ($)						
Seven pulp and paper mill counties	936	2524	5291	13235	22114	Na
Other non-MSA counties	1025	2604	5538	13369	23563	Na
Alabama	1580	3937	7266	16353	28688	41,657
USA	2619	5660	9590	19917	35225	50,046
Families below poverty (%)						
Seven pulp and paper mill counties	76.4	57.7	31.8	24.8	25.5	27.9
Other non-MSA counties	74.4	56.3	30.0	19.9	19.1	23.3
Alabama	56.3	39.1	20.7	14.8	14.3	16.1
USA	36.2	21.4	10.7	9.6	10.0	12.4
Adults with high school diploma (%)						
Seven pulp and paper mill counties	9.8	23.8	34.7	48.4	58.0	Na
Other non-MSA counties	8.2	21.2	31.0	44.9	55.6	Na
Alabama	12.4	30.3	41.3	56.5	66.9	75.3
USA	33.3	41.0	52.3	66.5	75.2	80.4
Unemployment Rate (%)						
Seven pulp and paper mill counties	N/A	5.8	4.8	8.4	10.2	Na
Other non-MSA counties	N/A	5.0	4.3	8.1	7.8	Na
Alabama	4.2	5.7	4.5	7.5	6.9	6.2
USA	4.8	5.1	4.4	6.5	6.3	5.8
Population change rate (%)[a]						
Seven pulp and paper mill counties	-6.5	-4.8	-3.7	2.5	-6.0	-0.6
Other non-MSA counties	-7.5	-9.1	0.5	13.1	2.1	10.7
Alabama	8.1	6.7	5.4	13.1	3.8	10.1
USA	14.5	18.5	13.4	11.4	9.8	13.1

Notes: The seven pulp and paper mill counties are non-MSA counties in southwest Alabama: Choctaw, Clarke, Dallas, Escambia, Marengo, Monroe, and Wilcox. "Other non-MSA counties" are the remaining thirty-seven non-MSA counties without pulp and paper mills.

[a]Data are for decades ending in year indicated.

Sources: Alabama Department of Economic and Community Affairs (multiple years), U.S. Bureau of the Census (multiple years).

Race and Class

The pulp and paper industry in Alabama is concentrated in the Black Belt, a string of counties stretching from Virginia through Louisiana, where African Americans make up 40 percent or more of the population. This region once prospered as the center of the cotton kingdom, but today it is known primarily for endemic poverty, low levels of educational achievement, and high rates of out-migration (Wimberley and Morris 1996; Duncan 1999; Joshi et al. 2000). The average poverty rate in 1997 for the sixteen rural non-metropolitan Black Belt counties in Alabama was 28 percent, nearly double the state average of 16 percent (U.S. Census Bureau 2000). In 1998, eight counties in Alabama's Black Belt were among the one hundred poorest counties in the nation. Wilcox County, home to a large pulp and paper mill, had the highest poverty rate in the state (33 percent) and was ranked as the twenty-second poorest county in the nation.

Social and political life in Alabama and other Deep South states is dominated by considerations of race. The rural South continues to be home to millions of African Americans, a high proportion of whom live in poverty. As eloquently attested to by Duncan (1999), African Americans and whites in the rural South live remarkably separate lives, reflecting a complex set of racial and class distinctions that affect social, economic, and political life throughout the region. These divisions present major obstacles to any efforts designed to overcome problems associated with persistent poverty. In the Black Belt, where African Americans have gained a measure of political power in recent decades, racial divisions continue to manifest themselves in a number of ways, including the continued segregation of school-age children in white-only private schools established immediately after federal courts mandated desegregation. In five Alabama counties, over 95 percent of students in public schools are African American. The unwillingness of white parents in some counties to send their children to public schools represents the continuation of a deep and long-standing division between the races.

In the economic realm, the legacy of slavery and farm tenancy has left its mark in numerous ways. African Americans own a small and shrinking share of all agricultural and forest lands in the rural South. The number of black-owned farms in Alabama declined by 98 percent from 1910 to 1987, and the acreage in black ownership declined by

96 percent (U.S. Census Bureau 1920-1987). This means that African Americans gain little direct benefit from the growth and sale of timber. Moreover, where agricultural land has been converted into forests, the resultant decline in employment opportunities in row-crop production has had a particularly serious impact on those whose only economic resource was their labor.

African Americans have gained relatively few employment opportunities in the forest products sector. At one time African Americans were well represented in logging operations, but the introduction of new technologies (feller bunchers, skidders, and loaders) led to greatly increased capital demands that usually could be met only through commercial credit at local banks. Whether through simple discrimination or because they had little business experience or collateral, few African Americans could qualify for loans of the size necessary to be competitive with highly productive logging outfits in the current industry. No longer was it possible to become an independent pulpwooder with only a chainsaw, an old truck, and a few strong workers. Most mills now require delivery of "long wood"—de-limbed whole trees that require specialized loaders in the woods and cranes at the mills. Modern logging equipment is far more efficient in terms of the amount of time it takes to cut and transport a load of logs to the mill and in the number of workers it takes to do the job. Working conditions (in terms of safety, reduced physical demands, higher pay) are surely better than in the old "short-wood" days for those who are able to find employment on logging crews, but there are far fewer jobs available. There are no systematic data available on the racial composition of logging crews, but our observations and interviews indicate that almost all owners of logging outfits and most of their crewmembers are white.

Clearer evidence of racial discrimination exists with regard to employment opportunities in pulp and paper mills. Prior to the 1970s, African Americans were limited to certain jobs near the bottom of the "lines of progression" (Northrup 1969). The end of lawful workplace segregation in the early 1970s had a delayed impact on the employment prospects of African Americans. In 1966, African Americans accounted for less than 12 percent of the total workforce in Alabama's pulp and paper mills; virtually none were to be found in clerical, sales, or managerial ranks (Bailey et al. 1996). Comparable data for 1993 reflect a gradual opening of opportunity, with African Americans accounting for 23 percent of all jobs, including nearly 10 percent of clerical, sales, and management jobs. Despite this improvement, vestiges of past discrimination persist. The most serious obstacle facing African Americans seeking high-wage jobs in pulp and paper mills is systematic under-investment in public education, which has left many local residents under-qualified for good jobs that do become available.

Who Owns the Forestland?

The impressive growth of the pulp and paper industry in Alabama was fueled in part by a land-ownership pattern conducive to supplying the huge volumes of wood fiber required to sustain the industry. The dominance of private forestland ownership means that a large supply of fiber is available to companies free from the complications and expense associated with obtaining harvesting rights on public lands.

Second, much of the private land is owned in large blocks by a relatively small number of landowners, particularly in the Coastal Plain and Black Belt regions of Alabama, the center of today's pulp and paper industry. The relatively flat topography and deep soils encouraged development of the slave-based plantation agriculture that flourished there before the Civil War. After slavery ended, many landowning families retained ownership of their lands through sharecropping and leasing arrangements. The concentration of land ownership during the days of King Cotton was further exacerbated by the hard times following the Civil War, when many smaller farm operations went broke and owners left the land in a massive exodus (Daniel 1985). Many of the large cotton plantations of the 1800s are forest stands and pine plantations today, and some are still owned by descendants of the same families that owned the land before the Civil War (Walkingstick 1996).

This concentrated land-ownership pattern made it easy for the pulp and paper industry to purchase both land and wood. Pulp and paper companies in the region typically follow a balanced strategy of wood procurement that includes ownership of company forestland as well as purchases of harvest rights from other private owners. In Alabama, they found willing sellers of forestland, idle agricultural land suitable for pulpwood production, and a reliable supply of fiber in large volumes from large ownerships.

With the creation of large, fiber-hungry mills, landowners had strong incentive to convert idle or marginal agricultural land to pulpwood production. Landowners in the immediate vicinity of the mills faced several opportunities: they could sell wood to the mill, sell forestland to the mill, or increase their own holdings in forestland in order to supply the mill. For rural, land-owning Alabamians, the rise of the pulp and paper industry was of great benefit, providing markets for a new crop and a foundation to sustain their ownership. As one informant said, "These mills made millionaires out of a lot of local landowners." Although growth of the pulp and paper industry did not create the relatively concentrated landownership pattern in the region, it has certainly facilitated its persistence.

Negative effects of the concentration of land ownership on rural well-being have been a subject of scholarly research for decades, particularly in the developing world. The primary effect is unequal access to land resources. Secondary effects include poverty, out-migration, food deficit, and environmental degradation (Griffin 1981; Hall 1987; El-Ghonemy 1990; Tyler et al. 1993). Research on land concentration in the United States has focused on relationships between farm size and community well-being (Goldschmidt 1978; Swanson 1988; Labao and Schulman 1991). Gaventa and Horton (1984) argued that concentrated ownership in Appalachia, combined with the failure of local and state governments to capture land and mineral wealth through taxation, led to underinvestment in human and physical capital and lack of economic-development opportunities. Kusel and Fortmann (1991) found that concentration of private timberland ownership in California was associated with low family income.

To explore relationships between the concentration of ownership of forestland and well-being in rural Alabama, Sisock (1998) utilized six measures of land concentration and a well-being index reflecting percent of families below the poverty level in 1989, net migration 1980-1988, average unemployment in 1990, and percent population with high school education in 1990. Sisock's analysis clearly demonstrated that significant levels of land concentration exist in rural Alabama, and that land concentration was significantly and negatively correlated with well-being. Counties in which land concentration was more pronounced achieved lower well-being index scores, even when controlling for race. Land concentration was significantly higher in counties having pulp and paper mills.

Many of the benefits from natural resource-based development (e.g. timber harvest revenues) flow to resource owners. Where ownership is highly concentrated, such as in Alabama's pulp and paper counties, these benefits are captured mainly by large forest owners, who are also the primary beneficiaries of the state's low property-tax rates. Industrial owners benefit further from generous tax abatements. Repeated attempts to reform Alabama's property-taxation policies to generate revenue for public education have been successfully resisted by strong forestry and agricultural interests. Alabama's property-tax burden was more than 60 percent below the national average in 1997 (Public Affairs Research Council 2001). Forestland in Florida that would be assessed $7,000 in property taxes would be assessed only $1,200 in Alabama (Benn 2001).

Abating Taxes, Neglecting Schools

Industrial-recruitment policies have had mixed impacts on the social and economic development of communities in which large forest products companies operate. The linchpin of Alabama's aggressive industrial-recruitment initiative, the provision of property-tax abatements, has had perhaps the most obvious effects on development of counties with pulp and paper mills. Industrial-development boards were authorized to issue revenue bonds to finance industrial projects and acquire land for lease to corporations. Since title to such properties was held by municipalities, they were exempt from state and local property taxes. These tax abatements included school taxes, the primary source of revenue for public education in the state. For a detailed examination of the impacts of tax abatements on education in Alabama, see Joshi et al. 2000.

In 1993, the only year for which such data are available, $78.5 million in ad valorem property tax was abated through local industrial-development boards, $30.3 million of this to the sixteen pulp and paper mills then present in the state (Joshi et al. 2000). These abatements, combined with exceedingly low property taxes and a low state income tax, resulted in total state and local tax revenues that were, adjusted for population, the lowest in the nation (Public Affairs Research Council 1998). In southwestern Alabama, where the pulp and paper industry is concentrated, the effect of the abatements was even more profound; the abated school revenue was roughly one-half of all school revenue generated from property taxes. In two counties, school tax abatements exceeded total school revenue (Joshi et al. 2000).

Although the Industrial Incentive Reform Act of 1992 limited future tax abatements to noneducational taxes and a ten-year period, the pulp and paper mills recruited under the previous policies continue to receive all abatements (Ward and Pippin 1994).

The combined impact of low and abated property taxes on funding for public education in rural schools has been profound. Theoretically, investments in education yield improvements in workforce quality. A large, high-quality workforce attracts new industry, which, in turn, contributes additional tax revenues for further investment in human capital. Tax abatements in rural counties hosting large industrial facilities such as pulp and paper mills represent a drain of revenue otherwise available for investment in human capital development.

Establishing a direct link between student performance and school funding is problematic. It is clear, however, that Stanford Achievement Test scores from public schools in Alabama's pulp and paper counties are far below national averages. Moreover, in their responses to a mail survey conducted in 1996 (Joshi et al. 2000), pulp and paper mill executives and Industrial Recruitment Board members rated local public-school graduates poor in writing, verbal communication, math, and computer skills. Mill executives further reported that at least one-quarter of their high-school-graduate employees needed supplementary adult-literacy classes. One executive complained that "we can't trust a high school diploma" from the local high school, because graduates lack entry-level job skills.

Frustrated by unsatisfactory recruitment of local employees, recognizing the poor condition of local public schools, and responding to public criticism, some pulp and paper companies have made periodic donations of money, equipment, and volunteer time to selected public schools. Others have established literacy and remedial classes for employees and their children. The magnitude of such donations and efforts varies tremendously, as does the frequency and regularity of giving. All aspects of the gifts are determined by the companies themselves, with variable input regarding needs from school administrators, students, or parents. While the gifts are welcomed by local schools, their impact is spotty at best, and they are a poor substitute for adequately funded public schools (Joshi et al. 2000).

If judged solely on the basis of their effectiveness in attracting forest industry to rural Alabama, property-tax abatements are marginally successful at best. While they played virtually no role in the industry's decision to locate in the South—that decision was based on the abundance of fiber, water, and cheap labor (Oden 1974)—abatements may have influenced the site-specific decisions of individual companies. If judged as a rural-development strategy, abatements, especially in conjunction with Alabama's low property-tax rates, must be seen as detrimental to achieving the goals of rural development. They have contributed to the impoverishment of already poor school systems, they have rendered local graduates unemployable in the very industry recruited to offer employment, and they have severely hampered development alternatives for these communities. Abatements are a clear example of a policy intended to facilitate forest-based rural development that has had, at least as regards the human capital side of development, a pronounced undesirable effect.

An Uncertain Future

Questions of community stability have long interested those conducting research on social aspects of forestry and forestry resources (Kaufman and Kaufman 1946; Lee et al. 1990). A central concern has been resource depletion and decline of employment. In the context of isolated resource-dependent communities, employment losses result in persistent unemployment and out-migration, adversely affecting local businesses, schools, churches, and other social institutions. The connection between sustainable harvests and community stability became a touchstone for early work in the field.

The combination of a long growing season and rapidly growing species (especially the loblolly pine) greatly reduces the threat of resource depletion in Alabama and other Southern states (although there is concern over harvest rates and cumulative impacts of intensive silvilcultural practices). Most forestland in the South is in private hands, reducing the likelihood that a single federal agency could initiate a policy removing a significant amount of timber from the market, as has been done in areas of the western United States where state and federal ownership is concentrated. And yet the issue of community decline associated with forestry remains a concern in Alabama and other Southern states as well as in the West. On the surface the issues are much the same: out-migration saps community strength leading to gradual decline. In the classic scenario, the resource is depleted or otherwise becomes unavailable (e.g., through policy), leading to mills being closed, logging jobs being lost, and people leaving in droves. The familiar pattern of booms and busts leading to ghost towns has historically been linked to forestry and mining operations in the western United States.

In Alabama, however, the key issues relate to technological change and industrial restructuring, rather than to resource availability. As previously noted, technological changes tend to replace labor with capital. In logging, chain saws and manual labor have been replaced by heavy equipment requiring capital investments of $500,000 or more (Bliss and Flick 1994). Today's mechanized log crews not only are far more productive per unit of labor than their predecessors, but they are far more mobile, able to operate 200 miles or more away from their home base during certain seasons. Thus, the connection between local resources and local employment opportunities is far weaker than it was in the past. Entrepreneurs able to mobilize enough capital to establish a logging operation are unlikely to live in rural communities with high rates of poverty.

In sawmills, the introduction of laser-guided and computerized equipment has simultaneously increased productivity and decreased labor costs. Even more striking have been the technological advancement and massive capital investments in the pulp and paper sector of the industry, which have allowed production to increase while the number of employees has continued to decline. Between 1990 and 1999, a period of economic boom, total manufacturing employment in Alabama's forest products industry decreased by 25 percent, from 55,600 to 41,500 (U.S. Census Bureau 1990, 1999).

Despite these gains in labor productivity and resulting loss of jobs, the forest products industry continues to be one of the most important sources of employment opportunity in rural Alabama. Pulp and paper mills in particular offer very attractive wages and benefits. Those fortunate enough to get a mill job rarely resign before retirement. Limited turnover and a steady decline in numbers of production workers has meant that few new opportunities have been created in recent years. Those opportunities have largely gone to white workers, even though most mills are located predominantly in areas with high African-American populations. This unbalanced distribution of jobs was the product of conscious racial discrimination until local unions were forced to desegregate in the 1970s (Bailey et al. 1996). Yet despite the end of overt racial discrimination, relatively few African Americans have been able to gain access to jobs in this industry, partly because of the limited number of new openings, and partly because of weaknesses in the local school systems that have left many applicants unqualified for mill jobs, as noted above.

Globalization of the forest products industry presents additional uncertainties to the forest-dependent communities of Alabama. Consolidation in the pulp and paper industry has led to a perpetually shifting ownership of mills, fewer companies in the sector, and a reduction in the number of pulp and paper mills in Alabama from sixteen to fourteen in the past decade. Many mills in the South are aging and in need of massive upgrading or replacement. The Southern Hemisphere has become increasingly attractive for new investments in physical plants and land due to the region's excellent tree-growing conditions, inexpensive land and labor, and relatively lax regulatory environment. An executive of one prominent U.S. integrated forest products company remarked in the mid-1990s that the search for investment opportunities in South America was so widespread that stepping into the airport terminals of South American capitals was "like arriving at a Society of American Foresters convention"— representatives of all the major U.S. companies were there. Fear of losing pulp and paper mills to foreign shores is often cited as justification for maintaining Alabama's low tax and business-friendly regulatory climate.

Lessons for Forest-based Rural Development

Forest resources and public policy choices have played key roles in shaping contemporary rural Alabama. Forests fueled the phenomenal growth of the pulp and paper industry. It was the region's abundant forest resources, above all else, that attracted both domestic and foreign investment and led to the South's emergence as a world center of pulp and paper production. Establishment of the industry resulted in employment opportunities that had not existed in the region before, in the mills themselves, in the wood procurement network, and in other indirectly related jobs.

Establishment of the pulp and paper industry hastened the transition from an agrarian to an industrial society. Local landowners became producers of fiber for multinational corporations with headquarters in distant cities and abroad. But this transition occurred with minimal disruption of existing local social relations. It made it possible for the landed elite to maintain dominance in land ownership, and with it, local political power. Economies of scale encouraged large ownerships to grow larger, often at the expense of smaller ownerships and less-well-capitalized owners. The rapid decline in the number and acreage of land owned by African-Americans has continued unabated. Relatively few African Americans got jobs in the mills; fewer still obtained positions of leadership within the industry. Rather than fostering opportunities for the rural poor, both black and white, to escape poverty, growth of the industry appears to have contributed to, rather than slowed, the out-migration of poor from the region. Moreover, taxation policies designed to facilitate agriculture, forestry, and industrial recruitment have resulted in inadequate funding of essential public services, principally education. Chronic under-investment in education has resulted in a dearth of human capital available for local development.

The Alabama experience suggests that what is good for forestry is not necessarily good for communities. Minimal property taxes, generous tax abatements, and a business-friendly regulatory environment contributed to Alabama's attractiveness for industrial-forestry investment. Such institutional attractions, combined with the state's natural endowment, led the state to become a world center for pulp and paper production.

The growth of the forest-based economy has contributed to improvement in the well-being of rural Alabamians over the past three decades (Table 1). Many rural communities owe whatever economic activity they have to the forest products sector. However, Alabama's forest-dependent counties continue to lag the rest of the state and the nation in all key measures of well-being. Why has rural Alabama failed to "bloom like a rose"? What lessons does the Alabama experience offer to forest-based development efforts elsewhere around the globe?

First, although forest resources can provide a foundation for economic development, excessive reliance on forestry—or any other single sector—encourages dependency rather than development. The success of Alabama's recruitment of the pulp and paper industry, coupled with its failure to invest in human capital, has effectively, if inadvertently, foreclosed other development options. Economic diversification is fundamental to rural development.

Second, land ownership matters. Lewis's observation, "Land not only produces income but serves as a store of wealth and power" (1980,

1) has profound implications for land-extensive enterprises such as forestry. Unless investments in forest-based rural development target intended beneficiaries, the primary beneficiaries will be those who own land or processing facilities. Moreover, few owners will be willing or able to invest in forest stewardship without secure rights to long-term use of the forest.

Third, what is good for forestry isn't necessarily good for rural communities. Policies designed to attract forest-sector investment may have unintended negative consequences. Industrialization, while bringing a measure of economic growth, may contribute to undesirable changes in land ownership and land use. Forestry policies should not be considered in isolation from policies involving labor, support for vital social services, investments in human and social capital, and environmental protection.

Finally, if forests are to contribute to supporting healthy rural communities, the social institutions governing their ownership and use must receive as careful tending as the forest itself. Existing ethnic, racial, and class structures have profound influence over who benefits from forest-based development and who does not. Unless such structures are taken explicitly into consideration when planning and implementing forest-based development programs and policies, existing patterns of access to resources, programs, and decision-making processes are likely to be maintained or strengthened. Potential benefits are unlikely to "trickle down" to the poor or the politically marginal.

Acknowledgements

The research from which this chapter is drawn was conducted by the authors in collaboration with a great number of faculty and graduate-student colleagues, especially including Mark Dubois, Glenn Howze, Mahendra Joshi, Karni Perez, Peter Sinclair, Mary Sisock, Lawrence Teeter, and Tamara Walkingstick. The research was supported by the USDA Cooperative State Research Service National Research Initiative Competitive Grants Program, the USDA Forest Service SE Forest Experiment Station, the Alabama Agricultural Experiment Station, and the Starker Program in Private and Family Forestry at Oregon State University.

References

Alabama State Docks. 2001. Port Facts. Mobile: Alabama State Docks. http://www.asdd.com/Asd/portfacts.htm

Bailey, Conner, Peter Sinclair, John Bliss, and Karni Perez. 1996. "Segmented Labor Markets in Alabama's Pulp and Paper Industry." *Rural Sociology* 61(3): 475-96.

Benn, Alvin. 2001. "Pension Official Says Alabama Needs Economic Reform." *Montgomery Advertiser*, February 13, 2001, page A1.

Bliss, John C., and Warren A. Flick. 1994. "With a Saw and a Truck; Alabama Pulpwood Producers." *Forest and Conservation History* 38:79-89.

Bliss, John C., Mary L. Sisock, and Thomas W. Birch. 1998. "Ownership Matters: Forest Land Concentration in Rural Alabama." *Society and Natural Resources* 11(4):401-10.

Cobb, J. C. 1993. *The Selling of the South: The Southern Crusade for Industrial Development, 1936-1990*. Urbana: University of Illinois Press.

Daniel, Pete. 1985. *Breaking the Land*. Urbana and Chicago: University of Illinois Press.

Duncan, Cynthia. 1999. *Worlds Apart*. New Haven, CT: Yale University Press.

El-Ghonemy, R. 1990. *The Political Economy of Rural Poverty: The Case for Land Reform*. New York: Routledge.

Falk, William W., and Thomas A. Lyson. 1988. *High Tech, Low Tech, No Tech; Recent Industrial and Occupational Change in the South*. Albany: State University of New York Press.

Flick, W., and L. Teeter. 1988. "Multiplier Effects of the Southern Forest Industries." *Forest Products Journal* 38(11/12):69-74.

Gaventa, J., and B. Horton. 1984. "Land Ownership and Land Reform in Appalachia." Pp. 233-244 in *Land Reform American Style*, Charles C. Geisler and F. J. Popper (eds.). Totowa, NJ: Rowman & Allenhead.

Goldschmidt, W. 1978. *As You Sow: Three Studies in the Social Consequences of Agribusiness*. Montclair NJ: Allenhead, Osmun.

Griffin, Keith. 1981. *Land Concentration and Rural Poverty*, second edition. London: The Macmillan Press.

Hall, Anthony. 1987. "Agrarian Crisis in Brazilian Amazonia: The Grande Carajas Programme." *Journal of Development Studies* 23:522-52.

Jackson, Harvey H., III. 1995. *Rivers of Hhistory: Life on the Coosa, Tallapoosa, Cahaba, and Alabama*. Tuscaloosa: University of Alabama Press.

Joshi, Mahendra L., John C. Bliss, and Conner Bailey. 2000. "Investing in Industry, Under-investing in Human Capital: Forest-based Development in Alabama." *Society and Natural Resources* 13(5):291-319.

Kaufman, Harold F., and Lois C. Kaufman. 1946. "Toward the Stabilization and Enrichment of a Forest Community: the Montana Study." Pp. 27-39 in *Community and Forestry: Continuities in the Sociology of Natural Resources*, R. G. Lee, D. R. Field, and W. R. Burch, Jr. (eds.). Boulder, CO: Westview Press.

Kusel, J., and L. Fortmann. 1991. Well-being in forest dependent communities, Vol. 1. Sacramento: California Department of Forestry and Fire Protection, Forest and Rangeland Resources Assessment Program.

Labao, L., and M. Schulman. 1991. "Farming Patterns, Rural Restructuring, and Poverty: A Comparative Regional Analysis." *Rural Sociology* 56:565-602.

Lee, R. G., D. R. Field, and W. R. Burch, Jr. (eds.). 1990. *Community and Forestry: Continuities in the Sociology of Natural Resources*, Boulder, CO: Westview Press.

Lewis, J. A. 1980. Land ownership in the United States, 1978. Agricultural Information Bulletin No. 435. Washington, D.C.: U.S. Department of Agriculture, Economics, Statistics, and Cooperatives Service.

Miller, P. E. 1994. Southern pulpwood production, 1992. USDA Forest Service, Southern Forest Experiment Station, New Orleans, LA. Resource Bulletin SO-187.

Northrup, Herbert R. 1969. *The Negro in the Paper Industry: The Racial Policies of American Industry. No. 9.* Philadelphia: University of Pennsylvania Press.

Oden, J. P. 1974. Development of the Southern pulp and paper industry, 1900-1970. Ph.D. dissertation, Mississippi State University, Starkville.

Public Affairs Research Council. 1998. How Alabama's Taxes Compare. The PARCA Report, Number 42. Birmingham: Public Affairs Research Council, Samford University.

Sedjo, Roger A. 1999. Biotechnology and Planted Forests: Assessment of Potential and Possibilities. Discussion Paper 00-06, December 1999. Washington, D.C.: Resources for the Future.

Sisock, M. 1998. Unequal shares: Forestland concentration and well-being in rural Alabama. Unpublished M.S. thesis, Auburn University, Auburn, Alabama. 87 p.

Swanson, L. 1988. *Agriculture and Community Change in the U.S.: The Congressional Research Reports.* Boulder, CO: Westview Press.

Tyler, G. J., R. El-Ghonemy, and Y. Couvreur. 1993. "Alleviating Rural Poverty through Agricultural Growth." *Journal of Development Studies* 29:358-64.

U.S. Census Bureau. 1990. Annual Survey of Manufacturers 1990. Geographic Area Statistics. Washington, D.C.: Department of Commerce, Census Bureau.

U.S. Census Bureau. 1999. Annual Survey of Manufacturers 1999. Geographic Area Statistics. Washington, D.C.: Department of Commerce, Census Bureau. http://www.census.gov/prod/2001pubs/m99-as3.pdf

U.S. Census Bureau. 2000. County Estimates for People of All Ages in Poverty for Alabama: 1997. Released November 2000. Washington, D.C.: U.S. Department of Commerce, Census Bureau. http://www.census.gov/hhes.www/saipe/stcty/a97_01.htm.

U.S. Census Bureau. 2001. Small Area Income and Poverty Estimates, 1998. Released December 20, 2001. Washington, D.C.: U.S. Department of Commerce, Census Bureau. http://www.census.gov/hhes/www/saipe/stcty/sc98ftpdoc.html.

U.S. Census Bureau. 1920-1987. Census of Agriculture. Washington, D.C.: U.S. Department of Commerce, Census Bureau.

U.S. Forest Service. n.d. Forest Inventory and Analysis Timber Product Output
(TPO) Database Retrieval System.

Vissage, J. 2000a. Forest statistics for Southwest-South Alabama, 1999.
Resource Bulletin SRS-55. Asheville, NC: Southern Research Station, U.S.
Department of Agriculture Forest Service.

Vissage, J. 2000b. Forest statistics for Southwest-North Alabama, 1999.
Resource Bulletin SRS-56. Asheville, NC: Southern Research Station, U.S.
Department of Agriculture Forest Service.

Vissage, J., and P. Miller. 1991. Forest statistics for Alabama counties - 1990.
Southern Forest Exp. Station Resource Bulletin SO-158. New Orleans, LA:
U.S.D.A. Forest Service.

Walker, Laurence C. 1991. *The Southern Forest: A Chronicle.* Austin: University
of Texas Press.

Walkingstick, T. L. 1996. Pulpwood, dinettes, and doublewides: Comparative
case studies of forest dependency in Alabama. Unpublished Ph.D.
dissertation, Auburn University, Auburn, Alabama.

Ward, K., and T. Pippin. 1994. Alabama property tax administration revisited,
1994. Center for Governmental Services, Auburn University, Auburn,
Alabama.

Wimberley, Ronald C., and Libby V. Morris. 1996. The reference book on
regional well-being: U.S. regions, the Black Belt, Appalachia. Starkville.
Southern Rural Development Center, Mississippi State University.

CHAPTER 9
Occupational Community and Forest Work: Three Cases from the Pacific Northwest

Matthew S. Carroll, Robert G. Lee,
and Rebecca J. McLain

D espite seventy-five years of disagreement over its precise definition (and several premature pronouncements of its death), the concept of community as a mediating institution between individuals and the larger society remains powerful in both sociological and popular literature. In the world of natural resource social science, there are perhaps more books and articles appearing with "community" in the title than ever. Most of this literature assumes that community involves a specifically geographic dimension—that is to say that "community" is coincident with "town" or a territorially bounded residence area. However, there is a thread extending far back in the literature which views "community" as a social psychological phenomenon rather than a territorial one (Nisbet 1962; Bender 1978). This view holds that, while in pre-industrialized society most communal relationships were developed and maintained in limited geographic space, in a globalized world such relationships can exist independent of territorial boundaries. Thus one's fellow community member might happen to live next door, or she might live a half a world away.

One manifestation of the "non-territorial" concept of community is that of occupational community. The term was probably first coined in a classic study of a printers' union by Lipset, Trow, and Coleman (1956). The basic notion of occupational community is that members of some occupations come to share a common (or community) life set apart from others in society (Salaman 1974; Van Maanen and Barley 1984). This common life extends beyond the workplace and working hours and is, in many cases, independent of the particular neighborhood or geographic community in which the members reside.

A key defining characteristic of an occupational community is that its members' sense of identity and embeddedness are closely tied to the occupation: "The notion of an occupational community derives from two classical sociological premises. First is the contention that people bound together by common values, interests and a sense of tradition, share bonds of solidarity or mutual regard and partake of a communal way of life that contrasts in idyllic ways with the competition, individualism, and rational calculation of self-interest associated with persons organized on utilitarian principles" (Van Maanen and Barley 1984, 292). Members of occupational communities tend to spend a significant portion of their free time in the company of others in a similar occupation and members tend to look to each other as a primary reference group. Thus, the opinions and values of other "insiders" come to be seen as more important and valid than those of out-group members. The member of such a community looks to other members in developing and defining his or her own identity or sense of self (Blumer 1969). The individual's identity literally becomes, at least in part, a reflection of the group, as he or she is primarily subject to the influences of other group members. This socialization process is common in many groups, but in the case of occupational communities the distinctive values and worldview that result tend to center specifically around the occupation and its culture.

The focus of this chapter is a discussion of studies of three examples of occupational communities whose members have traditionally worked at least part of the year in the forests of the northwestern U.S.: loggers, fruit harvesters (who harvest huckleberries in the forest), and mushroom harvesters. The results of each of these cases have been published elsewhere. While we will give most attention to loggers, since we have studied them more intensively, comparison of these three occupations will illustrate the nature and importance of occupational communities to the use of forests.

Because each of these cases is described elsewhere, we will dispense with a detailed description of study methods other than to say that each was examined using qualitative methods, in-depth interviews and some level of participant observation (Glaser and Strauss 1980; Charmaz, 2000). Loggers were studied twice, once in the early 1980s and again in the late 1980s and early 1990s in the midst of the spotted owl controversy (Lee, Carroll, and Warren 1991; Carroll 1995). The study that included the fruit harvesters (actually a broader study of wild huckleberry harvest) was conducted in 1999 and 2000 (Carroll, Blatner, and Cohn 2003), although we also make reference to an earlier book on the subject (Sonnemann and Steigmeyer 1992). The mushroom study was conducted from 1993 through 1998 (McLain

2000), although we also refer to a similar study also conducted in the mid 1990s (Fine 1997).

Northwestern Loggers

The loggers studied in the early 1980s and again in the early 1990s were a classic fit to the occupational community troupe as described in the sociological literature. The studies found very clear social boundaries around the logger group. Individuals involved in any part of the process of moving logs from the stump to the mill were considered part of the occupation. This included four categories of work: those who cut the trees (fallers and buckers); individuals who moved the logs from the stump to the landing where they are loaded onto trucks (rigging crew members); logging road builders; and log truck drivers. Workers who were not considered loggers included those whose primary duties were to cut and pile brush, clear logging debris, or plant trees after the harvesting operations were completed. At first, these membership criteria seemed arbitrary, but further exposure to the loggers' value system revealed inherent logic; logging has historically been an extraction activity. Although the era of "cut and get out" logging is long over, some of the values that developed in that period seem to have survived in the group studied. One of the ideas that survived is that "real" logging involves getting wood to the mill. In addition to viewing themselves as highly individualistic and independent, a bond that linked this group of workers was the commitment to the task of "getting the logs to town." Would-be loggers who were seen by their co-workers as lacking this commitment rarely last in the job. Informants said that if a crew member displayed lack of commitment by failing to "pull his weight," he would either be "sent down the road" by a foreman or ostracized by his fellow workers.

For those studied, logging was clearly more than simply a means of earning wages; it represented a way of life complete with a set of highly developed traditions and shared values that have been cultivated and passed down through multiple generations. The boundary between loggers and non-loggers was very clear to members of these two groups, and they attributed considerable significance to group membership. The studies observed a strong sense of shared mission and an almost militant esprit de corps.

Despite the social boundary defining the loggers' community, the logging group was far from a seamless web. This finding parallels those of others who have studied occupational communities (see especially Miller and Johnson 1981; Strangleman 2001). There was clear role segregation and limited mobility between the four job categories comprising the occupation. Although individuals occasionally moved from one category to another (for example, a rigging crewman might try bucking in the hope of eventually becoming a faller), informants and observations indicated a tendency for a worker to stay in a category once having become established there. Truck drivers, for example, stated time after time in the interviews that they wouldn't want to "get dirty" on a rigging crew and rigging crew members rarely expressed interest in driving a truck.

Fallers and buckers occupied the symbolic center and the high status position of the loggers' world. They were followed by rigging crewmen, with roadbuilders and truck drivers located closer to the periphery of the community. This center-to-periphery phenomenon was revealed both in terms of the relative esteem expressed by others within the community for occupants of various positions and also by the degree of attachment to the occupation demonstrated by members of the respective categories. Although members of all categories expressed relatively high degrees of attachment to logging as an occupation and way of life, fallers, buckers, and rigging crew members exhibited stronger and more consistent attachments. The implications of this for adaptability to other occupations are discussed below.

The Logger Identity

Logging is not the only activity in a natural setting around which social actors formulate their identities (Statham 1995). However, it would be difficult to point to an example of a more highly developed or heartfelt case. As noted above, this highly developed identity was found to be particularly pronounced among fallers, buckers, and rigging crew members. The identities of those interviewed and observed tended to revolve around four interrelated themes: independence, pride in skill, pride in facing danger, and a sense of being in a unique category of workers. Loggers in all occupational categories were clearly fond of regaling listeners with stories of daring accomplishments with a chain saw, with a piece of heavy equipment, or behind the wheel of a truck.

These accomplishments invariably were achieved by some combination of superior skill, physical strength, and unblinking "nerve." The expression of independence and rugged individualism surfaced repeatedly in the interviewing process. "You can't tell a logger what to do" was a statement recorded in many interviews.

It became clear early in the participant observation that occupational identity was created and reinforced by in-group interaction. Logger-like behavior and attitudes were reinforced and non-logger-like ones were discouraged or even ridiculed. One example is the loggers' view of the U. S. Forest Service, which manages much of the land in the places we studied loggers. Nearly every logger interviewed made a negative statement about the agency. Perhaps the most direct insight into this was provided by an equipment operator on a rigging crew who tacitly admitted the existence of group influence by prefacing a monologue on the agency with the remark: "I'm a logger, so I'm supposed to hate the Forest Service . . ."

Occupational identity had two interrelated consequences for the logger. One was to foster what was often a very intense attachment to the occupation; the other was to provide the individual with an identity and its accompanying sense of empowerment and purpose. "Getting the logs to town" was seen as an important mission that is accomplished in spite of weather, steep ground, equipment failure, fires, and worst of all, interference from the Forest Service and assorted environmentalists. Possessing the skills and courage to accomplish this difficult task led the logger to set himself apart from ordinary people.

Shared Meanings

Loggers viewed themselves as extreme, rugged individualists (in both the physical and economic sense) whose survival and prosperity was based almost exclusively on individual initiative, skill, and hard work. Loggers favored compensation based on individual production. For example, fallers and buckers (including those who worked for a large unionized company) preferred to be paid on the basis of the volume of timber harvested rather than on the basis of day wages.

Loggers shared a "can-do" or "do what it takes to get the job done" ethic. Loggers regarded formal arrangements and abstract rules as unnecessary or impractical. They were also observed to be creative and innovative in solving the mechanical and logistical problems that often surfaced in moving the logs from the stump to the mill. Many loggers had become skilled mechanics by a process of trial and error. The ability to figure things out on one's own and to solve problems by improvising reflects common sense—a highly valued attribute in the loggers' world.

To the logger, the city represented a crowded, unhappy place where individualism and freedom were stifled. Many who were interviewed stated that they simply "couldn't" live in a city under any circumstances. One employee of a log trucking firm reported that he had turned down the offer of managing the maintenance of a fleet of trucks for a firm in Portland. He proudly stated that the offer included a doubling of his present salary and free helicopter rides to and from the city on Mondays and Fridays. He refused the offer because he valued his rural lifestyle and attachments to friends and co-workers.

One of the ways that loggers, particularly those who work for a "gyppo" (an independent contractor for woods work), maintained a sense of independence was to change jobs on a frequent basis. Job changing was a time-honored custom among loggers and was apparently a tradition passed down from the very early days of western logging (Holbrook 1934 Hayner 1945; Stevens 1979). In times of plentiful jobs, an individual would quit for no stated reason and be hired back at a later time with no hard feelings. Gyppo operations often expanded and contracted from year to year, occasionally leaving no openings for individuals who had performed entirely satisfactorily in the prior year.

Most loggers, and particularly the gyppo loggers, expressed confidence that, under ordinary circumstances, another job could be obtained should the need arise. The individual derived his sense of job security not from a long-standing relationship with a particular employer but rather from his marketability based upon his reputation in the occupational community. This reputation, reflected back to the individual from his peers, contributed to his occupational identity and sense of personal empowerment. In a sense, the logger's reputation was the primary product of his work and provided the basis of both identity and job security.

Information for job references made its way between employer and potential employee almost entirely by word of mouth: experienced loggers had developed reputations that were passed on through informal networks. Many of those interviewed indicated that jobs would be offered to them rather than their having to look for work. Informants stated that in the late winter employers would begin calling around "to put a crew together" and those with reputations as the best workers were likely to have multiple job offers. In the case of larger company operations, union rules often would dictate who would be offered job slots first, but even in the case of larger companies, the remaining unclaimed job slots usually would be filled through the use of informal networks.

Worker Adaptability

In the early 1980s, the labor market for loggers in the study area depressed as the industry experienced the worst economic slump since the 1930s. This was followed by a brief boom period that was, in turn, cut short by harvest restrictions on public lands relating to the protection of habitat for the northern spotted owl and associated species. In retrospect, it is clear that the early study years marked the beginning of a transformation in which the industry permanently reduced employment substantially below levels common in the 1960s and 1970s.

The occupational community served a variety of very useful purposes in the lives of loggers. Mutual support and helping behavior within the community were strongly evident. Members, for the most part, believed in their work and the group tended to reinforce the sense of independence and empowerment in its individual members. Experienced hands taught new members the tricks of the trade and helped one another adapt to technological developments in the industry. The community had even developed its own internal job-referral network.

The community evolved over well more than fifty years, during which there were periodic shifts in the forest products economy but few questions about the long-term prospects of employment (except, possibly, during the Great Depression). Loggers, in our observation, were extraordinarily adept at finding innovative and more efficient ways to "get the logs to town," but it is not at all apparent that they were equipped to adapt to circumstances under which the logs were unavailable, no longer needed, or harvested with fewer workers. Rather, the very mechanisms that had embodied and maintained the loggers' community seem in some ways to impede problem-solving behavior that could possibly lead to the creation of alternative livelihoods.

A highly developed and narrowly focused occupational identity can very quickly be transformed from an asset to a detriment. Many of the loggers observed and interviewed had been taught since childhood to believe that logging is the only acceptable way to make a living. A typical individual may have followed in his father's footsteps, devoting ten or twenty years to developing skills and a reputation as a good logger. In the course of that time he would have received numerous affirmations from those around him that served to strengthen his identity and commitment to the occupation. He would have developed a circle of friends largely from the occupational group and many of his leisure-time activities would be, in one way or another, related to logging. If such an individual were suddenly faced with the fact that working in the woods was no longer a viable alternative, he not only lost a means of earning a wage, but an important part of his identity and a sense of personal empowerment as well. The more firmly attached an individual was to this occupational identity, the more traumatic and disorienting this kind of an experience was likely to be.

None of the loggers' strategies for getting a job adequately prepared them to cope with the set of conditions in the western forest products political economy in the post-spotted owl period The intergenerational transmission of values and shared meanings, group influences, the tradition of hard physical work, the attachment to rural life, and the job-information networks all evolved under conditions of relatively predictable demands for labor. These strategies did not prepare loggers to look outside the occupation for work. Rather, the net effect seems to have been that of fostering and encouraging attachment to an occupation and a way of life that, for many, was no longer viable.

The most difficult problems of adjustment were often faced by those relatively high-status individuals closest to the "center" of the occupation—fallers, buckers, and rigging crew members. This was due largely to two factors: their characteristically higher degree of attachment to the occupation and the relatively lower transferability of their skills to other jobs. Logging road builders and truck drivers generally shared strong preferences to work in logging, but their occupational identities as loggers tended not to be as strong and their skills were more readily transferable to other occupations. It was a less difficult transition (both in terms of identity and applicability of skills) for a log truck driver to take a long-haul truck-driving job or for a roadbuilder to hire on to a general construction crew (assuming such jobs were available) than it would be for a timber faller or a rigging crew member to find alternative employment. Chain saw operation for example, is not a skill in great demand outside of logging.

Harvest restrictions resulting from spotted owl habitat protection had an impact on the loggers' occupational community beyond the loss of jobs. The controversy itself, fought through the media on a national (and at times even international) stage, was vitriolic, with charges and countercharges between the forest industry and environmental interests appearing in the press on an almost daily basis. In those exchanges, and particularly in editorial cartoons, the industry was often portrayed as a logger, thereby conflating the roles of decision makers and workers. The following is exerpted from a field interview and illustrates how workers experienced the way they were protrayed as destroyers of the forest: "[He] said that he felt as though the media has treated the people of ——— like 'shit.' He said that 'they are depicting us as barbarians and idiots and that we are raping the forest,' and he said that he 'feels really angry at this depiction of his community.' " The result was a struggle not just over the disposition of the forest and job impacts, but also over how the loggers' occupational community was defined in the larger society. What was once largely seen as a romantic occupation was now being portrayed as "dirty work." As Ashforth and Kreiner (1999) state: "Everett Hughes . . . invoked the term 'dirty work' to refer to tasks and occupations that are likely to be perceived as disgusting or degrading. Hughes . . . observed that society delegates dirty work to groups who act as agents on society's behalf, and that society then stigmatizes these groups effectively disowning and disavowing the work it has mandated" (413).

The idea that logging might be dirty work rather than a romantic occupation did not originate with the controversy surrounding the habitat of the spotted owl. The famous logger historian Steward Holbrook alluded much earlier to "polite society's" distaste for logging (1934). However, the rhetoric around the spotted owl issue brought the alternative conception of the occupation into sharp (and for its members, often painful) relief (Moore 1993).

Fruit (Huckleberry) Harvesters

In a recent study of wild edible huckleberry harvest in the vicinity of the Colville National Forest in northeastern Washington (Carroll, Blatner, and Cohn 2003), the senior author was initially surprised to discover that a small but significant subset of those harvesting berries in the study area were more or less full-time, migratory fruit harvesters. Interviewees stated that they traveled a regular pattern each year harvesting citrus fruits in California (and in some cases Florida), apples and cherries in north-central Washington, and huckleberries in eastern Washington, northern Idaho, and western Montana. Some also reported harvesting mushrooms but, as we will describe later in this chapter, mushroom harvest tends to be a specialized activity. Several interviews later, it became clear that these self-described "fruit tramps" constitute an occupational community with intergenerational traditions, a large stock of occupational knowledge, a distinct worldview, and well-articulated occupational identities.

Writing about this group in another context (and referring specifically to one of her key informants), Toby Sonneman states:

> Rosie's argument moved me, bringing back all my years of living among fruit pickers and getting to know their ways. It reminded me why after reading John Steinbeck's Grapes of Wrath in my youth I was so attracted to the migratory life and so glad to find the people Steinbeck wrote about still existed. For all its hardships—low pay, low status, back-breaking work, and often poor conditions in the field and inadequate housing—most of the people who work in the fields and orchards are not downtrodden individuals. "Fruit tramps," they call themselves, mockingly aware that mainstream society has derogatorily labeled them "tramps." Although they are regarded with disdain and encouraged by schools, communities, and government organizations to leave agricultural work rather than to improve it, these people have miraculously clung to their self-respect, believing in the dignity and value of their work. A sense of pride sustains them (Sonneman and Steigmeyer, 1992, 4-5).

The following is an excerpt from interview notes describing a typical group interviewed in the Colville huckleberry study:

> This is a family group contacted at their camp in the Lightning Creek drainage. This group consists of the parents, their two adult sons, and their girlfriends/ spouses. They are camping with friends. They described themselves as "fruit tramps." They pick cherries in the Yakima Valley . . . and then move to Idaho to pick huckleberries. The parents said they had picked fruit in Washington and Florida with their families since childhood. The father said his family had been fruit tramps forever, but now, out of nine siblings, only two are still picking.
>
> . . . They had heard about huckleberry picking from other fruit tramps, but had never tried it. Then, about ten or fifteen years ago, a friend brought them to the area and they got into berry picking. They enjoy being outdoors. One son said, "It beats working by the hour." The mother said picking huckleberries was better than picking cherries because "there's no boss standing over you all the time." She complained about the costs of picking cherries—housing, food, etc, vs. what pickers were paid. She thought the owners could pay more, considering the price they (owners) received. With huckleberries, you get to keep it all and it is good money.

Other interviewees specialized in picking huckleberries only. One, an older man, described growing up in Montana in a "berry" family. His father began picking berries in the 1920s and taught him to pick at a young age. His uncles and brothers also picked all their lives. Although he was retired from a career as a truck driver, this interviewee clearly linked his identity to berry harvest and extolled the virtues of a good berry camp and the traditions of picking passed down through generations. Another, a woman in her twenties, said she was born in West Virginia and picked fruit with her family all over the West as a child and teenager. She also described having chronic seizures as a child that she attributed to pesticide use in orchards, and said her family had won a $5,000 court settlement over the problem. She stated that her father picked fruit to within six months of his death.

Other themes from interviews with fruit tramps included pride in skill and knowledge, valuing freedom and outdoor work, and experiencing tension with regulators or potential regulators (in this case the Forest Service), particularly over access issues, especially the use of roads.

Although fruit harvesters working in the forest have not, as have some other forest workers, been the subject of the years of research and policy debate, the evidence uncovered in the huckleberry study clearly points to an occupational-community dynamic at work with some commonalities with loggers (described above) and mushroom harvesters (to be described below). We believe these communities merit more scholarly attention as social scientists endeavor to examine what have been heretofore virtually "invisible" groups who depend on the forest for at least part of their livelihood.

Mushroom Gatherers

The fruiting characteristics of forest fungi have created conditions condusive to the emergence of occupational communities organized around the cycles of commercial mushroom gatherering opportunities (McLain 2000). Different species of forest fungi fruit in different phases of different seasons, and the timing of their emergence from the ground cannot be predicted. Moreover, the places mushrooms can be found at a given time cannot be precisely known. Mushroom production is governed by biological processes that seldom conform to mechanistic government rules and regulations governing where and when harvesting is permitted. A flexible and voluntaristic foraging strategy has proved to be the most successful way of finding mushrooms. Historically, these aspects of mushroom production have contributed to the formation of self-organizing communities of commercial mushroom gatherers who maintain close communication with one another.

McLain (2000) has studied mushroom pickers at Sisters, Oregon. Some members of this community will scout out promising patches at times associated with past crops. A good crop will be communicated to other members of the community, since success in commercial mushroom gathering requires a sufficient number of harvesters to supply buyers' requirements. Picking will be concentrated on "flushes," pockets where mushrooms fruit in relative abundance. Mushrooms are highly perishable commodities and vary in value depending on their size and condition. Small, over-mature, or worm-eaten mushrooms have little market value.

Buyers learn of good "picks" and establish stations nearby where they can set up a booth as a collection point; mushroom gatherers congregate here to sell what they have found. These stations are nodes in an extended communication network reaching far beyond the forested region where a good pick has been established. Buyers are key sources of information about the abundance and quality of mushrooms in a given location. A good crop will draw several mushroom buyers who then compete with one another for quality mushrooms. Since mushroom crops are episodic, mushroom gathering communities do not occupy a particular location for more than several weeks. As such, they function as mobile information networks, and tend to move on to other regions or forests where mushrooms have been found in the past or have been reported by trusted others.

Like loggers and fruit harvesters, mushroom gathering communities are united by shared meanings and identities. But unlike loggers, mushroom gatherers tend to group around a shared ethnic identity and language, facilitating interpersonal communication. The first mushroom gatherers relied on this activity to supplement incomes and enjoy a relaxing family time in the woods. They often lived in small towns in rural locations near the forests where mushrooms were found. With the growth of national and international mushroom markets, several ethnic groups, especially Mexicans and Asians, have taken up mushroom gathering as one source of income in a multi-resource economy. Communication networks tend to be segmented by ethnic groups, with each group having its own foraging strategy and communication network. Yet separate ethnic groups come together at buying stations and may share information provided by buyers.

Mushroom gatherers have also exhibited considerable adaptability in response to increasing competition among picker communities, as well as in response to tightening surveillance and regulation by state and federal government agencies. Information about good patches is carefully guarded by pickers, and is only shared with others whom they consider part of their community. Pickers tend to "farm" particular patches, often returning several times during the fruiting season to pick mushrooms as they mature. Pickers historically relied on self-policing and voluntary deference to others by staying out of patches they perceived to be farmed by others. The secretive nature of mushroom picking is legendary, with pickers carefully guarding knowledge of favored patches. Many pickers further limit such information by seeking out dispersed camp locations and only appearing at stations when they have a crop to sell.

Mushroom gathering has recently come under the regulation of state and federal agencies. The U.S. Forest Service has established a permit system and imposed regulations on where and when people can harvest mushrooms. They have also designated camps where harvesters are to stay when visiting a national forest. This has brought mushroom harvesting under the close surveillance of the federal government. State and local law-enforcement agents have joined federal officers in enforcing these regulations, as well as monitoring the transport of mushrooms to make sure that harvesting was done under the appropriate federal permits.

Grouping of mushroom gatherers in one camp where they can be efficiently watched by law-enforcement officers has reduced their opportunity to maintain knowledge of secret patches and foraging strategies and led to increasing antipathy and distrust of the government. The watchful eye of the government, utilizing the latest technologies developed for surveillance of those engaged in illegal drug production and distribution, has further alienated mushroom harvesters from government agencies. Like loggers and berry pickers, mushroom harvesters have increasingly come to view the U.S. Forest Service as a hostile police force rather than as an agency dedicated to land and resource stewardship.

Conclusion: Commonalities and Differences

Loggers, berry pickers, and mushroom gatherers all exhibit the characteristics of occupational communities. Their personal identities were found to be integrally related to their work; work and leisure were not experienced as separate social worlds; and community bonds emerge from sharing a common enterprise and espirit de corps. None of these communities as we studied them exhibited the sort of economic individualism characteristic of modern work settings where individuals are directly dependent on the state or a business. Thus we conclude that our evidence suggests that occupational communities serve as mediating structures, standing between the individual and larger governmental and business organizations. In this sense, they are some of the last vestiges of earlier forms of economic organization, in which a person's first obligations were to a family, parish, guild, and/or geographic community.

Occupational communities help to assure economic security through extended, informal communication networks. A person in one of these ocupational communities acquires security by his or her identification with a group and reputation as a worker. Hence, individuals will look to others in their group for guidance or affirmation. Social approval from many larger institutions of society is not highly valued, and is often seen as a way of becoming disloyal to others in the occupation. Loyalty, trustworthiness, and hard work are key ingredients of a person's reputation within these communities.

Loggers differ from fruit, and mushroom pickers in the extent to which information is shared. Since permission to cut trees, unlike mushroom and berry foraging, is not related to a logger's skill, job security among loggers is enhanced by engaging in public rituals that display strength and skill. Gossip and storytelling are a central part of the heroics of logging. In this sense, logging shows at county fairs or community festivals are not just entertainment. They are also important opportunities to acquire and display status in the community. Privacy, rather than public display, is a key feature of fruit and mushroom pickers. As foragers, they rely on arcane information shared only in closed networks. Job security is contingent upon the careful harboring of information about the location of berries or mushrooms, as well as on one's ability to gather these resources.

The tension between the U.S. Forest Service and loggers, berry pickers, and mushroom gatherers is not just about competing objectives. At its core rests a contest between the claims of the state and the claims of a group mediating the relationship of the state to the individual. The U.S. Forest Service, as an agent for the nation-state, seeks to create and administer individual rights so that it can efficiently regulate the behavior of individuals. Members of occupational communities resist these attempts of the state to make individuals directly dependent upon it, since their identities, economic security, and social worlds are embedded in mediating relationships within their communities. The U.S. Forest Service's use of regulations and law enforcement threatens forms of association that have assured meaning and security for these communities. Hence, the most important underlying issue involving the use of federal lands by occupational communities may be threats to freedom of association. Full imposition of state ideology and control may require that past understandings, accepting the role of occupational communities, be supplanted by the creation and regulation of individual rights to access and use natural resources on federal lands.

The future of occupational communities in forests is increasingly uncertain. Uncertainty is also felt by members of rural residential communities occupied by a wide variety of occupations, including small numbers of loggers, mushroom gatherers, and fruit pickers that may have a permanent residence from which to travel. Community forestry in general must address a common issue. Social control by the nation-state is increasing in almost all social domains. Concerns with environmental protection and public safety, especially the protection of endangered species on federal lands, has accelerated this trend in agencies such as the U.S. Forest Service. The goal of environmental security is pursued by expanding the role of government in regulating the lives of individual citizens. As mediating social structures, occupational communities and residential communities have maintained the allegiances of individuals to groups other than the nation-state. Advocates for expanding the role of the state appear to have little appreciation for the role of occupational communities or local communities, and generally favor their replacement by individual rights that tie persons to the state. While residential communities may be more successful in accommodating growing articulation of social activity through allocation of individual rights, occupational communities will face increasing challenges to their capacity for self-regulation and a continuing role in the use and management of forests.

References

Ashforth, B. E., and G. E. Kreiner. 1999. " 'How Can You Do It?': Dirty Work and the Challenge of Constructing a Positive Identity." *Academy of Management Review* 24(3): 413-36.

Bender, T. 1978. *Community and Social Change in America*. Baltimore. The Johns Hopkins University Press.

Blumer, H. 1969. *Symbolic Interactionism*. Englewood Cliffs, NJ: Prentice Hall.

Carroll, M.S. 1995. *Community and the Northwestern Logger: Continuities and Change in the Era of the Spotted Owl*. Boulder, CO. Westview Press. Rural Studies Series.

Carroll, M. S., K. A. Blatner, and P. Cohn. 2003. "Somewhere Between: Social Embeddedness and the Spectrum of Wild Edible Huckleberry Harvest and Use." *Rural Sociology* 68(3) 319-42.

Charmaz, K. 2000. "Grounded Theory: Objectivist and Constructivist Methods" Pp. 509-535 in *Handbook of Qualitative Research*, N. K Denzin and Y. S. Lincoln (eds.). Thousand Oaks, California; Sage.

Fine, G. A. 1997. "Naturework and the Taming of the Wild: The Problem of 'Overpick' in the Culture of Mushroomers." *Social Problems* 44(1):68-88.

Glaser, B. G., and A-L. Strauss. 1980. *The Discovery of Grounded Theory: Strategies for Qualitative Research.* New York: Aldine Publishing Company.

Hayner, N. S. 1945. "Taming the Lumberjack." *American Sociological Review* 2:217-25.

Holbrook, S. 1934. *Holy Old Mackinaw: A Natural History of the American Lumberjack.* New York. The Macmillan Company.

Lee, R. G., M. S. Carroll, and K. K. Warren 1991. "The Social Impacts of Timber Harvest Reduction in Washington State." In *Revitalizing the Timber Dependent Regions of Washington*, P. Sommers and H. Briss (eds.). Northwest Policy Center, Seattle. University of Washington.

Lipset, S. M., M. Trow, and J. Coleman. 1956. *Union Democracy: The Internal Politics of the International Typographical Union.* Garden City, NY; Anchor Books.

McLain, R. J. 2000. "Controlling the Understory: Wild Mushroom Politics in Central Oregon." Ph.D. Dissertation College of Forest Resources, University of Washington, Seattle.

Miller, M. L., and J. C. Johnson. 1981. "Hard Work and Competition in the Bristol Bay Salmon Fishery." *Human Organization* 40 21:131-39.

Moore, M. P. 1993. "Constructing Irreconcilable Conflict: The Function of Synecdoche in the Spotted Owl Controversy." *Communication Monographs* 60: 258-74.

Nisbit, Robert A. 1962. *Community and Power. A Study in the Ethics of Order and Freedom.* New York: Oxford University Press.

Salaman, G. 1974. *Community and Occupation. An Exploration of Work/Leisure Relationships.* London: Cambridge University Press.

Sonneman, T. F., and R. Steigmeyer. 1992. *Fruit Fields in My Blood. Okie Migrants in the West.* Moscow: University of Idaho Press.

Statham, A. 1995. "Environmental Identity: Symbols in Cultural Change." *Studies in Symbolic Interaction* 17:207-40.

Strangleman, T. 2001. "Networks, Places and Identities in Post-Industrial Mining Communities." *International Journal of Urban and Regional Research* 25 (2):253-67.

Stevens, J. B. 1979. "Six Views About a Wood Products Labor Force, Most of Which May Be Wrong." *Journal of Forestry* 77:717-20.

Van Maanen, J., and S. R. Barley. 1984. "Occupational Communities: Culture and Control in Organizations." *Research in Organizational Behavior* (6) 287-365.

CHAPTER 10
Communities and Forestry in Canada:
A Review and Analysis of the Model Forest and
Community Forest Programs

Gary Bull and Olaf Schwab

Introduction

F orests provide timber that can be used locally or processed
into commodity or finished products; non-timber forest
products that can meet the material needs of community
members or provide the opportunity for economic development; a
place to meet recreational or spiritual needs; and play a particularly
important role in the cultural lives of many aboriginal peoples (Duinker
et al. 1994). Among the world's forested nations, Canada holds a
unique position: 94 percent of Canadian forests are publicly owned,
with 71 percent owned by the provinces and 23 percent by the federal
government. By and large, forest products companies operate on these
lands under a system of tenure agreements, which allow industry to
conduct harvesting operations in exchange for commitments to invest
in and develop an infrastructure based on the extraction and utilization
of forest resources. Over sixteen hundred communities depend upon
the forest industry for employment; in 337 of these communities, the
forest industry accounts for more than 50 percent of employment
(Global Forest Watch 2001).

Globally and nationally there has been a trend in recent years toward
concentration of forest tenures among relatively few large forest
companies driven by a need to improve financial returns from the
forest resource. However, this trend has been matched by growing
public criticism of forest management practices and increased awareness
of the environmental role that forests play in the global ecosystem. To
address this criticism, the provincial governments have initiated a variety
of measures. Alterations to provincial codes of practices and other
regulatory measures have led to a larger portion of the productive

forest land base being set aside as protected areas. The impact of harvesting has been reduced by altering the shape and size of clearcuts, utilizing more selective harvesting systems and replacing chemical herbicides with biological alternatives. New sites are evaluated for the potential production of non-timber forest resources in an effort to diversify the uses to which we put forests (Natural Resources Canada 1999). Despite these and other efforts, current confrontations between some environmental groups and the forest industry demonstrate that concerns over the ecological and social impact of conventional forest management practices have not been resolved. It is necessary to redefine an appropriate balance between the environmental, commercial, social, and cultural needs, reflecting the changing demands of Canadian citizens from this publicly owned forest resource.

Two programs have emerged in Canada as a means of finding ways to address some of these conflicts and to work toward a new balance: the Model Forest Program and Community Forestry. The main aim of both programs is to involve the relevant communities in the decision-making processes in order to increase the chances of economic survival for forest-dependent communities and to promote the sustainable management of a wide range of non-timber forest products (Evans et al. 2001). The purpose of this chapter is to review and analyze the potential role of community involvement in forestry, using the Canadian Model Forest and British Columbia's Community Forest programs as examples. We will also highlight the significant impact of defining the community and the changing nature of property rights associated with each program.

Community: A Canadian Viewpoint

Most Canadian studies exploring the relationship between communities and their resource base have used economic indicators to define and assess the status of communities. However, recent research has indicated that the relationship between communities and forests goes far beyond a direct economic dependency (Nadeau et al. 1999). Therefore, one of the first decisions that has to be made when either developing or assessing a community forestry program is to define what a community is. In the Canadian literature, six common definitions are proposed (Duinker et al. 1994):

(1) Geographic Location—a human settlement with a fixed and bounded territory; sometimes referred to by economists as a functional economic area (economic approach);

(2) Way of Life—defined by a set of common values and interests around which institutions are developed and with which residents identify themselves (cultural approach);

(3) Social System—involving interrelationships between and among people living in the same geographic location (sociological approach);

(4) Type of Relationship—pertaining to a sense of shared identity (psychological approach);

(5) Source of Energy—a place from which a human population obtains the energy it needs to live and survive (ecological approach); and

(6) Holistic Approach—a setting in which the people have some sense of place, as well as common interests and goals, and are willing to cooperate or work together to achieve these goals (all of the above).

We will explore the relevance of community forestry to the Model Forest Program using the Holistic Approach definition and the Community Forest Program using the Geographic Location definition.

Model Forest

In 1992, the Canadian government launched the Model Forest Program to develop, test, and share best sustainable forest management practices across Canada. The program was one of the first local adaptations of the Agenda 21, an international U.N. strategy, introduced at the Rio Summit in 1992. The Agenda 21 was designed to provide governments and resource managers with some guidelines on how to find a balance among the often-competing objectives of economic growth, social stability, and environmental integrity.

It is impossible to find a single approach to sustainable forest management in Canada, since ecological, economic, and social conditions vary considerably throughout the Canadian forests. In such a diverse environment, top-down solutions such as legislative or regulatory changes are very limited in their ability to provide guidance for making specific changes to the management of a resource on a local level.

In response to both Agenda 21 and such diversity, the Canadian Forest Service determined that a multi-stakeholder process would be the most effective means of finding local solutions to sustainable forest management. Eleven Model Forests in eight provinces were established (Natural Resources Canada 1999): the Long Beach Model Forest and the McGregor Model Forest in British Columbia; the Foothills Model Forest in Alberta; the Prince Albert Model Forest in Saskatchewan; the Manitoba Model Forest in Manitoba; Eastern Ontario Model Forest and Lake Abitibi Model Forest in Ontario; the Waswanipi Cree Model Forest and the Bas-Saint-Laurent Model Forest in Quebec; the Fundy Model Forest in New Brunswick; and the Western Newfoundland Model Forest in Newfoundland. Although the majority were established on public forestland, some contain a substantial percentage of private land. This made it necessary to integrate a very diverse group of stakeholders, ranging from forest licensees over private landowners to local governments and special interest groups.

The first phase of the Model Forest Program (1992-1997) was designed to initiate a shift from sustained yield to sustainable development in managing the forest by integrating the knowledge, perspectives, and resources of all forest stakeholders in a given community (Carrow 1999; Natural Resources Canada 1999). For example, in British Columbia, the MacGregor Model Forest is working with thirty-four different organizations and the Long Beach Model Forest with forty-five partners (The Canadian Model Forest Network 2001; Scott 2001).

During the initial period a group of equal partners representing a broad range of interests formed within each Model Forest, including community and public-interest groups, Aboriginal groups, environmental non-governmental organizations (ENGOs), educational institutions, and local, provincial, and federal governments. The early years were awkward for most model forests, since people had to leave their entrenched positions to try to reach consensus about what constituted sustainable forestry (Naysmith et al. 2000). Despite these early difficulties, a program evaluation done in 1996 revealed several major achievements (Carrow 1999):

• Effective partnerships have been created through the Model Forest Program;

• In addition to the well-established timber supply interests, several new forest values have been addressed;

• First Nation communities have been involved in the majority of Model Forests;

• The Model Forests have provided a platform for research on social, economic, cultural and ecological topics related to sustainable forestry.

The following section will examine how the Model Forests have contributed knowledge about the integration of community interests into forest management.

Special Interest Groups

Developing a working relationship between forest managers and local community and public-interest groups is an important step in resolving some of the conflicts around the management of forest resources. In the Lake Abitibi Model Forest, it was possible to bring together the Iroquois Chamber of Commerce, the Town of Cochrane Community Development Corporation, the Abitibi-Black River Outdoor Association, and the Jackpine Snowmobile Club (Naysmith et al. 2000). These organizations had not previously coordinated their policies on sustainable forest management.

As could be seen from the confrontations between special interest groups and the forest industry, ENGOs play a special role in promoting public awareness about contentious aspects of traditional forest operations. Although it was not possible to resolve all disagreements, the Model Forest Program was successful in integrating some of these groups in the process of developing rules and guidelines for sustainable forest management. Examples include the Ontario Maple Syrup Producers' Association in the Eastern Ontario Model Forest, where special forest sites were established to demonstrate the effective management of sugar maple; and the Hinton Fish and Game Association in the Foothills Model Forest, where a study of grizzly bear habitat was initiated in 1999. Other examples of successful cooperation include the Cochrane and Area Fur Council of the Lake Abitibi Model Forest, and Time To Respect Earth's Ecosystems in the Manitoba Model Forest (Naysmith et al. 2000).

Individual Citizens and Youth

Although a wide range of community interests are represented through the participation of the aforementioned community and special interest groups, agencies involved in the management of the model forests also realized that there is a need for the involvement of non-affiliated citizens. In both the Fundy and the Lake Abitibi Model Forest a "citizen at large" seat was designated on the board or management committee. A similar procedure allows interested individuals to participate in the decision-making process in the Western Newfoundland Model Forest (Naysmith et al. 2000).

The structure of the Model Forest Program provides many opportunities to initiate programs with a strong social component. One of the major concerns for youth in resource-based communities is a lack of educational and career opportunities, as well as a belief that they cannot influence decisions that affect their environment. Programs such as the Internship and Trainee Program in the Long Beach Model Forest were designed to provide the local youth with opportunities both to gain valuable personal and career skills and to participate in resource management decisions (Naysmith et al. 2000).

Private Woodlot Owners

Building a working relationship with private woodlot owners presents the managers of model forests with a special challenge, since in many cases decisions to alter traditional forest management practices have a direct impact on the financial and non-financial benefits these landowners can acquire from their forestlands. For example, designating a forest area as a special conservation area within a land use planning process at the landscape level may limit the ability of the landowner to convert his or her land to uses other than protection or extensive forestry. Although the title to the land in most of the model forests in western Canada is held by the Crown, with harvesting rights and management obligations embodied in industry leases, some of the model forests in eastern Canada contain a significant percentage of private land. For example, 88 percent of the Eastern Ontario Model Forest, 62 percent of the Fundy Model Forest and 57 percent of the Bas-Saint Laurent Model Forest are owned privately (Naysmith et al. 2000).

Industry

As mentioned earlier, the forest industry plays an integral role in the development and continuous operation of the Model Forest Program. Not only do the forest companies own the harvesting rights on a large percentage of the Model Forests land base, but in many communities they also are a major contributor to the local economy through employment and direct and indirect spending. Continuing their involvement in these communities, companies such as Abitibi-Consolidated in the Bas-Saint Laurent Model Forest support many of the model forest's projects through cash and in-kind contributions.

In addition to these timber-based companies, several enterprises from the oil, gas, and coal sector became involved in the Model Forest Network. In the case of the Foothill Model Forest this presented a significant opportunity to resolve conflicts among competing users of natural resources, especially forest products and fossil fuels (Naysmith et al. 2000).

Aboriginal People

More than 80 percent of the Aboriginal communities in Canada are located within the productive forest zones, and many of these communities rely on the forest for their economic and social survival. There is increasing evidence that traditional and contemporary Aboriginal knowledge is not only complex and sophisticated but also relevant to understanding how to manage forests sustainably.

Although Aboriginal groups have been involved in ten of the eleven Model Forests, the partnership structure was not always able to resolve the conflicts between Aboriginal groups and other interest groups. First Nations are not simply another stakeholder in a Model Forest, since under the Constitution Act and other legislation they have special rights and title. First Nation groups have participated extensively at the grassroots level of the McGregor Model Forest, although there have been serious conflicts about the appropriate representation of First Nations on the various boards and committees. However, there also are examples where participation of First Nations in the Model Forests evolved without significant problems. In the Prince Albert Model Forest, three levels of First Nation's governing bodies are now participating as partners, the Montreal Lake Cree Nation, Prince Albert Grand Council, and the Federation of Saskatchewan Indian Nations (Naysmith et al. 2000).

The Model Forest Program and the Community Forestry Program evolved as two different approaches to the same problem: how do we sustainably manage natural resources while meeting the wide range of demands that Canadian citizens place on their forests? The Model Forest Program is an extensive system of "field studies", designed to test new approaches in a relatively controlled environment to evaluate concepts that may be of importance under substantially different social and economic conditions. The economic viability of these enterprises is only of secondary importance since an overly strict focus on the financial performance may exclude promising concepts from being tested and evaluated.

The Community Forestry Program places much more importance on economic viability. Designed to generate both financial and non-financial benefits to the local communities, these community forests are more closely aligned with the traditional property rights system in Canada. The next section describes in some detail how the Community Forestry Program has fared in British Columbia since its inception.

Models of Community Forestry in British Columbia

Eight different models of community forests developed in British Columbia as alternatives to the traditional control of the forestland and resources by companies headquartered outside of the community. These are Tree Farm Licenses held by the local community, Community Forestry Pilot Projects, Industry-First Nation Partnerships, Joint Ventures, Cooperative Business Arrangements, Forest Products and Service Contracts, Socioeconomic Partnerships, and Industry-Non-aboriginal Community Partnerships. This diversity of approaches is the result of the differing characteristics of the forests throughout the province and the wide range of objectives that went into developing and implementing these community forestry initiatives.

Tree Farm Licenses

Three well-established community forests are in the communities of Duncan, Mission, and Revelstoke. For the sake of brevity we will limit the discussion to the Revelstoke Tree Farm Licence. In the early 1990s over half of the timber cut in the Revelstoke Forest District was shipped to mills outside of the area, creating an unstable timber supply for the three local sawmills and providing relatively few employment opportunities for people from the community. During this period the City of Revelstoke and community groups lobbied for greater influence on the way the local forests were managed. Because of the strong opposition from these local groups, the provincial government rejected a proposal to transfer cutting rights for the Revelstoke Forest District to companies outside of the community (Revelstoke Community Forest Corporation 1994). Instead, in 1993 the Revelstoke Community Forest Corporation, with the City of Revelstoke as its only shareholder, was established to manage an area of Crown forest now known as Tree Farm License (TFL) 56.

The most important difference between a TFL held by a community and one held by a corporation is that the community retains most of the benefits related to timber production, notably revenue and local employment. In the case of the Revelstoke Community Forest Corporation, it was possible to achieve many of the socioeconomic objectives of a community forest. Although pulp logs are still processed outside of the community, approximately 80 percent of the saw logs are processed locally. Through the introduction of alternative harvesting methods, currently three times more people are employed than with conventional logging. The corporation is maximizing the revenue generated from the forestland base by selling 50 percent of the timber through a competitive bidding process, which became possible with the establishment of a central log yard, where the harvested timber is scaled and sorted into conventional assortments as well as special orders (Evans et al. 2001).

Community Forest Pilot Project

In December 1998, the Government of British Columbia initiated the Community Forest Pilot Program, cooperating with the forest industry and local communities to maximize the revenue generated from the forestland base while increasing the involvement of communities and First Nations in local forest management. The Community Forest Pilot Program was designed to reflect local community's priorities to:

- Sustain and enhance the existing economic structure;

- Provide business opportunities for value-added manufacturing and non-timber forest products;
    - Provide employment opportunities for local youth; and
    - Maintain visual, recreational and environmental values of the local forests (British Columbia Ministry of Forests 2001a).

The Community Forest Pilot Agreement is also an area-based forest tenure that is awarded by the Minister of Forests for a term of five years with provision for extension or replacement, with a long-term agreement of twenty-five to ninety-nine years if the initial stage of the community forest is successful. The main portion of the land base available for this program is public forestland; however, municipal, Indian reserve, and private land can be co-managed as part of the agreement. The most important difference between conventional forest tenures and Community Forest Pilot Agreements is that the latter does not only transfer timber harvesting rights to the licensee, it also may include rights to botanical and other non-timber forest products (British Columbia Ministry of Forests 1998). Due to the strong community support for this program, the British Columbia Government decided to expand the program by up to eighteen new tenure holders in addition to the ten community forest pilot agreements already in place in October 2000 (British Columbia Ministry of Forests 2001b).

Partnership: Industry–First Nation

Partnerships between Aboriginal communities and companies from the forest products sector are becoming a very important component of the economic development prospects of many First Nations people. The main benefits for First Nations entering into such a partnership are that they can utilize some of the companies' resources to obtain the capital, resources, and skills necessary to successfully pursue that particular business opportunity. At the same time, building a partnership with First Nations communities benefits the forest products company by providing secure access to forest resources despite ongoing Aboriginal land claims and treaty settlements, as well as providing the company with a source of employees, suppliers, customers, and contractors (Giardini 2001). Entering a partnership with Aboriginal communities also benefits a forest company in the process of forest certification, since most internationally recognized forest-certification schemes require recognition of and respect for Aboriginal rights. Depending on the resources available within the Aboriginal community and the purpose of the partnership, four different partnership models have proven effective in British Columbia: joint ventures, cooperative business arrangements, forest service contracting, and socioeconomic partnerships.

Joint Ventures. A joint venture is a partnership where profits, risks, management, and growth potential of a business opportunity are shared between Aboriginal and non-Aboriginal partners. This kind of relationship is relatively rare because it requires a complex and stable commitment from all parties involved as well as a suitable business opportunity (Giardini 2001). Both partners have to contribute substantially to the joint venture; the forest company usually provides access to markets, expertise, and technology, while the most important contributions from the Aboriginal partner are access to forest resources, traditional knowledge, a labour force, and an improved corporate image. Examples of First Nation-industry joint ventures in British Columbia include companies such as Isaak Forest Resources in Port Alberni, Tl'oh Forest Products in Fort St. James, and Eco-Link in Alkali Lake (National Aboriginal Forestry Association and The Institute on Governance 2000).

Cooperative Business Arrangements. Cooperative business arrangements are quite similar to joint ventures, but do not involve joint ownership. In the case of industry-First Nation partnerships, independent companies enter into a mutually beneficial cooperation that usually provides the Aboriginal partner with access to established distribution channels while providing the non-Aboriginal partner with some additional revenue through commission fees for products sold through these channels. Examples of this type of partnership in British Columbia include companies such as Toquaht Enterprises in Ucluelet and Ditidaht Forest Products in Ladysmith (National Aboriginal Forestry Association and The Institute on Governance 2000).

Forest Products and Service Contracts. These contracts are a relatively common form of business relationship where products and services are provided for an agreed price. One example could be an industrial forest company providing wood from its licenses to processing or manufacturing facilities owned by Aboriginal groups. As Aboriginal groups gain access to an increasing portion of the forestland base, this type of business arrangement will likely develop into a business relationship where timber is exchanged between both members of the contract in order to optimize the utilization of processing facilities (Giardini 2001). Another example of this type of partnership is where an independent First Nations business enters into a contract with the industry partner to carry out silviculture or harvesting work. Good examples of First Nation-owned silvicultural contracting companies in British Columbia include SIB Forestry Inc. in Sechelt and the Cheslatta Carrier Nation in Burns Lake. Once again, as the relationship matures and Aboriginal groups gain control of forest resources, cases may develop where First Nations are contracting out services such as large-scale inventory work (National Aboriginal Forestry Association and The Institute on Governance 2000).

Socioeconomic Partnerships. Some partnerships such as Agreements on Principle or Memoranda of Understanding are difficult to classify as commercial at all. A typical goal of this type of partnership is the recognition of existing First Nations rights, and increasing the involvement of First Nations in resource planning and management of the forest in the industry partner's license area (Giardini 2001). This type of partnership is most important in situations where the Aboriginal group lacks experience and expertise in forestry-related issues, since it provides a starting point for cooperation at a higher level such as training, employment, or access to resources through the industry partner. In British Columbia examples of this type of relationship can be found at Inkameet Forestry, owned by the Osooyos First Nation in Oliver, and the West Moberly First Nation in Moberly Lake (National Aboriginal Forestry Association and The Institute on Governance 2000).

Partnership: Industry–Non-Aboriginal Communities

Partnerships between the forest industry and non-Aboriginal communities most frequently are in the form of socioeconomic partnerships. In many situations, signing an Agreement on Principle or a Memorandum of Understanding is sufficient to ensure that forestry-related community objectives, such as establishing a process for public consultation as a platform for discussions about resource management, are met. Since most forest companies are relying heavily on the skills and expertise readily available within these resource-based communities, there is generally no need to formalize agreements concerning training and employment.

Analysis

From a conceptual point of view, significant differences exist between the Model Forest and Community Forestry. These programs use very different definitions of the term "community," thus selecting a different segment of society as relevant to their mandate.

The Model Forest Program uses a very broad, holistic definition of community (the Holistic Approach explained earlier in this chapter), which allows for the incorporation of a broad range of interests into the decision-making process when developing a sustainable forestry management framework for the local conditions within each Model Forest. This holistic definition of a community integrates those people living within the area as well as those economically or socially connected to local forestry to participate in the decision-making process; it also allows for input from all interest groups concerned about forest management in that particular area and willing to participate in developing solutions for managing the forests sustainably. This creates significant opportunities, especially for nationally or internationally operating ENGOs, since in many cases they would not have the human and financial resources to establish a permanent presence in all regions where they feel that conventional forest management practices are not fully able to meet the requirements of sustainable forest management.

Integrating such a large number of potential partners into the decision-making process can be a time-consuming and frustrating experience, especially if some of the partners are not fully committed to making the Model Forest a success. Although the "partnership of equals" employed in the Model Forest Program ensures that smaller partners have a fair representation in the process, this consensus-based approach can constrain opportunities to operate a profitable enterprise. In a sector where demands are changing quickly and where the average margin of profit is relatively low, a successful enterprise must be able to respond quickly to changing market conditions and business opportunities.

Community forestry programs, such as found in British Columbia, employ a narrower definition of "community" (the Geographic Location approach). As mentioned earlier, being able to respond quickly to changing market conditions and business opportunities is essential for wood products enterprises operating in current economic conditions. Defining the relevant community as those people living in a specific geographic location significantly reduces the number of potential stakeholders seeking to influence decisions about how to manage local forests. In community forestry, financial success has first priority, since operating a profitable forest enterprise provides the platform on which the stakeholders can work towards examining and integrating new components of sustainable forest management. The formal partnership agreement as well as the extent of cash and in-kind contributions by each stakeholder provide a clear structure for who should be involved in the decision-making process and what priority should be given to the concerns of particular stakeholders. This arrangement does not mean that concerns about forest management practices voiced from outside of the immediate community will be ignored; what this arrangement implies is that the objectives determined by the local community have first priority while other issues will be addressed in a way that does not constrain the financial and social viability of the community forestry project.

The answer to the question of which definition of "community" is most appropriate depends on local conditions. The Model Forest Program provides an excellent opportunity to explore a wide range of options for alternative forest management practices, especially in the area of community-controlled forest management on a relatively small scale. Individual community forestry projects would not have the financial and human resources necessary for exploring issues ranging from wildlife habitat protection, or the development of locally adapted harvesting methods, to developing frameworks for meaningful public participation. Through the Model Forest Network, the individual initiatives can combine their resources and exchange knowledge, thus becoming a very effective catalyst for change, developing concepts and solutions for issues that would be too complex to address within the setting of conventional forest operations. Model Forests are able to integrate input from stakeholders and stakeholder groups that do not have the resources to cooperate with established forest companies directly, although their ideas and concepts may prove to be very important for the development of sustainable forest management practices that reflect the new balance between economic, social, and cultural needs of the forest. Therefore, the most important function of Model Forests is to provide testing grounds for the development of these new concepts, which in turn may be integrated into forest management practices throughout Canada.

But not only does the broad definition of "community" used in the Model Forest Program impose restrictions on the creation of profitable businesses through the relatively slow decision-making processes, the lack of property rights allocation also limits the possibilities for creating business opportunities. As shown in the case of the Model Forests with a significant percentage of private forestlands, coordinating the objectives of different categories of land ownership imposes special challenges on resource managers. For example, while the most important objective for private lands held by forest companies or individuals may be the generation of a constant stream of revenue, governments might choose conservation or protection of natural resources as the main objectives for public forest lands.

The more focused definition of "community" used in Community Forestry programs allows for the rapid implementation of change. By using a clear, more businesslike structure designed to meet the objectives of the population within a well-defined geographic location, it becomes possible to test the applicability of concepts such as those developed by the partners within the Model Forest Program. Such testing is evident in the wide range of frameworks employed within the broad category of Community Forestry (community forests on TFLs, Community Forest Pilot Projects, and the different categories of company-community partnerships). Local conditions, in terms both of natural resources and of community structure and goals, vary to such an extent that it becomes necessary to adapt forest management practices to the changing social and environmental conditions in a step-wise approach. Starting community forestry enterprises based on a relatively small, well-defined community provides the first stepping-stone toward integrating alternative approaches into everyday forest management.

Concluding Remarks

We have argued that there are, at least in the context of the nation of Canada, no right or wrong definitions of "community." The appropriate definition depends on the intended outcome. Some may say that the Community Forestry Program is defining community too narrowly; however, these community forests are able to meet their goal of providing some economic stability for local communities as well as a foundation for addressing broader resource and environmental concerns. Some argue that the Model Forest Program has attempted too much, that it got caught in the struggle to accommodate the interests of too many stakeholders. But it was not the goal of the program to create concepts that were directly transferable to other forest operations. The program achieved what it was intended to do: promote ". . . living laboratories where people with a direct interest in the forest, supported by the most up-to-date science and technology, could participate in decisions about how the forest could be sustainably managed" (Naysmith et al. 2000).

As related earlier, community forestry will solve some local economic problems; but without broad support, this approach would be unable to address all the issues relevant for developing new concepts in sustainable forest management. The loose definition of community used in the Model Forest Program offers the opportunities to explore broad issues with more resources than what would be available within an isolated project. Combining these two approaches, using the Model Forest Program as a catalyst for change and Community Forestry for testing the implementation of the concepts developed, has been effective in bringing Canada into a leadership role in the global dialogue on sustainable development.

References

British Columbia Ministry of Forests. 1998. Request for Proposals for Community Forest Pilot Agreements [Web Page]. Accessed Dec 10, 2001. Available at: http://www.for.gov.bc.ca/pab/jobs/community/rfp.pdf.

British Columbia Ministry of Forests. 2001a. Community Forest Pilot Agreement Facts [Web Page]. Accessed Dec 10, 2001. Available at: http://www.for.gov.bc.ca/pab/jobs/community/Commfor200203.pdf

British Columbia Ministry of Forests. 2001b. New Opportunities for Community Forests [Web Page]. Accessed Dec 10, 2001. Available at: http://www.for.gov.bc.ca/pab/jobs/community/factsheet02.htm.

Canadian Model Forest Network. 2001. Long Beach Model Forest [Web Page]. Accessed Dec 7, 2001. Available at: http://www.modelforest.net/download/fact_sheets/lbmf_eng.pdf.

Carrow, Rod. 1999. "Canada's Model Forest Program: Challenges for Phase 2." *The Forestry Chronicle* 75(1):73-80.

Duinker, Peter N., Patrick W. Matakala, Florence Chege, and Luc Bouthillier. 1994. "Community forests in Canada: An Overview." *The Forestry Chronicle* 70(6):711-19.

Evans, Bryan, Cheri Burda, and Samantha Song. 2001. Community Forestry in Canada [Web Page]. Accessed Jul 25, 2001. Available at: http://www.forestsandcommunities.org.

Giardini, Anne. 2001. Practical Advice for Structuring Business Relationships with First Nations. Forestry Forum 2001; Vancouver. Toronto: Insight Information Co.; Section III.

Global Forest Watch. 2001. Quick Facts Canada [Web Page]. Accessed Dec 8, 2001. Available at: http://www.globalforestwatch.org/english/canada/quickfacts.htm.

Nadeau, Solange, Bruce Schindler, and Christina Kakoyannis. 1999. "Forest Communities: New Frameworks for Assessing Sustainability." *The Forestry Chronicle* 75(5):747-54.

National Aboriginal Forestry Association and The Institute on Governance. 2000. Aboriginal - Forest Sector Partnerships: Lessons for Future Collaboration. Ottawa: National Aboriginal Forestry Association.

Natural Resources Canada. 1999. Canada's Model Forest Program: Achieving Sustainable Forest Management Through Partnership. Ottawa: Natural Resources Canada, Canadian Forest Service.

Naysmith, J., L. LaPierre, and Future Directions Committee of the Canadian Model Forest Network. 2000. Beacons of Sustainability: A Framework for the Future of Canada's Model Forests . Ottawa: Model Forest Network.

Revelstoke Community Forest Corporation. 1994. Annual Report 1993-1994. Revelstoke, Canada.

Scott, Anne (editor). 2001. The McGregor Story - Pioneering Approaches to Sustainable Forest Management. Prince George, Canada: McGregor Model Forest Association.

CHAPTER 11

The National Community Forestry Center—
An Experiment in Institutionalizing Community Forestry
in the United States

Ajit K. Krishnaswamy

Introduction

Thousands of forest communities in the United States—in the coastal forests of the Pacific Northwest, in Native American reservations, in the woods on the Mississippi Delta, in towns in the midst of Maine's corporate plantations, and in and around the nation's forests—are becoming increasingly impoverished, both socially and economically (National Network of Forest Practitioners 1999). In the past, natural resources surrounding these forest communities have been managed with inadequate consideration for resource sustainability and community well-being (Poffenberger and Selin 1998).

Forest managers attempting to develop sustainable resource management strategies generally overlook the reciprocal relationship between forest degradation and community impoverishment. This oversight limits the likelihood of sustainable resource management, because sustainability requires the engagement of rural people whose knowledge, perspective, and experience can inform science, management, and policy (Chambers 1983; Arnold 1992). Forest communities are often ignored regarding forest management decisions that affect them. Their capacity to contribute to resource management and policy is limited by their lack of access to information, and this can be exacerbated by an assumption that rural residents have little to offer. Shut out of decision-making processes, and lacking an institutional mechanism for accessing and developing information pertinent to their needs, rural people in forested areas are often overlooked even though they are essential to sustainable management and stewardship partnerships (National Network of Forest Practitioners 1999). Lack of community involvement has contributed to environmental conflicts, stalemates over the use and management of natural resources, lawsuits, and escalating project costs that have often resulted in the failure of many initiatives for community development and natural resource management. In response to these problems, which have characterized forest management in the United States during the past two decades, community forestry has gained momentum as a means of supporting rural development and the sustainable management of natural resources. This growing interest has emerged from increased awareness of what is often a direct relationship between ecosystem health and community well-being, and the promise community forestry holds for helping communities achieve well-being through engaging them in solving their own problems.

Community forestry has been widely practiced in parts of Asia, Africa, and South and Central America since the mid-eighties through the participation of local communities in the protection, regeneration, and distribution of forest resources (Arnold 1992). In forested countries in these regions, governments, non-governmental organizations, and international agencies concerned with rural development are institutionalizing community forestry through prioritizing and supporting it (World Bank 1992; World Resources Institute 1992). In comparison, community forestry is relatively new in the United States, and there is a lack of widespread support for it among government agencies and private industry.

The National Community Forestry Center (NCFC) was established in 2000 to promote community forestry in the United States. This chapter examines the strategies used by the NCFC to promote community forestry, and the challenges to institutionalizing it in the United States, which I believe would entail greater support by government agencies, private industry, nonprofits, and funding agencies of its strategies, such as participatory research, use of local knowledge, and capacity building. Institutionalization would also require government agencies and private industry to promote and use community forestry as a part of their standard management practices.

Emergence of Community Forestry in the United States

Participation and collaboration have become part of the new paradigm of natural resource management since the late 1980s. Collaborative groups involving community residents, nonprofit organizations, federal agency officials, industry representatives, and others have formed all over the United States. These developments emerged from the forest management crisis in which forest communities became embroiled in the late 1980s and early 1990s.

The crisis in forest communities peaked and became very visible in the early nineties when communities, especially in the Pacific Northwest, were affected by resource degradation, environmental litigation, changing federal agency priorities for forest management, and industrial restructuring. These communities had little or no say in policy decisions. These changes caused widespread economic distress in many forest communities throughout the Pacific Northwest. Loss of jobs, migration, drop in school attendance, and increase in cases of alcoholism, domestic violence, and other crimes accompanied and followed this crisis in forest communities. Between 1989 and 1996, the closure of 273 western sawmill and veneer plants resulted in the elimination of 22,578 jobs (Poffenberger and Selin 1998).

A rapid growth of local community efforts in the Pacific Northwest took place in the early and mid nineties as a reaction to this situation. In other parts of the country, and during the same period of time, several nonprofit organizations were engaged in organizing, training, and providing technical assistance to forest communities and forestland owners (Brendler and Carey 1998; Poffenberger and Selin 1998). At that point in time, the term "community forestry" was rarely used in association with local community efforts and the forestry programs of nonprofit organizations. The general sense was that rural communities in the United States were well taken care of by traditional forest management policies and that community forestry was only relevant to situations in the developing world (Carey 2001).

The term "community forestry" gained popularity in the U.S. as people who had worked abroad, usually in international programs supporting community forestry in Asia and Africa in the early eighties, realized that though the context was different the issues in community forestry were common in the United States and overseas. The common issues were: (1) forest communities were being ignored regarding decisions that affect them; and (2) resource sustainability is best ensured if local communities participate in management decisions. The Ford Foundation, one of the major supporters of community forestry internationally, extended their support for efforts in the United States.

However, the concept of community forestry in the U.S. evolved to be broader than the place-based focus in other countries (see section below on Diversity of Community Forestry in the United States). Community forestry in the U.S. is broadly defined as efforts by people, united by place or interest, to use and conserve their local forest resource to their advantage (Brendler and Carey 1998; National Community Forestry Center Northern Forest Region 2001). The goal of community forestry is to enhance the ability of community members to guide the direction of economic, social and environmental change in their region—in essence to promote community self-determination (Wilmsen and Krishnaswamy 2003). Central to this goal is the participation of local community members in forest management and policy processes. Community forestry in the USA is, at least in part, a response to the frequently inequitable outcomes of traditional scientific forest management.

Diversity of Community Forestry in the United States

The wide range of groups, organizations, and individuals engaged in community forestry in the U.S. is due to diversity in communities of place, communities of interest, and types of forestland ownership in the United States. Forestland ownership is distributed between federal, state, and tribal governments, private industry, and nonindustrial private landowners. Most of the forestlands in the West and Southwest are federally owned, while most of the those in the East are privately owned.

The National Network of Forest Practitioners (NNFP) is a leading non-governmental organization that links about five hundred diverse groups and individuals involved in community forestry in different parts of the country. The sample of NNFP members below reflects the geographical diversity and the diversity of interests in the community forestry movement in the USA. The West has the most groups engaged in community forestry.

• The Alliance of Forest Workers and Harvesters in Eugene, Oregon, focuses on improving the working conditions of forest workers and non-timber forest product harvesters;

• Forest Community Research in Taylorsville, California, advances community-based approaches to ecosystem management and research;

• The Watershed Training Center in Hayfork, California, focuses on sustaining the local forest-based economy;

- The Maidu Culture and Development Group in northern California focuses on using Native American traditional ecological knowledge on forestland;
- The Redwood Community Action Agency in Arcata, California, focuses on issues of forest restoration;
- Forestry Action Committee in Cave Junction, Oregon, builds coalitions between local citizens and mobile non-timber forest product harvesters;
- The Jefferson Center for Education and Research in Oregon works to educate and empower migrant forest workers—especially those from Southeast Asia;
- The Forest Trust in Santa Fe, New Mexico, provides resource-protection strategies to environmental organizations, rural communities, and public agencies;
- The Las Humanas Cooperative, a Hispanic community-based organization at Manzano, New Mexico, has several activities that include involving its youth in the monitoring of forest-restoration work;
- Rural Action in Trimble in Appalachian Ohio promotes economic, social, and environmental justice with a strong forestry focus;
- Yellow Wood Associates, Inc., a consulting firm located at St. Albans, Vermont, offers services that include training programs in community capacity building;
- The Federation of Southern Cooperatives at Epes, Alabama, focuses on reducing minority land-ownership loss.

The National Community Forestry Center

Several institutions have emerged to support community forestry in the United States. A prominent example is the National Community Forestry Center (NCFC), one of the few institutionalized efforts in the U.S. that is geared specifically toward developing the capabilities of communities to engage in their own land stewardship through participatory research. The NCFC is a direct effort at bringing people into projects, where local people themselves lead and develop what they need.

The NCFC was established on the twin premises that the capacity of local communities to participate in forest management and policy is limited by their lack of access to information, and that local knowledge is the key to better forest management. Use of local knowledge assumes that the information, experiences, and perspectives of local people are crucial since they are an integral part of the functioning of the real world (Schon 1995).

The NCFC was established as a project of the National Network of Forest Practitioners (NNFP), a nonprofit national forum of groups and individuals involved in community forestry. The NNFP has been instrumental in increasing the visibility of community forestry in the U.S. and received a four-year grant from the USDA's Cooperative State Research Extension and Education Service (CSREES) in 2000.

During 1999, Henry Carey, Shanna Ratner, Lee Williams, Jonathan Kusel, and Michael Jenkins, all of whom were involved in community forestry in different parts of the country, conducted three site visits, in New Mexico, Vermont, and Kentucky. Each site visit included meetings in communities with rural people to discuss ideas for the design and function of the NCFC. They engaged people to share their ideas about how the center could build capacity to help solve rural community problems. Participants included large and small landowners, loggers, environmentalists, Native Americans, Resource Conservation and Development District staff, U.S. Forest Service staff, educators, consulting foresters, farmers, tree farmers, and community leaders from former Spanish land grants. These participants emphasized the need to bring rural communities into decision- and policy-making processes and contributed to the conceptualization of the NCFC.

The NCFC is a decentralized network of four regional centers in Appalachia, the Northeast, the Pacific West, and the Southwest:

• Appalachian Forest Resource Center, Trimble, Ohio (www.appalachianforest.org)

• National Community Forestry Center Northern Forest Region, St. Albans, Vermont (www.ncfcnfr.org)

• Pacific West Community Forestry Center, Taylorsville, California (www.pwcfc.org)

• Southwest Community Forestry Research Center, Santa Fe, New Mexico (www.theforesttrust.org/research.html)

The regional centers work collaboratively and intensively with local communities on a wide range of issues associated with community forestry, and related to the management of both public and private forestlands across the United States.

Bioregional Advisory Councils: The Heart of the NCFC

Bioregional Advisory Councils—BACs for short—guide the work of each regional center by setting research priorities and selecting partner communities. BACs range in size from ten to twenty people, representing a wide range of perspectives, cultures, and experience, and members play a critical role by providing information on community needs and keeping people in the region informed about center activities and services..

The functioning of each BAC determines whether the activities of each regional center are participatory, grassroots, and effective, and the NCFC regional centers have developed effective, strong, and representative BACs. The centers try to make their BACs diverse. In order to maintain a balance between advocates, policy people, experts, and researchers on one hand and practitioners on the other, at least half of the BAC membership is expected to represent rural communities of place or be working-class residents.

Strategies to Support Community Forestry

Regional centers adopt three strategies to support forest communities.

Strategy 1: Participatory research with partner communities. Each NCFC regional center partners with two to five target communities every year to build their capacity to conduct research. The NCFC's four regional centers use participatory research or PR (see box on page XX) when working collaboratively with communities. The PR process consists of several steps, including (1) selecting partner communities with the help of the center's advisory council; (2) identifying local cooperators who act as the community liaison for research projects; (3) helping communities identify goals and information needs; (4) developing a collaborative work plan; (5) assisting communities in collecting information; and (6) helping the community interpret and use the information.

In the PR process, community members identify research questions, carry out research activities and, during this process, develop research skills and techniques. Community members learn to analyze information they have collected and decide how to use this information. Most importantly, communities own their research.

During the PR process rural residents develop critical thinking skills for improved decision making and problem solving; new relationships within the community, and between communities and experts and resources from ouside the communitty; collective knowledge of their community; and the capacity to determine root causes of problems and issues by structuring information according to community need.

Because communities themselves shape the activities and priorities of the NCFC's regional centers, the centers' approaches reflect the cultural, social, and ecological diversity of the places where they work. A good example of these different approaches is the way centers identify partner communities and local cooperators. In the Northern Forest and Appalachia, for example, the centers invite applications from communities, and select partner communities with the help of their regional advisory councils. Center staff then work collaboratively with partner communities to help them recruit a local cooperator and develop a work plan. The community is primarily responsible for working with the local cooperator to see that the work plan is implemented.

The Southwest Center and the Pacific West Center, on the other hand, begin with a focus on building trust with potential partner communities in ways that are culturally sensitive and appropriate. The Southwest Center has partnered Hispanic and Native American communities, while the Pacific West Center has partnered Native American communities, and migrant Southeast Asian and Latino forest workers. The centers identify or help develop grassroots leadership within the community through interacting over a period of time with potential partners. The advisory councils guide the centers in selecting partner communities in which grassroots leadership has been clearly identified. The centers then recruit a local cooperator, and jointly develop a work plan with that person based on community-identified needs. Center researchers work collaboratively and intensively with the local cooperator and other community members to implement the work plan.

All of the regional centers have found that the PR process is lengthier and less definite than conventional research, observing that building trust takes a lot of time and patience. However, once people have identified their goals and developed a plan of work, they become excited about research, and feel empowered. Along the way, they develop skills that are valuable for future projects. For these reasons, many people involved in PR cite the process of conducting PR as one of its most significant products. At the same time, the results of PR projects, which are owned equally by everyone involved—a central tenet of PR—have enabled communities to use information to leverage change and become more active and informed stewards of the forest.

Participatory Research

Participatory research (PR) is the core of the NCFC's work with partner communities. This research method is based on the idea that people's knowledge, information, experiences, and perspectives are an extremely important part of their ability to solve problems, and uses community people as researchers in pursuit of answers to questions encountered in daily life (Tandon 1988). PR counters the traditional dependence on specialists and external experts to assess people's needs. It is research of the people, by the people, and for the people (Freire 1973; Park 1997).

PR differs from conventional research in a number of key areas, including: who initiates and controls the research; how the research question is defined; how and by whom research is conducted; how and by whom results are interpreted; and the ways in which research results are used (National Community Forestry Center Northern Forest Region 2001).

Development practitioners around the world have been using participatory approaches for creative rural development using labels such as participatory learning and action, participatory rural appraisal, participatory monitoring and evaluation—all driven by the democratic aims of PR (Williams 1998). In the field of forestry, the growing interest in PR is due to increased awareness of the reciprocal relationship between forest health and community well-being. PR helps achieve community well-being through engaging community members in helping to solve their problems.

The recent growth of community forestry in the U.S. has created space for the use of PR, resulting in the use of

PR as a tool in building the capacity of communities to access and use research for informed and effective participation in forest management and policy. PR has gained popularity in community forestry because of the recognition that ordinary citizens need good information in order to participate effectively in natural resource management, and because access to information is often otherwise controlled by resource management professionals. Thus, PR is a response to the rigidity and hierarchy in the flow of information in traditional forest management.

A major challenge to the use of PR in forestry lies in the fact that government agencies and private industry are not interested in PR, or do not have the institutional knowledge to share decision-making power with local communities (Wilmsen and Krishnaswamy 2003). They still try to retain and protect their right to forest-related decision making, while excluding communities in the process. Often, they are interested in public involvement to the extent that people in local communities can participate to a greater extent than before in decision-making processes. But this is not the same as actually devolving power so that people at the local level increase their own capacity to effectively share in the management of forest resources. This devolution of power is a central goal of participatory research.

Examples of NCFC's participatory research with target communities.

• The NCFC Northern Forest Region (NCFC-NFR) worked in partnership with the Starksboro Conservation Commission to develop indicators of forest health for use in local decision making. The project received an award from the Vermont Urban and Community Forestry Council, and NCFC-NFR is continuing to work with Starksboro and designed a workshop entitled "Giving the Forest A Voice in Community Planning: Creating Local Indicators of Forest Health."

• Working with the Southwest Community Forestry Research Center, Las Humanas Cooperative, in Manzano, New Mexico, has completed its research plan to monitor ecological and social effects of forest restoration work in the Manzano Mountain area. In the second phase of this project, youth worked with center staff to map the distribution of National Fire Plan projects in relation to traditional use areas and community wealth.

• The Pacific West Community Forestry Center is collaborating with the Crescent Lake Multi-Party Mushroom Monitoring Project, an effort initiated by mushroom harvesters at the Crescent Lake "pick," which spans five national forests in south-central Oregon. Harvesters represent five language groups and involve both local and mobile harvester communities. Mushroom "monitors" (experienced and respected harvesters) walk the woods and document harvesters' concerns and may also provide peer education on ecologically sustainable harvesting practices. In addition, weekly meetings are held in public campgrounds, where ecological and social concerns are discussed among harvesters, Forest Service personnel, local residents, law enforcement, representatives of non-governmental organizations, and other stakeholders. This project has resulted in a Forest Service review of the social, economic, and environmental impact of timber sales on mushrooms and the communities that depend on them.

• The Appalachian Forest Resource Center is working with the Blue Ridge Sustainable Woods Cooperative, in Hiwassee, Virginia, to establish a landowners' cooperative in the central Blue Ridge Mountains. The cooperative will demonstrate profitable alternatives to high-grading, forest fragmentation, and the selling of trees by landowners in economic distress. The first phase of the project involves educating the public and landowners about benefits of sustainable forest management.

Strategy 2: Center Research. The NCFC's four regional centers conduct research identified by the bioregional advisory councils on topics relevant to communities in the region.

Examples of research conducted by regional center researchers:

• The Northern Center conducted a land ownership and management study that provided an overview of how forestland ownership is changing in the Northern Forest, described the impact of ownership changes on local communities, and discussed what some communities are doing to manage change to maximize both economic and environmental benefits.

• The Southwest Center worked with the Zuni Pueblo and Las Humanas Cooperative to develop ecological monitoring protocols for forestry projects that recently received grants from the Collaborative Forest Restoration Program, a program under the National Fire Plan of the U.S. Forest Service. Center researchers worked with four community restoration projects, training twenty-five youth and seven community members in monitoring methods.

• The Pacific West Center has been involved in identifying rural environmental justice issues through a review of policies and the legal framework for environmental justice including compiling a database of rural environmental justice issues. Activities have included library and Internet research of financial, educational, and technical resources for environmental justice groups.

Strategy 3: Regional Resource Center. Regional centers function as a resource for communities in the region. They are a clearinghouse of information on community forestry and provide technical assistance to communities. This is done in a variety of ways including: a toll free telephone number, listservs, Web sites, databases listing technical assistance providers, newsletters, and publications on relevant research. Regional center staffs are available to provide information and referrals, and the centers also conduct workshops, training, and meetings with community groups.

Example of a Center as a regional resource:

• The Northern Region organized several workshops on PR throughout the country to help rural people conduct and use research to make informed decisions about forest resources. The highly interactive four-hour workshops were intended for a mix of community members and professional researchers, and explored the value of a PR approach to community problem solving.

Research themes in 2003 and 2004:

The regional centers are focused on different research themes identified with the help of their BACs. The themes that the Northern Center is focused on include: the use and marketing of "opportunity wood" (the term they prefer to use for "low-value wood") to benefit communities and landowners; the impact on employment from changes in land ownership; and making available databases on legislative initiatives, research, and demonstration forests to communities and the center's partners. The Southwest Center's research themes included: marketing of small-diameter wood, opportunities for communities provided by the national fire plan, and monitoring ecological restoration projects (with emphasis on youth involvement). The Pacific West Center's research themes included: environmental justice issues (especially issues concerning mobile forest workers such as Latino floral-green workers, and Southeast Asian mushroom harvesters) and the use of traditional ecological knowledge. The Appalachian Center staff has identified worker issues arising from the harvesting of non-timber forest products as a potential research theme; one example of a topic concerns conflicts involving migrant Latino mushroom harvesters on public lands in North Carolina.

Lessons Learned

NCFC researchers have found that communities want to participate in research. Shared ownership of research has resulted in communities using information effectively to their advantage and becoming more active and informed land stewards. Regional center researchers initially expected that PR on topics such as indicators of forest health, fire management, and forest restoration would be hard for rural communities to get involved with. They have been surprised that this has not been the case. Often, it has been natural and exciting for communities to participate in the research process.

Communities know the questions that are important to them, and are constantly looking for answers. They initially need help and facilitation in getting the answers. The regional centers have been able to create the space for the communities to find answers, and once they have them, they are excited about their capacity to solve resource-related problems. The communities with which the NCFC regional centers have partnered have learned to ask and answer questions about the type of information needed to make decisions that will allow a stronger stream of sustainable benefits back from the forest to the community.

NCFC activities have resulted in new learning by bringing together trained researchers with people from rural communities who are not trained researchers, and who have traditionally been the voiceless object of research. These people are now directly engaged in the learning process, and have become more active in land stewardship.

Interacting with the diverse groups engaged in the research process has been a valuable learning experience for participants. One regional center advisory council member said "I was excited because it was the one place in forestry in America where I saw the confluence of different people across various sectors. I saw workers, I saw landowners, I saw professionals, as well as academics sit down together to solve a problem relevant to community needs."

Challenges

The NCFC faces several challenges. One important challenge is working with underserved communities such as migrant forest workers and Latino brush-harvester communities. Building trust, identifying leadership, and organizing within these communities for PR has been difficult and time consuming. This is due to a long history of distrust and fear sustained by these communities. A discussion has emerged amongst NCFC researchers about the balance between organizing and participatory research when working with communities such as these. Some Native American communities with which the centers are currently partnering are also historically distrustful of external researchers, especially concerning the dissemination of traditional knowledge outside their community.

In awarding the grant that funded the NCFC to a nonprofit organization, the USDA CSREES simultaneously recognized the legitimacy of community forestry and, through the establishment of the NCFC, helped to further its institutionalization. Awarding the grant to a nonprofit was significant because historically grants of this nature have been awarded only to land grant universities. Nevertheless, while the NCFC was a more appropriate recipient of the grant (since the primary focus of the center's work has been building research capacity in communities they partner), a consequence has been that NCFC researchers, who all work for nonprofits, have had little or no direct institutional links with academic researchers. There is little incentive for them to present their research in academic conferences or publish their research in academic journals. Most of the publications of the centers are targeted to local communities and the general public. However, in order to advance knowledge in community forestry, it is important for NCFC and academic researchers to share their experiences and learn from one another.

Due to with low levels of awareness and support for PR and grassroots capacity building, the NCFC faces the challenge for sustaining its funding. The USDA CSREES funding for the NCFC ended in December 2004. Currently, there are a comparatively few government and private funding agencies that support community forestry and PR. Funding agencies that would support the NCFC's work are often the same as those that support several other community forestry organizations and programs. The reality is that nonprofits involved with community forestry are limited to looking for funding from a small group of funders. The NCFC has been successful in building a relationship of trust with local communities, and if the organization does not get further funding support, then the support to participatory research that the NCFC has provided to communities may be lost. This may be a setback to the institutionalization of community forestry.

Conclusion

There is broad support for the type of capacity-building work the NCFC has been doing among communities as well as among government agencies at the state, regional, and federal level that are aware of the participatory and grassroots strategies used by the regional centers. Government agencies recognize that the NCFC has played an important role in building the capacity of community forestry practitioners thus promoting the mutual well-being of forests and communities through research and outreach.

While NCFC research projects address specific needs of communities, community members also increase their capacity to gather their own information and generate their own knowledge for meaningful engagement in resource management. However, this cannot be sustainable unless there is an incentive for the government agency or private industry involved with the particular community in question to heed the community's input, or if there is no built-in mechanism for holding them accountable for facilitating achievement of community goals. Currently, there are two major incentives for government agencies and private industry to work collaboratively with communities: (1) avoiding political conflict (i.e., lawsuits and appeals); and (2) finances (reduced budgets for government agencies and effects of globalization on competitiveness of private firms) (Wilmsen and

Krishnaswamy 2003). But government agencies still retain the ultimate decision-making authority, and private industry still has disproportionate economic and political clout. Thus, NCFC's efforts in institutionalizing community forestry might not be successful in the long run if these fundamental, underlying relations of power are not addressed.

Institutionalization of community forestry in the United States is critical for forest sustainability. Resource sustainability increases if local people, using their knowledge and experience, have an opportunity to participate in decisions that affect their lives. Community forestry, after emerging in developing countries about two decades ago, has grown into a worldwide phenomenon due to clear evidence of the reciprocal relationship between community involvement and forest sustainability. The community forestry movement in the United States, partly drawing on the principles and inspiration of the international movement, has rapidly grown, due to local communities organizing to gain more influence over the ways the priorities of forest management are set. Their efforts are being supported by several nonprofit social movement organizations operating at the local, regional, and national levels by focusing on social change as a way to sustain forest health. However, government agencies and private industry have been slow to adjust to these changes in civil society. Institutionalization of community forestry in the United States remains a challenge unless government agencies and private industry actively promote community participation in forest management.

References

Arnold, J. E. M. 1992. *Community Forestry: Ten years in Review.* Rome: U.N. Food and Agriculture Organization.

Brendler, T., and H. Carey. 1998. "Community Forestry, Defined." *Journal of Forestry* 96(3): 21-23.

Carey, H. 2001. *National Network of Forest Practitioners: A History (and Work in Progress).* Santa Fe, NM: The Forest Guild.

Chambers, R. 1983. *Rural Development: Putting the Last First.* Burnt Mill, Harlow, Essex, England: New York: Longman Scientific & Technical.

Freire, P. 1973. *Pedagogy of the Oppressed.* New York: Continuum.

National Community Forestry Center Northern Forest Region. 2000. What is Community Forestry and Why Does it Matter? St. Albans, VT: NCFC-NFR.

National Community Forestry Center Northern Forest Region. 2001. What is Participatory Research and Why Does it Matter? St. Albans, VT: NCFC-NFR.

National Network of Forest Practitioners. 1999. National Resource Center for Rural People in Forest Communities. FRA Grant Application. Santa Fe, NM: The Forest Trust.

Park, P. 1997. "Participatory Research, Democracy and Community." *Practicing Anthropology* Vol. 19, No. 3.

Poffenberger, M., and S. Selin, eds. 1998. *Communities and Forest Management in Canada and the United States. A Regional Profile of the Working Group on Community Involvement in Forest Management.* Berkeley, CA: Forests, People and Policies.

Schon, Donald A. 1995. "Knowing-in-Action: The New Scholarship Requires a New Epistemology." *Change* November/December:27-34.

Tandon, R. 1988. "Social Transformation and Participatory Research." *Convergence* 21 (2-3): 5-18.

Williams, L. 1998. "Participatory Research: Science for the People." *Practitioner:* Newsletter of the National Network of Forest Practitioners 10: 1-2, 9.

Wilmsen, C., and A. Krishnaswamy. 2003. Institutionalizing Participatory Research in Forestry in the United States—A Study of Two Programs (Draft). Working Paper 8: National Community Forestry Center. Providence, RI: NCFC-NNFP.

World Bank. 1992. *World Development Report 1992: Development and the Environment.* New York: Oxford University Press.

World Resources Institute. 1992. *World Resources 1992-93: A Report by the World Resources Institute.* New York and Oxford: Oxford University.

CHAPTER 12
Another Look at Private Forestlands: America's Forest Landowners

James C. Finley, A. E. Luloff, and S. B. Jones

Introduction

Implementing forest stewardship on private forestlands (PFLs) is no small task (Finley et al. 2001). Despite decades of efforts by foresters, most PFLs are not well managed. This inability to bring more PFLs under sound management may be due to foresters' failure to gain a true understanding of the PFL owner. The tendency is to frequently characterize them (Wiant 1997; DeCoster 1998; Wenger 1998; Heissenbuttel 2001) in a way that mirrors professional and personal biases, and thereby creates a PFL myth.[1] In this paper we address a critical question: can the forestry community (defined here as resource professionals, including agency and industry foresters and academics) abandon perceptions of forest landowners based on myth, and help empower PFL owners to practice forest stewardship?

This problem is most evident in the East of the U.S. and particularly in the northeastern states where private forest landownership is dominant. In Pennsylvania, for example, 75 percent of the state's 18 million acres of forestland are held by more than five hundred thousand PFLs (Table 1). Moreover, on the basis of information drawn from Birch's studies (Birch and Dennis 1980; Birch and Stelter 1993; Birch 1996), it is clear that private forestlands change hands every thirteen years. This suggests that the state has about forty thousand new forest landowners every year.

PFL's management situation in Pennsylvania is typical, at least throughout the eastern United States (e.g., Bliss 1993). Only 3 percent of the Commonwealth's PFL owners have a written management plan, accounting for just 16 percent of PFL acreage (Table 2: Birch and Stelter 1993). Less than 20 percent of PFL timber harvests involve a forester. Without a plan or a forester, highgrading practices prevail (Nyland 1992; Fajvan et al. 1998; Pell 1998). Along with the removal

Table 1. Distribution of private forest landowners and acreage, nationally, northern region, Pennsylvania.

Area	1978		1994	
	Owners (000)	Acres (000,000)	Owners (000)	Acres (000,000)
United States	7,757.9	333.094	9,901.7	393.389
North	3,289.5	114.054	3,931.2	129.551
Pennsylvania	492.8	10.677	513.9	12.508

of the largest, fastest-growing, highest-value trees, highgrading often results in damage to the residual trees and soils (Egan 1993). But the practice of highgrading is common on PFLs, due to landowners' inadequate knowledge of forests and forestry. Woodlot-management decisions are made too often with less information than is necessary to make sustainable decisions.

Understanding PFL Owners

Education can be a powerful motivator for landowners, but unless we know our PFL clientele better, we cannot help them realize their full potential. Getting to know PFL owners requires collaboration with nonforesters, including sociologists. We can no longer operate as though PFL forestry is simply the application of science to small woodlots. It is much more than that and includes the process of engaging PFL owners in an active management role so that they can implement informed sustainable forestry actions.

A number of "market analyses" have carefully examined PFL owners. These geographically based studies include surveys conducted throughout the eastern United States—in Pennsylvania, Alabama, the Tennessee Valley (Mississippi, Alabama, Georgia, Tennessee, Kentucky, Virginia, North Carolina), Illinois, and Indiana—and a separate study of five southern states (Alabama, Mississippi, Oklahoma, Tennessee, Texas). Evidence from these surveys suggests that foresters have constructed an image of PFL owners that is rationalized, in part, by characterizing them as members of the forestry community, distinct from the general public (Bliss et al. 1994). Ticknor (1986) lamented foresters' tendency to attribute their own views to landowners, only then to puzzle about why they "don't see the world the same way we do."

Table 2. Forest landowners with written management plans, nationally, regionally, and by state.

	Owners (000)	Percent	Acres (000,000)	Percent
United States 1994				
Owners with written plans	531.2	5.3	153.6	39.0
PFLs	528.8	99.5	88.1	57.4
Owners with no written plan	8594.1	86.8	226.2	57.5
No Answer	784.9	7.9	13.6	3.5
North 1994				
Owners with written plans	206.5	5.2	38.1	29.4
PFLs	205.5	99.5	25.2	66.1
Owners with no written plan	3,449.5	87.8	86.2	66.4
No Answer	275.2	7.0	5.3	4.2
Pennsylvania 1992				
Owners with written plans	15.4	3.0	2.0	16.0
Owners with no written plan	436.1	85.0	10.0	80.0
No Answer	61.6	12.0	0.5	4.0

In retrospect, Haymond's 1994 observation was prescient. At that time, she said that a major barrier to promoting forest stewardship was "foresters' ignorance of our customers." This ignorance is reflected in the continued characterization of PFL owners by foresters as rural dwelling and land connected, anti-environmentalist, timber oriented, and intensely in favor of private property rights. For example, Sedjo's chapter in Frederick and Sedjo (1991) mentions private forestland resources, but its emphasis is squarely on timber production from public lands, ignoring the magnitude of private land resources for both timber and a plethora of other valued assets. This focus reflects a long-term trend perhaps best captured nearly twenty years earlier in Royer and Risbrudt (1983). This book riveted attention on foresters' need to focus on managing private forestlands to meet growing timber demand. Their suggestions paid little or no attention to the fact that PFL owners own land for myriad reasons.

Similarly, the commodity values commonly associated with forests(for example, timber and consumptive wildlife) are often emphasized (e.g., MacCleery 1992), but many of the forest-related amenities that society broadly values (for example, songbirds, aesthetics, non-consumptive recreation, solitude, and water) are not recognized. In more recent literature, this failure has been reflected in calls for increased citizen and community participation in forest decision making, on both public and private lands, with the emphasis on maintaining product flow (Poffenberger and Selin 1998; Moore 2000). This continued focus on traditional forest production, colored by whatever current phraseology is popular in Washington, D.C. (multiple use, forest stewardship, ecosystem management, and/or sustainable forestry), continues to pervade discussions on how to best manage and use our private (and public) forests. Indeed, if we listen carefully we might even hear Gifford Pinchot describing what he saw as the proper role of the federal government in the management of the private forests for the greater good (Pinchot 1974).

These problems led us to examine each of the myths foresters continue to hold about PFL owners.

Rural and Land Connected?

Two states, geographically dispersed, serve as reference points for the examination of this first myth—Alabama and Pennsylvania. Both states have about 70 percent of their commercial forestland in PFL ownership (Birch and Stelter 1993; Bliss 1993). The 1978 and 1992 USDA Forest Service surveys of Pennsylvania landowners (Birch and Stelter 1993) revealed that the percentage of PFL owners who were farmers declined during this period from 16 percent to 10 percent. In Alabama, however, farmers owned a greater percentage of the state's forestland in 1992 (22 percent; Bliss 1993), but the percentage of Alabama PFL owners who considered themselves of "farm origin" declined by almost 50 percent over the period 1971–1991 (from 90 percent to 50 percent), indicating that the current owners are further removed from their farm heritage—and less connected to it. Similarly, over the same twenty-year period, the percentage of PFL owners who were residents on their woodlots decreased from 75 percent to 40 percent (Bliss 1993). In a related study, Bliss et al. (1993) found that 45 percent of PFL owners in a seven-state Tennessee Valley area resided on their property. This pattern has been documented in a range of states.

Other rapid shifts are occurring in landowner demographics. The proportion of Pennsylvania landowners who are white-collar workers or retirees has increased by 50 percent since 1978—from 18 percent to 27 percent and from 17 percent to 26 percent, respectively. In Alabama, the percentage of owners with a college education increased from 16 percent in 1971 to 42 percent in 1991 (Bliss 1993), while one in four owners in the Tennessee Valley had completed college (Bliss et al. 1993). In 1991, 47 percent of all Alabama owners were retired.

The evidence from these studies lead to a very different conclusion about today's PFL owners. Clearly they are not necessarily rural or land connected. Instead, the multigeneration, farm-based owners characteristic of the 1950s have morphed into a set of well-educated, white-collar or retired owners, who are either nonresident or of urban, nonfarm origin.

Anti-environmentalist?

In the Pennsylvania Forest Stewardship survey (Luloff et al. 1993), landowners and the general public were each asked to note any of eight environmental actions they had engaged in during the previous year. These actions included: (1) reducing their use of lawn and garden chemicals; (2) contributing time or money to an environmental or wildlife group; (3) no longer buying a product because of perceived environmental problems associated with it; (4) attending a public hearing or meeting about the environment; (5) contacting a government agency to get information or to complain about an environmental issue; (6) reading a conservation or environmental magazine; (7) watching a television special on the environment; and (8) voting for or against a political candidate because of his or her position on the environment (Table 3). Those who had engaged in more of these environmental behaviors were seen as exhibiting a higher degree of pro-environmental behavior (Luloff et al. 1993; Nord et al. 1998).

PFL owners indicated higher levels of activity for all eight environmental actions (and were significantly more likely to have taken such action for six of the eight) than the general public. Despite the common complaint of various forestry professionals (Wenger 1997), i.e., if only those damn environmentalists would get out of the woods, we could do our jobs, the "typical" Pennsylvania PFL owner is more of an environmental activist than the general citizen.

PFL owners often do not have the capacity to translate such belief systems—including the belief that environmental concerns are more essential than timber—into responsible management (Egan 1993). As a result, they often turn to forest professionals for assistance.

Table 3. Comparison of Pennsylvania PFL owners and general public on environmental activism (Luloff et al. 1993).

Environmental action	% General public	% Landowners	Significance
Reduced their use of lawn and garden chemicals	57	64	<.01
Contributed time or money to an environ-mental or wildlife group	38	45	<.01
Stopped buying a product because of perceived environmental problems	57	64	<.01
Attended a public hearing or meeting about the environment	11	24	<.01
Contacted a government agency to get information or to complain about an environmental issue	16	24	<.01
Read a conservation or environmental magazine	56	66	<.01
Watched a television special on the environment	84	86	NS
Voted for or against a political candidate because of position on the environment	34	35	NS

Unfortunately, forest managers, with their propensity to timber, are often unable to translate a landowner's desires into land management plans and action, despite the apparent need for forestry advice as expressed by PFL owners (O'Hara and Reed 1991).

In a related discussion of such divergences between foresters and PFL owners, Bliss (1994) stated that foresters were ". . . seriously out of sync with the views prevailing among forest owners." This disjuncture has contributed to the rise of interest in community-based forestry in the United States. Here, frustration over the anger between environmentalists and traditional forestry interests has led communities and PFL owners to a new level of dialogue about their relationships to the land. PFL owners can and do identify with the environmentalist position more easily than forestry professionals because they share a level of understanding that has broader foundations than timber (Gray et al. 2001).

Evidence supporting this view was generated at a November 1993 task force meeting (composed mostly of foresters) to address the proliferation of local timber harvesting ordinances in Pennsylvania. The tone of the meeting was that environmentalists wanted to keep foresters from harvesting timber and that they intended to use local regulations as a means to accomplish this goal. Moreover, the chairman's column in the fall 1993 Allegheny Society of Foresters (SAF) newsletter referred to environmentalists as "our worthy adversaries." These "adversaries" are the individuals who own 58 percent of the nation's commercial forestland!

Timber Oriented?

Bliss (1994:43) observed that the "forester's obsession with the timber supply questions, while producing much useful information, has also prevented researchers from understanding PFL owners as real, three-dimensional people." Most landowners are not particularly timber oriented, even though many of them do sell timber at some point in their tenure. An Indiana survey team (Ticknor 1986) characterized the primary reason for forestland ownership as "rebuilding the spirit"— a metaphor for reconnecting owners to all of the reasons they hold land. Echoing this, Hodge and Southard (1992) found that the top three reasons Virginia respondents gave for owning forestland were "preserving nature," "maintaining scenic beauty," and "viewing wildlife." Ticknor (1993) presented similar findings for owning land using a survey of Illinois PFL owners. Many owned their land to provide shelter for wildlife (87 percent), preserve natural beauty (81 percent), and reserve a heritage for future generations (80 percent). About half indicated they owned their land for family recreation (56 percent) or a place to hunt (55 percent). Only 16 percent mentioned timber sale income as a primary reason for owning land.

Pennsylvania respondents also identified the forest values they perceived as important (Luloff et al. 1993; Table 4). Interestingly, landowner responses were not significantly different from those given by the general public. And Pennsylvania's percentage of landowners who viewed timber production as a very important forest benefit was similar to the 28 percent of landowners in Doolittle's (1993) five-state southern region who listed income from timber sales as the primary benefit of their ownership.

Table 4. Usual results of cutting down trees (Luloff et al. 1993).

Impacts of Cutting	% General Public	% PFL Owners	Significance
Wildlife habitat destruction	92	77	<.01
Residential and commercial development	87	77	<.01
Muddy streams	86	76	<.01
Soil erosion	81	71	<.01
Recreation space loss	78	66	<.01
Permanent forest loss	75	62	<.01

Table 5. Percentages of Pennsylvania PFL owners and the general public perceiving forest benefits as very important (Luloff et al. 1993).

	General Public	Landowners
Clean air	94	96
Clean water	94	96
Soil protection	85	85
Wildlife habitat	85	82
Timber production	20	27

That landowners are not timber oriented does not imply that they oppose harvesting. The Virginia survey found that 56 percent of PFL owners harvested timber (Hodge and Southard 1992), while Bliss (1993) reported that 43 percent of Alabama PFL owners had sold timber in the previous ten years and 50 percent planned to sell it in the future. Fifty-five percent of Pennsylvania PFL owners (accounting for 71 percent of PFL) had harvested timber; 37 percent (52 percent of acreage) intended to harvest (Birch and Stetler 1993). And 70 percent of Tennessee Valley PFL owners agreed that trees are "like any other crop and should be cut and replanted to provide consumer products" (Bliss et al. 1993).

Such pro-harvest attitudes and actions are not unconditional. For instance, PFL owners do not generally view clearcutting with favor. A majority of Tennessee Valley respondents (both landowners and the general public) felt that clearcutting was unacceptable on PFLs, forest industry lands, and public lands (Bliss et al. 1993). Alabama PFL owners' views of clearcutting were similar; only 53 percent agreed that the practice was acceptable and 8 percent were uncertain (Bliss 1993). Pennsylvania respondents expressed even stronger sentiments: 62 percent of PFL owners and 66 percent of the general public believed that clearcutting should be banned (Luloff et al. 1993).

Why are landowners and others opposed to clearcutting? Tennessee Valley respondents offered several reasons, including loss of forests, soil erosion, destruction of wildlife habitat, other environmental effects, and a conclusion that clearcutting is "immoral." The majority of Pennsylvania landowners and the general public believed that cutting trees usually results in destruction of wildlife habitat, residential and commercial development, muddy streams, soil erosion, loss of recreation space, and permanent loss of forests (Luloff et al. 1993; Table 5). So the third myth—private landowners are timber oriented— is also untrue. But they are not averse to cutting trees.

Extremists for Private Property Rights?

The furor over SAF's Task Force Report on Sustaining Long-Term Forest Health and Productivity was in large measure spurred by foresters' fear that ecosystem management on mixed ownerships threatened private property rights (e.g., Larson 1993). Yet Tennessee Valley survey respondents (86 percent) thought that private property rights were important only if the environment was not harmed (Bliss et al. 1993). Indeed, 76 percent indicated that private property rights should be limited, when necessary, to protect the environment. Only 21 percent of PFL owners said that they had the right to do as they pleased regardless of environmental consequences. In fact, 61 percent felt that protecting scenic beauty on private lands was important enough to justify harvesting regulations. But more than two of three respondents (68 percent) also indicated that landowners so regulated should be compensated for the "loss."

The Tennessee Valley survey findings revealed only minor differences in the answers given by PFL owners and the general public. In Alabama, 42 percent of landowners said that forestry practices on private lands should be regulated to protect the environment; 57 percent felt that timber harvesting should be strictly controlled in wetlands; and 64 percent indicated that timber harvesting practices should be regulated, where necessary, to protect the habitat of endangered species (Bliss et al. 1993).

Landowners are willing to accept some measure of regulation, with its consequent diminution of private property rights, provided the justification is environmental protection. Although many landowners are concerned about a potential loss of property rights, they also accept the social responsibilities that accompany land ownership.

Defending the Myth—"Large Landowners Are Different"

When presented with this information on PFL owners, many foresters cling to their long-held beliefs, mythologizing an image of this group that does not exist. In defense of their actions, these foresters often assert that the data are skewed and misleading because they aggregate all PFL owners, regardless of acreage owned. These same foresters often insist that they know most landowners hold just a few acres and that the attitudes and practices of such owners are different from "real" landowners who own more than one hundred acres.

Such sentiments constitute a fifth myth—that large landowners are different. Among Pennsylvania landowner groups, the largest landowners were most likely to support banning clearcuts: 64 percent of those owning at least 200 acres and 60 percent of those holding 10-199 acres (Luloff et al. 1993). And large landowners' views of cutting trees were only slightly less skeptical than the opinions of smaller landowners and the general public (Table 6).

Although large landowners are more timber oriented than those owning fewer than ten acres acres, few hold their property for the sole purpose of generating income (Luloff et al. 1993). Even the belief that large landowners are more likely to conduct harvesting and implement management practices warrants scrutiny. Cleaves and Bennett (1994) attributed differences due to ownership size to an "available acres artifact." That is, large landowners may be no more likely to harvest or actively manage their property; they may simply

Table 6. Percentages of both PFL owners (by acres owned) and general public agreeing that various effects usually result from cutting trees (Luloff et al. 1993).

Perceived environmental impact	General public	PFL owners (acres owned)			All PFL owners
		1-9	10-199	>199	
Wildlife habitat destruction	92	74	69	57	70
Residential and commercial development	87	82	72	76	77
Muddy streams	86	78	74	70	76
Soil erosion	82	74	69	57	71
Loss of recreation space	78	72	60	59	66
Permanent loss of forests	75	71	52	61	62

have more acreage available on which to operate. The linear relationship between tract size and harvesting tendency may not reflect an inherent tendency on the part of larger landowners.

Foresters' general view of PFL owners clearly tends to be incorrect. Forest landowners are environmentally aware and are concerned about perceived negative consequences of timber harvesting, even as they continue to sell timber. Landowners believe in protecting the environment, even if it means living with additional regulations. And, large landowners' views differ little from those held by smaller landowners and the general public.

Can Education Make a Difference?

Once such myths are dispelled, what can foresters do to connect with PFL owners? Will more information for landowners lead to greater adoption of responsible natural resources management? Egan and Jones (1993) found limited correlation between landowners' attitude (their expressions of a land ethic) and actual practices associated with harvesting, but substantial correlation between knowledge (what they know about forests and forestry) and post-harvest site conditions. Their research revealed an even stronger relationship between assistance from a forester and such impacts. This suggests that without adequate knowledge and/or assistance from a forester, many landowners do make timber harvesting decisions that damage the site and residual stand (Pell 1998; Fajvan et al. 2000).

The relationship between knowledge and action is clear (Jones et al. 2001), but do uninformed PFL owners really want to know more? Ninety-four percent of Pennsylvania's PFL owners said they needed more information to properly manage their land. Both PFL owners and the general public selected one or more strategies they thought

Table 7. Strategies for promoting forest management preferred by both Pennsylvania PFL owners and the general public (Luloff et al. 1993).

Strategy	% General public	% PFL owners
Government cost share	77	43
Local regulation	85	59
State regulation	91	61
Tax incentives	79	69
Education	99	98

could effectively encourage PFL owners to practice forest management (Table 7). Overwhelmingly, both preferred education. The 150 invited PFL owners who attended the First National Forest Stewardship Conference (the Circle of Stewards; April 1994) developed very similar, prioritized recommendations for increasing the number of forest stewards. The list included improving the tax climate, educating landowners and the general public, and fostering a friendly regulatory environment.

Recommendation

What have we learned from this collection of experiences and evidence? First, we recognize that not all foresters embrace every one of the "myths"; we also concede that PFL owners represent tremendous diversity. Ticknor (1986) noted that "real" people are a lot different from "typical" people. There is no question that some foresters work with clientele who are anti-environmentalist, extreme proponents of private property rights, aggressively timber oriented, and resident on their property. However, our intent has been to examine the composite, representing foresters and PFL owners broadly, so that we can encourage foresters to rethink their relationship to the owners of a critically important resource (Finley and Jacobson 2001).

PFL owners and the general public alike are committed to environmental objectives. We must, therefore, thoughtfully repackage and deliver the information needed by PFL owners to implement responsible forestry and wildlife management procedures. The Forest Stewardship Program (a Forest Service partnership with individual states) encourages PFL owners to develop plans that integrate multiple values. But even within the Forest Stewardship context, a myth-led forester can slip into an old comfort zone. For example, one central Pennsylvania couple, who are adamant about not cutting trees on their property, was recently surprised to see that their forester had prescribed a timber-stand improvement harvest in their Forest Stewardship plan.

Foresters and educators must discard historical stereotypes about PFL owners. We must abandon the tendency to speak with authority about what "our" PFL clientele believe and what information they need. It is time to reexamine both our audiences and our messages.

Yvan Hardy, assistant deputy minister of the Canadian Forest Service, offered a parallel caution regarding our belief that we could solve many forest policy problems if only the public were more knowledgeable. Speaking to the joint SAF/Canadian Institute of Forestry convention in Anchorage, he advised foresters to forget about educating the public (1994). Instead, he said we should start listening to the public and remember that we are their servants. He observed that being technically correct is not necessarily the most important thing.

Bliss (1994) suggested that we spend "less time defending unpopular practices and more time demonstrating practices which satisfy silvicultural and environmental goals in socially acceptable ways." Fortmann and Fairfax (1991) urged the forestry profession to overcome the presumption that resource management is a technical, not a social, undertaking. Regardless of whose proscription makes foresters most comfortable, it is incumbent upon them to first listen to PFL owners and then provide them with science-based information in an atmosphere of respect and participatory learning. As long as we continue to base our outreach efforts on mythical characteristics, foresters will fail to capture the full benefit of engaging PFL owners in a shared learning experience, one that will result in a forest that provides for all of society's resource needs.

Note

1 Myth is defined by the *Merriam-Webster's Ninth Collegiate Dictionary* as: "a popular belief ... that embod[ies] the ideals and institutions of a ... segment of society." We believe this definition nicely reflects work in this area. Another myth, not addressed in this paper, is the one associated with nonindustrial private forest landowners or NIPFs. The NIPF moniker suggests that industry is the standard of choice and those who do not identify with industry are at odds with the perspective held by foresters. Why the professions would chose to lump non-industry owners into one category remains unclear and perverts the range of reasons why private citizens, corporations, Native American tribes, organizations, and NGOs own land. For clarity, we refer to this group of owners as PFLs.

References

Birch, T. W. 1996. Private Forest-land Owners of the Northern United States, 1994. USDA Forest Service Resource Bulletin NE-136. Radnor, PA: USDA Forest Service.

Birch, T. W., and D. F. Dennis. 1980. The Forestland Owners of Pennsylvania. USDA Forest Service Resource Bulletin. NE-66. Broomall, PA: USDA Forest Service.

Birch, T. W. and C. M. Stelter. 1993. "Trends in Owner Attitudes." Pp. 50-60 in *Penns Woods—Change and Challenge*, J. C. Finley and S. B. Jones (eds.). University Park: The Pennsylvania State University.

Bliss, J. C. 1993. Alabama's Nonindustrial Private Forest Owners: Snapshots from a Family Album. ANR-788. Auburn: Auburn University, Alabama Cooperative Extension Service Center.

Bliss, J. C. 1994. "Unidentified Forest Owners." Pp. 43-48 in Proceedings of the First National Forest Stewardship Conference: Circle of Stewards. St. Paul: University of Minnesota, Minnesota Extension Service.

Bliss, J C., R. T. Brooks Jr., and M. D. Larsen. 1993. Attitudes in the Tennessee Valley Region Toward Forest Practices and Policies. Final Report to the Tennessee Valley Authority. Auburn, AL: Auburn University and the Gallop Organization, Inc.

Bliss, J. C., S. K. Nepal, R. T. Brooks, and M. D. Larsen. 1994. "Forestry Community or Granfalloon?" *Journal of Forestry* 92(9):6-10.

Cleaves, D. A., and M. Bennett. 1994. Holding Size and Behavior of Nonindustrial Private Landowners: A Cautious Second Look. Paper presented at The 24th Annual Southern Forest Economics Workshop, Savannah, GA.

Decoster, L. A. 1998. "The Boom in Forest Owners – A Bust for Forestry?" *Journal of Forestry* 96(5): 25-28.

Doolittle, M. L. 1993. "Future Availability of Nonindustrial Private Timber in the South. Pp. 56-69 in *Proceedings: Nonindustrial Private Forests in the 1990s.* Auburn, AL: Auburn University Press.

Egan, A. F. 1993. Forest Stewardship: The Relationship between the Articulations and Actions of PFL Owners. Unpublished Ph.D. Dissertation. University Park: The Pennsylvania State University.

Egan, A. F., and S. B. Jones. 1993. "Do Landowner Practices Reflect Beliefs?" *Journal of Forestry* 91(10):39-45.

Fajvan, M. A., S. T. Gurhseckey, and C. C. Hassler. 1998. "The Effects of Harvesting Practices on West Virginia's Wood Supply." *Journal of Forestry* 96(5):33-39.

Finley, J. C., S. B. Jones, A. S. Reed, M. G. Jacobson, and G. R. Glover. 2001. "Finding a Name to Fit the Owner." *Journal of Forestry* 99(3):48.

Finley, J. C., and M. G. Jacobson. 2001. "Extension in Pennsylvania: Diverse Partners Working Together." *Journal of Forestry* 99(3):9-13.

Fortmann, L., and S. Fairfax. 1991. "Forest Resource Policy." Pp. 270 -80 in *Rural Policies for the 1990s,* C. B. Flora and J. A. Christenson (eds.). Boulder, CO: Westview Press Inc.

Frederick, K. D., and R. A. Sedjo. 1991. *America's Renewable Resources: Historical Trends and Current Challenges.* Washington, DC: Resources for the Future.

Gray, G. J., M. J. Enszer, and J. Kusel. 2001. *Understanding Community-based Forestry: Forest Ecosystem Management.* New York, NY: Food Products Press.

Haymond, J. L. 1995. Achieving Harmony with NIPF Owners and Society Selecting the Right Timbre? Paper presented at Society of American Foresters National Convention, Portland, Maine.

Heissenbuttel, J. F. 2001. "Ending the Cold War." *Journal of Forestry* 99(2):1.

Hodge, S. S., and L. Southard. 1992. "A Profile of Virginia PFL Landowners: Results of a 1991 Survey." *Virginia Forests* 47(4):7-9, 11.

Jones, S. B., G. R. Glover, J. C. Finley, M. G. Jacobson, and A. S. Reed. 2001. "Empowering Private Forest Landowners: Lessons from Pennsylvania, Alabama, and Oregon." *Journal of Forestry* 99(3):4-5.

Larsen, L. R. 1993. "Why the SAF Task Force Report is Invalid." *The Consultant* (fall).

Luloff, A. E., K. P. Wilkinson, M. R. Schwartz, J. C. Finley, S. B. Jones, and C. R. Humphrey. 1993. Pennsylvania Forest Stewardship Program's Media Campaign: Forest Landowners' and the General Public's Opinions and Attitudes. Final Report to the USDA Forest Service. University Park, PA: Department of Agricultural Economics and Rural Sociology.

MacCleery, D. W. 1992. *American Forests: A History of Resiliency and Recovery.* Durham, NC: Forest History Society.

Moore, P. 2000. *Green Spirit: Trees Are the Answer.* Vancouver, BC, Canada: Greenspirit Enterprises Ltd.

Nyland, R. D. 1992. "Exploitation and Greed in Eastern Hardwood Forests." *Journal of Forestry* 90(1):33-37.

O'Hara, T. J., and A. S. Reed. 1991. "Timber Market Development on Private Forests in Minnesota." *Northern Journal of Applied Forestry* 91(8): 153-55.

Pell, J. A. 1998. Variables Characterizing Timber Resource Sustainability of Recently Harvested Tracts Across Pennsylvania. MS Thesis. University Park: The Pennsylvania State University.

Pinchot, G. 1974 (1947). *Breaking New Ground.* Washington, DC: Island Press.

Poffenberger, M., and S. Selin. 1998. Communities and Forest Management in Canada and the United States. Working Group on Community Involvement in Forest Management. Ford Foundation and United Kingdom's Department for International Development.

Royer, J. P., and C. D. Risbrudt. 1983. Nonindustrial Private Forests: A Review of Economic and Policy Studies: Symposium Proceedings. Durham, NC: School of Forestry and Environmental Studies, Duke University.

Society of American Foresters. 1994. Managing Forests to Meet People's Needs: Proceedings of the 1994 Society of American Foresters/Canadian Institute of Forestry Convention. Anchorage, AK.

Ticknor, W. D. 1986. "A Forestry Love Affair." *National Woodlands* (Jan./Feb.):5-7.

Ticknor, W. D. 1993. A Survey of Selected Forestland Owners in Southcentral Indiana. Orient, OH: Forestry Consultants, Inc.

Wenger, K. F. 1997. "The Public's Interest is Our Opportunity." *Journal of Forestry* 95(10):3.

Wenger, K. F. 1998. "Why Manage Forests?" *Journal of Forestry* 96(1):1.

Wiant, H. V. 1997. "Off-ramp on the Road to Ruin." *Journal of Forestry* 95(1):3

SECTION III

Community and the Urban Forest
Demographic Cycles and the Future of Urban and
Exurban Forests

Donald R. Field and Robert G. Lee

This third section examines forests in an urban setting. Metropolitan communities and the urban fringe possess some of the most abundant forest fragments in the United States. Overlooked in forest assessments, these places are home for many plant and animal species that provide diversity to the urban community. Urban forests have meaning in the daily lives of urban dwellers. These forests are sources of pride, symbols of place, objects of neighborhood attachment, and remarkably in some cases, contested spaces. Forests have likewise been reinvented or recreated in the city by urbanites in their own image, reflecting their culture and building attachment to a place. As we will see in the chapters in this section, the dynamic nature of urban nature changes with the face of community and the actors therein. Forests or plots of trees in the city, as in the country, ebb and flow as the community of people maintaining these forests changes over time. The chapters in this section represent a matrix of urban forest connections from the urban center to urban wildland fringe. The application of community forestry in each human setting requires adaptation to the social, cultural, and natural resource environment present.

Mcdonough and Vachta, in their intensive case study research in urban Detroit, provide an opening statement on the connection of urban people and forests. They describe how a local, low-income community was empowered by a community forest initiative. Use rights and management responsibility for vacant city lots in Detroit were transferred to local groups of volunteers. The authors recount the processes by which these groups were formed and gained control over unused land. Principles common to community forestry in general are illustrated by how local people assumed control, developed pride in their accomplishments, and improved the quality of their lives by participating in shared reinvention of forest space, parks, and gardens. The authors remind us that community is not always coterminous with a given place. Community emerges through collective interest, occupational commonality, and an interactive field of common interest and goals. This study exemplifies the latter. Here, intersections of social organization or activity by a group of people signals the potential of community. This chapter illustrates how community emerges from empowerment of people.

Grove, Burch, and Pickett portray a community forestry program in a slightly different manner from the other authors in this section. Clearly, social goals of community forestry, including group formation, collective action, institutional development, and sustainable social structures are central to the authors' undertaking. They take an ecological approach to studying human society, and apply these principles to understand the interaction of people and forests through collective actions across "ecological landscape transects" from the central city to the suburban edge to the urban fringe. In the case of a single Baltimore watershed, the authors draw on the community forestry tradition originating in lesser-developed nations to address communities as vehicles for constructing, managing, and maintaining urban vegetation mosaics of water supply, stream water quality, biodiversity, and recreation. The authors also discuss communities of people in terms of natural social units—groups specifically organized to conduct a specific forest activity or groups organized for purposes other than forest management. The combination of groups and their interaction at the different scales of urban center, neighborhood, or stream valley, for example, provide us with the picture of social networks shaping the Baltimore urban region. Lodged within an ecosystem analysis, a configuration of human and biological communities in space and time allows us to appreciate the interaction and change occurring in both the social and biological system. The complexity of this urban project illustrates the dynamic nature of the vegetative mosaic of a city and what is required to improve human life and quality of natural resources in any urban metropolitan region.

Egan and Luloff return our attention to the urban/wildland fringe by summarizing and interpreting current literature. The migration of urban or suburban residents to forests surrounding cities or to remote rural locations dominated by forest vegetation has accelerated in the past fifteen to twenty years and continues today. This trend has created as complex a challenge for integrating people and forests as in the central city. The authors synthesize our knowledge of the migration patterns to the urban fringe, where people are attempting to capture a quality of life and environmental services unavailable in more-developed urban settings. They describe how such residential development creates new problems of incompatible land uses and environmental impacts for people who own and use these forests for purposes other than as a residential backdrop. Applying community forest principles at the fringe presents problems and issues in a different context from the city core. Here the emergence of community necessitates novel approaches to developing community forest programs suited to a diverse population with conflicting goals.

An ecological transition is placing forests, community, and people in a new set of relationships. The chapters in this section provide a prelude to a postmodern society, post-production forestry in which the democratization of forest management is unfolding. Across the nation, forests are gaining importance for human living whether in the city or on the bounds of public lands in the rural west. Communities of people are changing the composition and structure of forests within the city and in the country to mirror their expectations and values. Vegetation management, including forests and forest fragments, must meet human community goals as well as ecological requirements. In the last chapter we embed community forestry principles in an understanding of postmodern society to emphasize emerging ways people value and use forests. We suggest professional management of forest resources will take on a community forestry character within the context of postmodern forms of social organization and values.

CHAPTER 13

Community Empowerment and the Urban Forest

Maureen H. McDonough and Kerry E. Vachta

Introduction

Forests shape human communities. A commonly held stereotype is that a close relationship with forests is primarily common for members of rural forest-dependent communities or in the exurban setting where people have moved away from the city to find the higher quality of life perceived to be available in rural forested areas (Egan and Luloff 2000). In these settings, residents are perceived to have daily experiences with forests through employment, recreation and other aspects of their lives. A significant amount of work has been done on the importance of forest resources to rural communities (Humphrey et al. 1993; Peluso, Humphrey, and Fortmann 1994).

However, 80.9 percent of all Americans live in metropolitan areas, with 90.2 percent of people of color living in these urbanized settings (U.S. Bureau of the Census 2000). Dwyer et al. (2000) estimate that there are currently 3.8 billion *urban* trees in the United States—74.4 billion if entire metropolitan regions are taken into consideration. The average tree cover in U.S. urban areas is 27.3 percent but in metropolitan areas it is 33.4 percent. While the amount of urban tree cover varies by community, it is clear that most urban residents live in an urban forest. Such a widespread feature of the urban environment has a significant impact on the lives of its residents.

Numerous studies document the value of trees and forests in these communities and neighborhoods. For example, trees reduce urban pollution and moderate sometimes-extreme urban temperatures (Luley 1998). One study exploring the impact of trees and other vegetation on residents of urban public housing found that "compared to residents living adjacent to relatively barren spaces, individuals living adjacent to greener common spaces had more social activities and more visitors, knew more of their neighbors, reported their neighbors were more concerned with helping and supporting one another, and had stronger feelings of belonging" (Kuo et al. 1998). People's satisfaction with their neighborhoods is strongly affected by having views of trees as well as the number of trees near the residence (Kaplan and Kaplan 1989; Kaplan, Kaplan, and Ryan 1998). This is true across income levels as residents' evaluations of trees in their neighborhoods are positive even where housing stock is deteriorating. Large open spaces and designated parks do not contribute to satisfaction as much as trees near people's homes.

In a series of facilitated discussions held in ten metropolitan communities from Lincoln, Nebraska, to Newark, New Jersey, to Goodwater, Alabama, people who had never been engaged in forestry issues were asked to discuss trees in their communities. Without exception, people talked about the importance of trees in their daily lives, including aesthetics, property values, historical values, and environmental contributions (McDonoughet al. 2002).

The remainder of this chapter discusses the role of the urban and community forest in building urban communities. The focus is on the Urban Resources Initiative in Detroit, Michigan, where residents developed community forestry projects to reclaim vacant land in their neighborhoods.

A Sense of "Community"

Contested meanings of "community," especially "urban community," present a challenge to those who study contributions of forests to the lives of urban residents. Building on the work of such influential social theorists such as Durkheim and Marx, early community sociologists romanticized rural communities and were concerned with the social and psychological impacts of the perceived anomie thought to characterize urban centers (e.g. Vidich and Bensman 1958; Stein 1960; Redfield, as cited in Effrat 1974). While that tradition retains some adherents, more recent researchers have undertaken a more comprehensive approach to the study of urban communities. Their work indicates that a genuine sense of community, characterized by feelings of warmth and attachment and close neighboring relations, exists and, in some instances, flourishes in urban centers (Rivera and Erlich 1995; Green 1997; Minkler and Wallerstein 1997).

In an effort to dispel the notion of the city as the embodiment of anomie and social disorganization, these researchers have described the institutions and landmarks that make urban life meaningful for residents and explored the role of neighboring in urban communities. For example, Ahlbrant and Cunningham (1979) found that those who were most satisfied with their urban neighborhood viewed it as a small community within the larger city, and tended to have a stronger sense of loyalty to that neighborhood than to the rest of the city. Hummon (1990) further determined that while rural America represents an idyllic lifestyle for whites, African Americans are more likely to identify the city as a source of emotional and social fulfillment. In fact, Rivera and Erlich (1995) suggest that urban communities of color are "characterized by strong social support systems and relationships that are personal, informal and sentiment-based rather than formal, specialized, and utilitarian" as predicted by Marx's early writings and presumed by early community sociologists. While cities may appear to be alienating and isolating masses from the outside, people within them do not interact with "the city." Instead, they interact with one another within mediating structures such as neighborhoods, churches, and community organizations.

In urban centers, community organizations often take the form of block clubs and neighborhood associations. The term "community organization" refers to a group of concerned citizens engaged in self-help efforts to improve the quality of life in their immediate residential vicinity. Block clubs and neighborhood associations working toward progressive social change have proliferated throughout the United States, especially in low-income communities and communities of color, building locally on the work of the national civil rights and black power movements (Minkler and Wallerstein 1997).

As block clubs and neighborhood associations develop, the increasing interaction among residents through these organizations and their activities may provide an opportunity for building cohesion and a sense of community among residents. Often considered the first step in engendering political power by community organizers, cohesion fosters a sense of shared values and visions for the neighborhood (Sarason 1982; Sampson et al. 1997). Once established, community cohesion may be important in the development of a successful community organization, especially among traditionally underrepresented groups (Janowitz and Street 1978; Hirsch 1986; Fisher 1987). Therefore, prior to forming an organization and a collective voice, residents begin to establish neighboring relationships and recognize their mutual interest (Unger and Wandersman 1983; Weeniget al. 1990).

Participation in community forestry may provide an opportunity to build cohesion among local residents who are engaged in creating green spaces. The availability of gathering areas such as porches, courtyards, or other green spaces is an important factor in influencing community cohesion (Weenig et al. 1990; Bady and Lurz 1993; Louv 1995). By creating green spaces, residents have the opportunity to identify collective interests and concerns as well as the strengths and resources existing within the community. The Urban Resources Initiative in Detroit (URI/Detroit) was developed to explore this potential. URI/Detroit was a partnership between the Department of Forestry at Michigan State University and community groups in Detroit funded by the W. K. Kellogg Foundation, the USDA Forest Service and the Michigan Department of Natural Resources. Through URI/Detroit, Detroit communities began to reclaim some of the city's vacant land for use in forestry-based projects and, by doing so, generated economic, social, and environmental benefits.

Community Forestry in Detroit: The Urban Resources Initiative

A Brief History of Detroit

Detroit was first settled by French traders in 1701 and served as a center for trade and commerce. The waterfront site provided access to transportation routes for export and served as a departure point for expeditions further north into Canada and west across the northern forests. While Detroit grew steadily through the earlier years, its major expansion took place during the boom of industrialization between 1910 and 1930 during which the city grew to its current size of 132 square miles, while the population reached a high of approximately 1.5 million.

As in other northern cities, industrialization was followed in the period between 1940 and 1960 by the advent and growth of suburbanization (Darden al. 1987). During World War II and the post-war industrial boom, migrants from the South in pursuit of factory jobs, coupled with the migration of whites to the suburbs, resulted in a concentration of African Americans within the city. The African American population of Detroit grew from 9.2 percent to 63.1 percent.

In addition, Detroit was among the last cities in the U.S. to prohibit segregation and, as documented by Massey and Denton (1993), the city continues to be among the most hyper-segregated of all metropolitan areas in the nation. Detroit's segregation index was well above the "hyper-segregation cutpoint" and, often, well above those of the other fifteen identified hyper-segregated regions (Massey and Denton 1993).

Tensions fueled by questionable economic development decisions, coupled with the historical lack of interaction between racial groups resulting at least in part from the city's extreme segregation, have had a variety of impacts on Detroit and its history. Among the most dramatic and influential was the 1967 rebellion following a police raid on a popular nightclub patronized primarily by African Americans. In the decade following the rebellion, the city lost 311,000 residents, primarily through continued "white flight" to the suburbs (Dardenet al. 1987) and that depopulation continues. Census figures show the loss of an additional 45,000 families between 1980 and 1990 (U.S. Bureau of the Census 1990).

At the time of the 1990 Census, 26 percent of the population of Detroit was living below the poverty line. With an average family income of $18,740 (Detroit Empowerment Zone Development Corporation 1997), the city had the highest poverty rate of the seventy-seven cities with populations above two hundred thousand in the United States. While Detroit's unemployment rate was about 15 percent (Detroit Empowerment Zone Development Corporation 1997), unemployment among African Americans was ranked first in the nation at 33 percent (U.S. Bureau of the Census 1990). Such a high unemployment rate more closely approximates the 45 percent unemployment rate of blacks in South Africa at the end of Apartheid (James 1992) than that of New York City at 10 percent (Johnson 1997). Detroit's infant mortality rate of 21 per 1,000 live births (U.S. Bureau of the Census 1990), fell between that of Northern Ghana (at 23.9/1,000) (Rosset al. 1995) and Chile (at 19.5/1,000) (Potts 1990). Finally, Detroit had the highest concentration of African Americans in any city in the United States at 75.7 percent of the population (U.S. Bureau of the Census 1990). While this, along with the history of African-American leadership in Detroit, is a source of tremendous pride within the city, Greenberg (1990) notes "the morbidity and mortality rates of black people in the U.S. exceed those of any other industrialized nation."

Detroit has certainly faced tremendous political and economic challenges. Through it all, Detroiters have responded with concerted efforts for local control and social justice, often related to the well-documented labor movements born in the city. With the support of local progressive black churches, residents of the city responded to segregation by establishing black-owned and -operated hospitals, insurance companies, credit unions, and newspapers, which were vital to the growing social consciousness in Detroit. By 1912, the Detroit Chapter of the United Negro Improvement Agency was established by Marcus Garvey followed by the Booker T. Washington Trade Association and the Housewives League of Detroit, both founded in 1930. In the late 1930s, protest and conflict-oriented strategies came to the fore and provided the seeds for building political power among African Americans. This empowerment was realized through the efforts of the NAACP and the strikes of black workers throughout the 1930s and '40s (Thomas 1992).

The heritage of local organizing and self-help lives on in Detroit. In addition to a host of block clubs and neighborhood associations and a large number of faith-based and community-service organizations, several regional and citywide citizens' organizations struggle to rebuild the city along a number of dimensions—to take neighborhoods back from drug dealers, regenerate hope among local youth, challenge youth violence, and work to create a climate of support for the city's young people (Boggs 1998).

The Urban Resources Initiative in Detroit

In 1987, then-Mayor Coleman Young ordered a massive demolition program to clear the "vacant and dangerous" buildings left behind by depopulation. At that time, approximately one of every twelve housing units in the city was classified as "vacant or abandoned" (Detroit Empowerment Zone Development Corporation 1997). By 1991, when Michigan State University's Department of Forestry first launched the Urban Resources Initiative, Detroit's demolition program had generated more than sixty-five thousand vacant lots (Fitzgerald 1991). Given that the average lot in Detroit measures 110 feet by 70 feet, those lots would, if contiguous, have made up approximately twenty-six square miles of vacant land or about one-fifth of Detroit's entire land area. The demolition has continued into the present, leaving increasingly vast areas of the city devoid of buildings or residents.

Budgetary constraints often prevent the city from providing adequate maintenance of the vacant lots, with the result that they become illegal waste dumps. Many Detroit neighborhood groups have identified problems with vacant lots as among the most important concerns in their communities. But the vacant lots also presented an opportunity for Detroit communities to build on their long and rich history of organizing to confront economic and social concerns.

Participants in the URI/Detroit program were members of neighborhood organizations who were already working toward mutually defined goals of community development. Over the eight years the pilot initiative was active in the city, partnerships were established with seven block clubs and neighborhood associations to reclaim eleven vacant lots, and convert these dangerous and abandoned lands to such community-building projects as community nurseries, agroforestry gardens, and orchards. These community groups identified local needs, interests, skills, existing resources, and future goals, and designed forestry-based projects that were appropriate for each individual community. Goals for URI/Detroit projects were determined by each individual community organization in collaboration with and with technical assistance from URI/Detroit personnel and their network of professional contacts and resources. Groups designed projects on the basis of their own collective assessment of their interests, abilities, resources, and visions for their neighborhoods, as well as for the areas in which capacity-building activities would make the greatest contribution toward achieving those visions. These efforts were constrained only by funding and biological/environmental considerations.

In introductory meetings with community groups, organizers explained the community forestry approach and the purposes of the URI/Detroit program, including both its community-centered objectives and its status as a research project of Michigan State University. Participants were introduced to the research process and informed of the related activities that would be asked of participant groups. The program took place in three overlapping phases: collective determination of project objectives and assessment criteria; planning and design; and a multi-level, multi-method evaluation.

Needs assessments. Determination of project objectives and assessment criteria took place early in the URI process. Members of the organization were asked to reflect on the existing resources and skills available to the group within the community, their ideal vision of the community, and the types of activities and resources that might be necessary in order to achieve this vision. Based on this assessment, groups identified their goals and objectives for participating in the URI program, and began to identify forestry-based projects that might facilitate achievement of those objectives. In addition to addressing economic, environmental, educational, and subsistence needs, many groups cited local organizing objectives as an important purpose of developing a community forestry project. Many community groups had a small core of people who did most of the work and had had great difficulty getting younger residents to participate in their activities. These groups sought solutions to attract teens and young adults who had not previously participated in block clubs and neighborhood associations. Since the projects required regular maintenance and provided participants with a constant reminder of the contribution they are making to the community, group members hoped that those involved in planting the projects would remain committed over the long-term (McDonough and Vachta 1997).

Project implementation The planning and design phase built on this work through more detail-oriented activities. These included determining the specific project to be implemented, selecting appropriate tree and shrub species, identifying and contacting supporters who could be helpful (such as church groups, neighboring block clubs, and other groups that might be willing to participate in planting day activities or local businesses that might contribute refreshments or tools), scheduling the planting day event, and making the necessary arrangements with the Department of Public Works and other pertinent agencies.

Evaluation. The evaluation procedures were designed to be collaborative and participatory and consisted of two parallel processes:

quarterly group interviews assessing achievement of group-specific project objectives and semi-annual focus groups exploring group building and other more broad-ranging outcomes of participation in the URI program. The focus groups were preceded by distribution of anonymous individual questionnaires to group participants to ensure the agenda for the focus group meeting reflected the interests and concerns of participants and to provide an opportunity for those with underrepresented views to express themselves freely.

The quarterly group interviews assessed the extent to which participants felt they had achieved their project objectives. The group interviews were held during regularly scheduled group meetings for one year following the planting of the community forestry project. The data reported are a summary of group consensus rather than a compilation of individual responses. During these meetings, the group was asked to recall its initial objectives for the project and to assess how well each objective had been achieved to date.

Additional items explored whether or not groups encountered any unintended consequences (either positive or negative), whether they were gaining increased access to technical assistance through networking with related agencies and organizations, and any organizational changes, such as increased or decreased participation of men or women, older or younger residents. All of the participant groups took part in this process, although local events occasionally precluded a group from completing the procedures for a particular data-collection point (Table 1).

The quarterly assessment was complemented by more in-depth biannual assessments of organizational development and capacity-building outcomes. Assessment of these factors was more complex; there were two steps in this process. First, the purposes and processes of the additional assessment were explained during a regularly scheduled organizational meeting where potential and interested members were invited to volunteer their participation. Although most participants were recruited at these meetings, non-attendees who had been highly involved in the project development and/or implementation were contacted directly if they were not present. In those cases where the group was no longer meeting, contact was made through the group president who typically provided contact information for those members who had been active when the project was implemented and initially evaluated.

Table 1. Number of participant groups completing quarterly assessments.

Group	Data point				Total quarterlies completed by group
	Q1	*Q2*	*Q3*	*Q4*	
1			x	x	2
2	x	x	x	x	4
3	x	x	x		3
4	x	x	x		3
5	x	x	x	x	4
6	x	x	x	x	4
7	x	x	x	x	4
Total # groups completing data point	6	6	7	5	24

In any case, those members who indicated interest in participating were mailed copies of individual questionnaires exploring the issues of group and community development, political and social empowerment, and community participation. Approximately two weeks later, follow-up calls were made to ensure return of mail surveys and to remind participants of the scheduled focus group meeting. Responses to these questionnaires allowed the researchers to develop an agenda for each focus group discussion that represented the specific interests and concerns raised by participants and allowed group members holding dissenting or underrepresented views to express them anonymously if they did not feel comfortable doing so during the group discussion.

During the second step, participants gathered for an in-depth discussion of the issues raised by questionnaire responses in an effort to generate a collective assessment of how participation in the program had impacted the group and community. Specifically, focus group guidelines included opportunities to explore:

• The group's original vision for the project and assessment of the program to date;

• Participants' vision of the ideal community organization and the role the program played in the organization's becoming more or less like their ideal—this section typically included issues such as leadership, membership development, and strategic planning skills;

• Suggestions about how the program could improve on its approaches and processes in the future; and

• Opportunities to explore other issues not already discussed.

Table 2 illustrates the number of participants from each group taking part in each component of the focus group procedure. For the neighborhood associations, the assessment procedures were integrated into the ongoing quarterly evaluation process at the six- (Time 1) and twelve-month (Time 2) data-collection points. However, because this assessment was instituted several years following the planting of the block clubs' community forestry projects, members were asked to participate in one long-term follow-up meeting (Time 2), four to five years following the initial project implementation.

Focus group meetings, which were videotaped for later coding, were typically held in the same place where regular meetings took place. Most often, participants were those members who had been most active in the planning and implementation of the community forestry project. In smaller groups, this typically included most if not all members. However, in some of the larger groups, such as the neighborhood associations, this group represented either a core membership or a group that had indicated particular interest in planting and beautification efforts, constituting a subcommittee of the organization. The meeting agenda followed similar topics to those included in the mail surveys. Discussions, leading to consensus about the implications of participating in the URI program, were initiated through presentation of the aggregated responses from the individual mail surveys.

Data from the quarterly group interviews were recorded as numeric responses along predetermined scales. For example, participants were asked to rate how dangerous the vacant lots in their neighborhood had been before participation in the URI program along a one to five scale and then to rate how dangerous they felt the sites were following planting their community forestry project. The responses agreed upon by group-interview participants were recorded on a single questionnaire form. Because of the limited number of groups, analyses of these data were limited to means.

Focus group transcripts were coded and then analyzed using the computer program Ethnograph v 5.0. Primary categories were determined theoretically based on the literatures in community organization, community building, social and political empowerment, and participation as discussed above. Additional categories for discussions specific to the URI experience and related issues were also

Table 2: Number of Participants Responding to Quantitative Measure at Each Assessment by Organization.

Group	T1 Mail	T1 FG	T2 Mail	T2 FG	Subtotal Mail	Subtotal FGs	Total
1	X	X	X	X	X	X	0
2	X	X	X	X	X	X	0
3	X	X	X	1	X	1	1
4	X	X	4	5	4	5	9
5	4	11	1	1	5	12	17
6	5	5	5	1	10	6	16
7	4	6	6	6	10	12	22
Subtotal	13	22	16	14	30	35	
Total		T1 = 35		T2 = 30			65

T1 = Time 1, 6 months; T2 = Time 2, 12 months; FG = Focus Group.

included. Secondary categories included an assessment of whether each coded comment represented a positive or negative sentiment on the particular issue and the demographic categories of the speakers. Thus, excerpts could be identified, for example, as illustrative of "positive discussions of participation," or "negative assessments of lot safety."

Project outcomes as discussed below result from the quarterly assessments, mail surveys, and focus groups. Data sources for each outcome are identified.

Project Outcomes

Empowerment can be defined as people, organizations, and communities gaining mastery over issues of concern to them. In the needs-assessment phase of URI/Detroit, community members identified common concerns that they hoped to address through community forestry projects. Did they gain mastery over these issues through participation in URI/Detroit? Two themes that address this question emerged as project outcomes from the evaluation process: increased community cohesion, and impacts on organizational capacity (including achievement of collective objectives and access to resources).

Community Cohesion. Erosion of community cohesion due, in part, to high resident turnover, was a commonly identified concern among program participants. There were, however, signs of consistent improvement in this factor throughout the duration of the program, as illustrated by the increased sense of cooperation among neighbors.

Through the quarterly group interviews, the groups were asked to compare the levels of cooperation among neighbors prior to and following their participation in the URI/Detroit program. They reported improved cooperation among neighbors at each data-collection point project (pre-URI mean 2.67; 12-month post-URI mean 3.50). The groups also reported organizing special events or celebrations more frequently, holding such activities between two to four times a year (x = 2.54).

While few groups reported growing memberships as a result of their participation in the URI/Detroit program, most reported success in meeting their participation objectives (Table 3). In large part, their assessment was based on the number of community residents who participated in the community tree planting and project-maintenance activities who had never participated in organization activities before. In some cases, these participants became integral members of the groups (including one who eventually became president of her neighborhood association). In other cases, the impacts on participation centered on shifting formerly peripheral members to core-member status, creating a more equitable distribution of workload among the membership, and building the cadre of potential future leaders. For example, one participant reported: "There were four members who were previously not involved or only superficially involved who became highly active through the project."

Despite these successes, some groups did report that responsibility for the ongoing maintenance of the projects continued to fall on a small number of core members. However, positive and enduring outcomes were often reported even when the burden of designing and implementing the initial project was shouldered by relatively few members: "People have cooperated more in our park since doing this program—I've been really pleased with the results. Even though it

Table 3. Mean group responses to whether participation objectives had been met (n = 7). Scale: 0 = not all, 4 = completely.

Variable	Time	Mean response
Participation	3 months	3.00
	6 months	2.00
	9 months	3.00
	12 months	4.00

was a small group that was involved it united them and gave them pride in their accomplishment."

There was also a fairly strong sense that the program contributed to improved organizational and strategic development skills, which may contribute to further membership development and task sharing in the future. One leader, for instance, reported that: "This discussion and the last one has helped us to think through . . . it's almost like that, in the long term, may be of more help than the trees themselves."

Organizational Capacity. Changes in organizational capacity were measured by several characteristics including achievement of collective objectives and access to resources. Organizational empowerment, defined in this case as the realization of collectively defined objectives, was assessed as a direct measure of the extent to which community forestry activities could contribute to the realization of a shared community vision.

One overarching measure of perceived community control in URI/ Detroit was provided by responses to a scale completed during the bi- annual evaluations assessing participants' initial impression of the URI/ Detroit program and sense of the likelihood of achieving community- defined objectives through their participation. The mean score on the four-point scale across groups at Time 1 was 3.08 and at Time 2 was 2.99, indicating participants' general belief that their interests were driving the project in their community and their objectives could be achieved through the program.

Achievement of collective objectives. The groups shared a number of common concerns they hoped to address through their community forestry projects. Figure 1 illustrates the number of groups citing each major goal area for their project: aesthetic, social, economic, participation, subsistence, and safety. Because most cited multiple purposes, the number reported is greater than the number of participant groups. All seven groups hoped to improve the appearance of their communities and of the lots they were working to reclaim. Five groups reported an interest in economic, social, and other benefits (including creating more play spaces for children and gathering areas for adults). Four sought to increase or improve participation. Three of the participant organizations chose subsistence goals among their purposes for participating in the URI/Detroit program and the same number

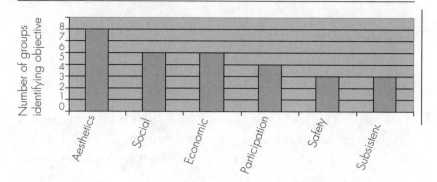

Figure 1. Group goals for URI/Detroit community forestry projects.

wished to improve the safety of the vacant lots and of their neighborhoods.

In assessing the outcomes of these collectively identified objectives, participants consistently reported that the lots were safer after planting the URI community forestry project than they had been before. However, as illustrated by Table 4, there were changes in perceptions of how great the improvement was over the course of the evaluation process.

The groups universally reported improvements in the appearance of their project sites (aesthetics) (Table 4). Despite the tremendous effort required to bring about such changes, given the prevailing conditions of the lots prior to their involvement in the URI/Detroit program, members of these groups often reported a dramatic change in the appearance of the project sites as illustrated by one participant who remembered: "There was a hell of a lot of work; there were about four lots together that were vacant. No six, I'm sorry, six together that were vacant over there and when we did that and uh there was a transformation from being overgrown full of junk and everything to clean, we got it cleaned, we got it cut, and it looked nice, it really did, and we planted the trees and that looked nice."

Subsistence and economic objectives were not achieved through the community forestry projects within the evaluation period. However, two groups did hold plant sales and were able to recoup their maintenance-related expenses, while others chose to redistribute the plants to beautify additional vacant lots in the community rather than focusing on maximizing the group's monetary gains. Furthermore, the leader of one group reported a rather dramatic improvement in property values in the neighborhood which she

Table 4. Mean group responses to whether group objectives had been met (n = 7).

Variable	Time	Mean
Social	3 months	1.50
	6 months	3.00
	9 months	3.00
	12 months	2.50
Aesthetic	3 months	3.17
	6 months	2.80
	9 months	3.00
	12 months	3.50
Safety	3 months	2.00
	6 months	2.00
	9 months	2.50
	12 months	3.50
Subsistence	3 months	1.00
	6 months	1.00
	9 months	2.00
	12 months	1.33
Economic	3 months	1.00
	6 months	1.00
	9 months	2.00
	12 months	1.00

Scale: 0 = not all, 4 = completely.

attributed, at least in part, to the group's participation in the URI/ Detroit program:"With the trees, with the painting of the trees and the curbs and even with our fruit trees, in this neighborhood, the property values have just about doubled; I found that out today, the house next door here, two years ago it was on the market for $10,000. It's for $32,000 now."

Access to resources. Successful implementation of sustainable community forestry projects requires access to technical information about trees and forests. This has been clearly demonstrated in international development projects where access to technical resources has been demonstrated to be a limiting factor on a community's ability to be successful (McDonough and Wheeler 1998). While access to information and other resources was not a stated community objective in URI/Detroit, the largest percentage of the focus group discussions (29 percent) centered on such access. Although the URI/Detroit participant organizations were located in economically disadvantaged areas of the city, few reported financial limitations to implementing their projects. The majority focused on educational materials and the need for informational resources.

Groups acknowledged the value of the resources and contact information provided through the URI/Detroit's community-resources manual provided to each participating group. However, that resource was insufficient to ensure adequate accessibility to technical assistance. Although few groups reported establishing relationships with potential sources of information, most felt comfortable contacting the Wayne County Cooperative Extension Service (CES) because of the personal contact they had with Extension personnel who offered workshops on composting, project maintenance, and other project-specific issues. One participant reported: "When we first started with the program, there was always information as to who to call, we had numbers as to if we had problems with the trees or whatever, we had numbers to call. It wasn't like we were just 'hey, here's a project, you go for it,' there were numbers, there were other outlets for us to reach out to."

Such direct interpersonal connections led to the formation of mutually supportive ongoing relationships among several URI/Detroit participant organizations as well as between those groups and other community-based organizations. One leader who made exceptionally effective use of these network resources reported:

> We're trying to set up a tree-moving day and we're
> planning on calling on the Wayne County alternative
> workforce, our own membership of course, and uh, we're
> planning on requesting help from some of the
> neighborhood churches and, uh, I am planning on also, I
> think, requesting help from the [Quince] group, one of
> their officers suggested that we send them a letter asking,
> and that's especially good from our point of view because
> they have experience and . . . oh yes, Mr. Bricault [Wayne
> county CES Consumer Horticulturist] told me to send in
> a letter requesting help from the master gardeners, so if
> we can get that diverse a group out there it may work.
> (Bracketed text added for clarification)

Another reported benefit of participation in URI/Detroit was the development of the skills and information necessary to allow for entrepreneurial use of the plant resources while meeting important local needs. One group member stated that the program "has increased our knowledge about trees and shrubs, about different types of plants and a greater sensitivity toward our environment. An awareness of what kind of shrubs do people like and use, and what has economic potential in our neighborhood."

Participants also believed that the project provided an opportunity for environmental education to build a sense of responsibility and awareness among neighborhood children, as supported by the following participant's quote: "Education, just those kids we do come across, educate them on what the real usefulness of trees are. If they learn this, they'll never break another branch in their lives."

Participants also suggested the addition of a more formal environmental education component in the future in order to enable communities to achieve project objectives and to recruit additional participants.

Conclusions

The URI/Detroit project demonstrates that forests are an integral part of communities in urban settings. Active participation in community forestry projects not only contributes to an improved urban environment in terms of air quality and climate management (McPherson 2000), but also contributes to community building and community empowerment.

What needs to be done is clear: plant more trees in cities.

But tree planting in Detroit was successful only because it empowered communities. Community involvement and control rather than professional or governmental control produced sustainable community projects because social capacity and commitment were created. It is not enough to have municipal forestry or tree-planting programs without community participation. The international development literature documents that the success of tree-planting projects requires community ownership (McDonough and Wheeler 1998). Social and environmental sustainability is a product of community participation and development of community access to resources and information. Community capacity and empowerment cannot be achieved without community participation and control.

A second lesson learned in URI/Detroit is the need to create direct interpersonal contact between partner organizations and potential sources of future technical assistance in order to establish access to additional resources for communities. Groups felt comfortable contacting sources of technical assistance only after personal relationships had been established through activities organized by the project. This finding parallels findings from community forestry projects in Thailand (McDonough and Wheeler 1998).

The kinds of community benefits resulting from URI/Detroit are seldom derived from conventional approaches to urban and community forestry and demonstrate the unique opportunities presented by recognizing and harnessing the powerful relationships between urban residents and their forested environment. Utilizing participatory approaches to urban resource development may be one important tool in that process.

References

Ahlbrant, R. S. Jr., and J. V. Cunningham. 1979. *A New Public Policy for Neighborhood Preservation.* New York: Henry Holt & Company, Inc.

Bady, S., and W. H. Lurz. 1993. "Gathering Places Fulfill the Desire to be Connected." *Professional Builder and Remodeler* 58(5): 108-9.

Darden, J. T., Child Hill, R. Thomas, J. and R. Thomas. 1987. *Detroit, Race and Uneven Development.* Philadelphia, PA: Temple University Press.

Detroit Empowerment Zone Development Corporation. 1997. http://detez.com/index.html.

Dwyer, J. F., D. J. Nowak, M. H. Noble, and S.M. Sisinni. 2000. Connecting People with Ecosystems in the 21st Century: An Assessment of our Nation's Urban Forests. Gen. Tech. Rep. PNW-GTR-490. Portland, Oregon: USDA Forest Service, Pacific Northwest Research Station.

Effrat, M. P. 1974. "Approaches to Community: Conflicts and Complementarities," In *The Community: Approaches and Applications,* M. P. Effrat (ed.). New York: The Free Press.

Egan, A., and A. E. Luloff. 2000. "The Exurbanization of America's Forests." *Journal of Forestry* 98 (3): 26-30.

Fischer, R. 1987. *Let the People Decide: Neighborhood Organizing in America.* New York: Macmillan Library Reference.

Fisher, R. 1995. "Improving Health through Community Organization and Community Building: A Health Education Perspective." In Community Organizing and Community Building for Health, M. Minkler (ed.). New Brunswick, NJ: Rutgers University Press.

Fitzgerald, M. 1991. "A Mammoth Task." *Detroit News* 122(32): 17-19.

Green, C. 1997. "Globalization, Challenge and the Black Diaspora." In *Globalization and Survival in the Black Diaspora*, C. Green (ed.). New York: State University of New York Press.

Greenberg, D. S. 1990. "Black Health: Grim Statistics." *The Lancet* 335(8692): 780-82.

Hirsch, E. L. 1986. "The Creation of Political Solidarity in Social Movement Organizations." *The Sociological Quarterly* 27: 373-87.

Hummon, D. M. 1990. *Commonplaces: Community Ideology and Identity in American Culture.* Albany: State University of New York Press.

Humphrey, C. R., G. Berardi, M. S. Carroll, S. Fairfax, L. Fortmann, C., Geisler, T. G. Johnson, J. Kusel, R. G. Lee, S. Macinko, N. L. Peluso, M. D. Schulman, and P.C. West. 1993. "Theories in the Study of Natural Resource Communities and Persistent Rural Poverty in the United States." In *Persistent Poverty in Rural America*, Rural Sociological Society Task Force on Persistent Rural Poverty (eds.). Boulder, Colorado: Westview Press.

James, J. H. 1992. "Haunting Images of South Africa Point to Dismal Prospects for Equality." *The Masthead* 44(3): 36-38.

Janowitz, M. and D. Street. 1978. "Changing Social Order of the Metropolitan Area." In *Handbook of Contemporary Urban Life*, D. Street (ed.). San Francisco, CA: Jossey-Bass Publishers.

Johnson, J. H. Jr., W. C. Farrell, Jr., and G. R.Henderson. 1996. "Mr. Porter's 'Competitive Advantage' for Inner-City Revitalization: Exploitation or Empowerment?" *Review of Black Political Economy* 24(2/3): 259-89.

Kaplan, R., and S. Kaplan. 1989. *The Experience of Nature: a Psychological Perspective.* New York: Cambridge University Press.

Kaplan, R., S. Kaplan, and R. L. Ryan. 1998. *With People in Mind: Design and Management of Everyday Nature.* Covelo, CA: Island Press.

Kuo, F. E., W. C. Sullivan, R. L. Coley, and L. Brunson. 1998. "Fertile Ground for Community Inner City Neighborhood Common Spaces." *American Journal of Community Psychology* 26:823-51.

Louv, R. 1995. "What Makes a Great Neighborhood? How Some Families have Turned Their Streets into True Communities." *Parents Magazine* 70(8): 125-27.

Luley, C. J. 1998. "The Greening of Urban Air." *Forum for Applied Research and Public Policy* 13: 3-35.

Massey, D. S., and N. A. Denton. 1993. *American Apartheid: Segregation & the Making of the Underclass.* Boston, MA: Harvard University Press.

McDonough, M. H., and K. E.Vachta. 1997. Urban Resources Initiative: Community Forestry in Detroit. Final Grant Report to the W. K. Kellogg Foundation.

Minkler, M., and N. Wallerstein. 1997. "Improving Health through Community Organization and Community Building: A Health Education Perspective." In *Community Organizing and Community Building for Health*, M. Minkler (ed.). New Brunswick, NJ: Rutgers University Press.

Peluso, N. L., C. R. Humphrey, and L.P. Fortmann. 1994. "The Rock, the Beach and the Tidepool: People and Poverty in Natural Resource-dependent Areas." *Society and Natural Resources* 8(2): 111-31.

Potts, M. 1990. "World Summit on Children: Mere Survival or a World Worth Living In?" *The Lancet* 336(8718): 866-69.

Rivera, F. G., and J. L. Erlich. 1992. *Community Organizing in a Diverse Society.* Boston, MA: Allyn and Bacon.

Ross, D. A., R. Kirkwood, F. N. Binka, P. Arthur, N. Dollimore, S. S. Morris, R. P. Shier, J. O. Gyapong, and P. G. Smith. 1995. "Child Morbidity and Mortality Following Vitamin A Supplementation in Ghana." *The American Journal of Public Health* 85(9): 1246-52.

Sampson, R. J., S. W. Raudenbush, and F. Earls. 1997. "Neighborhoods and Violent Crime: a Multilevel Study of Collective Efficacy." *Science* 277:918-24.

Thomas, R. W. 1992. *Life for Us Is What We Make it: Building Black Community in Detroit, 1915-1945.* Bloomington: Indiana University Press.

U.S. Bureau of the Census. 1990.

Unger, D. G., and A. Wandersman. 1982. "Neighboring in an Urban Environment." *American Journal of Community-Psychology* 10(5): 493-509.

Vachta, K. E. 1998. Community forestry as participatory development: Community outcomes of participation in the Urban Resources Initiative in Detroit, Michigan. Doctoral dissertation, Michigan State University, East Lansing.

Vidich, A. J., and J. Bensman. 1958. *Small Town in Mass Society: Class, Power, and Religion in a Rural Community.* London: Princeton University Press.

Weenig, M. W. H., T. Schmidt, and C .J. H. Midden. 1990. "Social Dimensions of Neighborhoods and the Effectiveness of Information Programs." *Environment and Behavior* 22(1): 27-55.

CHAPTER 14

Social Mosaics and Urban Community Forestry in Baltimore, Maryland

Morgan Grove, William R. Burch, Jr., and S. T. A. Pickett

Introduction: Rationale for Urban Community Forestry

Urbanization is a dominant demographic trend and an important component of global land transformation. By 2005, slightly more than half the world's population will reside in cities, and by 2025 this figure is projected to rise to more than 60 percent of the world's population (Gottdiener and Hutchinson 2000). The developed nations have more urbanized populations; for example, close to 80 percent of the U.S. population is urban. Urbanization has also resulted in a dramatic rise in the size of cities: over three hundred cities have more than ten million inhabitants and fourteen megacities exceed one hundred million. The increasing population and spatial prominence of urban areas are significant reasons for turning our attention to the environmental management of cities and to ensure they are reasonable places to live in the future (Pickett et al. 2001).

In addition to its global dimensions, urbanization has important relationships to regional landscapes. For example, in industrialized nations the conversion of land from wild and agricultural uses to urban and suburban settlement is growing at a faster rate than the population in urban areas. Cities are no longer compact; rather, they sprawl in fractal or spider-like configurations (Makse, Havlin, and Stanley 1995). Consequently, urban areas increasingly intermingle with wild lands. Indeed, even for many rapidly growing metropolitan areas, the suburban zones are growing faster than other zones (Katz and Bradley 1999). The resulting new forms of urban development include edge cities (Garreau 1991) and housing interspersed in forest, shrubland, and desert habitats. While these habitats were formerly controlled by agriculturists, foresters, and conservationists, they are now increasingly dominated by people possessing resources from urban systems, expressing urban habits, and drawing upon urban experiences.

Urban ecosystems are the dominant global human habitat of this century in terms of constituency, geography, and influence. This reality has important consequences for social and ecological systems at global, regional, and local scales, as well as for natural resource organizations attempting to integrate ecological function with human desires and behavior. Urban community forestry has a significant role to play in this effort. This chapter paints a broad-brush picture of some of the linkages between communities and forests.

Continuities From Rural to Urban Community Forestry

Community forestry projects typically address local needs and benefit local residents, and they work with people in a community to develop tree-based systems that meet their needs and interests. Historically, community foresters have worked mostly in developing nations to design projects in rural areas that increase access to firewood and fodder, prevent soil erosion, improve soils, and provide other benefits associated with trees. In addition to growing trees, some of the social goals of community forestry include group formation and collective action, institutional development, and the establishment of sustainable social structures and value systems to mobilize and organize groups and individuals (Cernea 1991). In practice, community foresters focus on assisting local people to plan and execute their own projects by providing advice, skills, and inputs to derive the desired goods, benefits, and services the community desires.

The application of community forestry principles in the United States, particularly in urban settings, is more often the exception than the rule for two reasons. First, many people in the U.S. believe that forestry primarily involves the growing and harvesting of trees for commercial wood utilization. Many foresters have perpetuated this relatively narrow definition. Yet forestry includes a much broader set of activities, and "the forestry community—including practicing foresters, forestry educators, and researchers—must expand its concern to understand and articulate the multiple functions of forests" (Lee et al. 1990), and this expanded view of the functions, values, and challenges of forestry is extremely relevant to urban areas. Second, when people accept the idea of forestry in urban areas, most people confuse urban forestry with arboriculture: the planting and maintenance of individual trees. But, as Smith (1984, 101) indicates, forestry in urban areas provides foresters with a number of challenges and opportunities that extend beyond either the production of pulpwood and sawlogs or the maintenance and care of trees:

> The urban forester seldom knows which problem is going to hit next and works in an environment that is full of them. . . . This means that urban forestry ought to be one of the best fields for foresters, who are, in the long run, esteemed most for the problems they solve and not for how well the trees grow. Physicians do not necessarily thrive in healthy communities, and it is worth noting that the urban forest is full of patients needing cures. The urban forest has opportunities as well as maddening problems. Foresters should not be put off by those who know only what cannot be done.

Urban community forestry activities can occur at several scales and include a variety of environmental, economic, and social goods, benefits, and services (see Box 1; Grove et al. 1994). The continuity from rural to urban community forestry is strikingly highlighted by the fact that the list in Box 1 could be applied equally well to either rural or urban areas. Indeed, our initial inspiration for this list is based upon rural community forestry publications such as Chambers (1985), Cernea (1991), and numerous publications from the U.N. Food and Agriculture Organization (FAO).

Organization of this Chapter

The goal of this chapter is to broaden the continuities of sociological study of communities and forests to include community forestry in urban areas. To achieve this goal, we use experiences gained since 1989 in Baltimore, Maryland, through:

• The Urban Resources Initiative, a partnership among the City of Baltimore's Department of Recreation and Parks, The Parks and People Foundation, and Yale University's School of Forestry and Environmental Studies to initiate research and development projects

Box 1. Environmental, Economic, and Social Goods, Benefits, and Services from Community Forestry

Goods

Forest Products	*Materials for Community Projects*
Fruits	Tree seedlings
Nuts	Saplings and small diameter trees
Craft materials	Mulch
Poles	Woodchips
Timber	
Christmas trees	
Firewood	

Infrastructure

Community land
Irrigation systems
Fencing
Vacant lots and vacant homes (reduce)

Benefits

Social
Improved community organization
Empowerment for collective action
Social bonding within and across generations and cultures, etc.
Improved community identity and pride
Immigration vs. emigration from urban areas
Safety (reduced crime)
Improved continuity and neighborhood stability
Development of microbusinesses based upon community gardens, greenhouses, agroforestry, and recycling

Environmental
Improved air quality
Reduced air temperatures
Improved water quality
Neighborhood beautification
Increased wildlife habitat
Identification of environmental hazards in the community

Services
Educational
Technical support and training
Tree planting and maintenance skills
Expansion of traditional educational skills (improvement in reading, writing, math, science, and history skills)
Identification of long-term job and career paths in environmentally related professions for local residents
Greater awareness and understanding of local links to regional resources such as the Chesapeake Bay (e.g. through the dumping of motor oil in storm sewers)
Organizational
Leadership skills
Community organization
Community cohesion
Collective action

for the department based upon international lessons in natural resource management and community development;

• Revitalizing Baltimore, a U.S. Forest Service-leveraged collaboration among federal, state, and local government agencies, community groups, and nonprofit organizations to link urban revitalization with environmental restoration; and

• The Baltimore Ecosystem Study, one of two urban Long Term Ecological Research Projects funded by the National Science Foundation in order to understand the long-term relationships among social and ecological patterns and process in urban areas.

We do not provide in-depth case studies. Rather, we give an overall view of the diverse types of forestry in the Baltimore metropolitan region. Second, we discuss community forestry strategies that have emerged through The Urban Resources Initiative and Revitalizing Baltimore. Finally, we describe four modes of social ecology thinking from the Baltimore Ecosystem Study that are important perspectives for a sociological understanding of communities and forests in urban areas.

A Typology of Forestry in an Urban Ecosystem

Forest landcover in the Baltimore metropolitan region ranges from 2.8 percent in Baltimore City to 35.4 percent in Baltimore County, with forestland cover defined as areas greater than 0.4 hectares, 10 percent stocked, and at least 40 meters wide (Jenkins and Riemann, 2001; Figure 1). There are five primary types of forestry in the Baltimore metropolitan area: (1) regional forestry; (2) stream valleys; (3) large, protected areas; (4) abandoned industrial areas; and (5) neighborhood areas.

Regional forestry activities focus on management for drinking-water supply, streamwater quality and quantity, biodiversity, recreation, wildlife habitat, and timber and non-timber forest products. For instance, the city has recently completed a comprehensive forest management plan for 6,880 hectares of city-owned watershed properties that addresses community issues associated with water supply, biodiversity, wildlife, recreation, and forest harvesting.

Forestry focusing on the city's 140 km of stream valleys addresses issues of streamwater quality and quantity and recreation, particularly greenway projects in the city's three primary watersheds: Gwynns Falls, Jones Falls, and Herring Run. Regional and streamvalley forestry are frequently assessed in the context of the Chesapeake Bay watershed.

Forestry in large protected areas, or parks greater than 15 hectares, deals extensively with reforestation and forest succession in order to promote aesthetics, particularly scenic qualities, water and air quality, and wildlife habitat. In these areas, forests are balanced with grass and picnic areas.

As manufacturing in Baltimore continues to decline, the extent of abandoned, industrial areas has grown. Many of these areas are along the city's harbor or adjacent to decommissioned rail lines and numerous sites are classified as brownfields, sites identified by the U.S. Environmental Protection Agency as having low-level toxic contamination. Forestry in these areas centers on site remediation, greenway recreation along the harbor or rail-to-trail lines, and wildlife habitat.

Finally, forestry in neighborhood areas attempts to address the city's 276 neighborhoods and a range of activities, including local parks, 6,500 abandoned lots, community gardens and tree nurseries, and approximately three hundred thousand street trees.

Community Forestry Strategies for Urban Revitalization and Environmental Restoration

Drawing lessons initially from rural community forestry activities in tropical countries, community forestry in Baltimore has emphasized the importance of three goals: sustainable productivity of the goods, benefits, and services associated with the five types of forestry listed above and included in Table 1; equity in the distribution of benefits and burdens of such productivity; and a sense of cultural and ecological continuity. Consequently, a significant aspect of urban community forestry must be tied to real gains in productivity, learning, leadership, health, security, housing, and employment. Also, various types of social units exist that might be predisposed to participate in urban forestry activities (Grove et al. 1994). These include:

• Natural (existing) social units, such as individuals, families, or tightly knit ethnic or kinship groups or subgroups;

• Groups organized specifically to plant, protect, or cultivate trees, such as local or national environmental organizations, participants in community gardens, and stream restoration groups; and

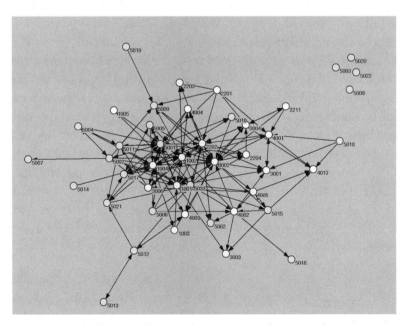

Figure 1. Organizational network structure of the natural resource management regime in the Gwynns Falls watershed, Baltimore, Maryland (Dalton 2001).

• Groups established for purposes other than forestry, but willing to undertake forestry-related activities as well. These might include religious organizations, block clubs, neighborhood associations, and parent/teacher associations.

Community forestry programs in Baltimore have responded to the five primary types of forestry discussed above by adopting and relating five dominant strategies for their programs: regional analysis, organizational networks, organizational change, community development, and information networks, education, and training.

Regional Analysis

Regional analysis has involved all three types of groups listed above in identifying forestry issues, collecting and analyzing data, and proposing policies, plans, and management strategies. Results from these efforts include the Gwynns Falls Human Ecosystem Atlas (http:// www.parksandpeople.org/gfatlas.pdf), hydrologic field measurements and modeling projects that incorporate social and ecological patterns and processes, and forest landscape analyses to address drinking-water supply, biodiversity, wildlife habitat, recreation, and forest products. For instance, Brun and Band (2000) have modeled the progressive effects of land use change on streamflow in the Gwynns Falls watershed over a twenty-year time frame. Band et al. (2002) have been measuring and modeling the effects of urban development and infrastructure on soil moisture patterns, and runoff and water quality in forested and suburban catchments, while Law et al. (forthcoming) have compared lawn extent and management practices in different neighborhoods as they affect catchment nitrogen budgets. In addition, Costanza et al. (2002) have developed integrated ecological economic models that examine the effects of historic and future scenarios of land use and policies—human settlements and land management practice—on hydrology, plant productivity, and nutrient cycling in the landscape (http://www.uvm.edu/giee/giee_projects.html).

Organizational Networks

Like community forestry activities in nonindustrialized nations, Revitalizing Baltimore has played an important role as a facilitator, connecting a variety of individuals and institutions that have common interests but little coordination in their efforts. In order to forge linkages, Revitalizing Baltimore works to build networks between formal social structures, within and between local, state, and federal public agencies, and to integrate formal structures with informal social structures, neighborhoods, nonprofit and civic organizations, and community associations (Figure 1). As these networks are knit together, projects become more sustainable and forestry activities become more linked to participants' needs. This enables participants to act upon the connections between themselves, their communities, and their environment (Dalton 2001).

Organizational Change

In many forestry projects, governmental and non-governmental agencies have tried to change or reform communities to conform to the goals of the planning organization. This strategy of community development has begun to change, and in many cases community forestry projects have recognized the importance of working to change the goals of governmental agencies to be more responsive to the needs and interests of the communities themselves (Whyte 1991; Dalton 2001). Community participation in urban forestry depends on the level of community organization. In some cases, the community already has a strong neighborhood association, church leadership, or informal neighborhood leaders. In other cases, the community forestry program works with selected individuals to help develop community leadership, training and education programs, and other community development activities.

Community Development

Revitalizing Baltimore works in partnership with community residents to determine the type of project most appropriate for each individual community. This is necessary since a number of diverse communities exist within an urban area, including geographically based communities and affiliation-based communities. Further, none of these communities are homogeneous and many might contain discrete interest groups.

Different types of property regimes—state, private, community, and open access—play a significant role in community forestry activities, since access to land and local rights enable the community to regulate local resources (Grove 1995; McManus and Steer 1998; Parker et al. 1999). Community members have used forestry projects such as tree nurseries, pocket parks, and sliver parcels to reclaim derelict properties from absentee landowners. Many neighborhood associations believe that these projects increase local control of the neighborhood, attract potential residents from outside the community, and decrease rates of vacancy. At the same time, local residents who are renters are more inclined to purchase a house in the neighborhood and to make a commitment to the area because they feel that the community is stable and a desirable place to live. This investment in the community has financial as well as social rewards, since property values will increase as more people choose to live in the area.

In one neighborhood, the community has received official permission to develop tree nurseries and community gardens on city-owned properties. After the neighborhood has developed a credible record and a sustainable organization for community management, the city will transfer the title to the community organization. In a similar example, a community has taken on the responsibility for the management of an entire stream valley park that runs through their neighborhood. The community's management of the area ensures that the park is maintained at a level higher than the city could afford (Burch and Grove 1993).

Information Networks, Education, and Training

A critical component to regional analysis, organizational networks, organizational change, and community development is information networks, education, and training. Revitalizing Baltimore has become a central node, helping to link consumers and suppliers of data, knowledge, education, and training in order to help the community forestry strategies listed above to be more effective, efficient, and equitable. Although it has not been broadly addressed, an underlying question from the rural sociology literature is the relationship between characteristics of public agencies, nonprofit organizations, and neighborhoods; different types of information networks and education and training programs; and the adoption of community forestry innovations (Burch and DeLuca 1984).

Framing Community Forestry in a Social and Ecological Context: Patches and Mosaics

The preceding sections focused on practical applications and experiences from our urban community forestry work since 1989 in Baltimore and our previous experiences in international rural community forestry. These strategies enhance existing approaches to community forestry by promoting a complex social-ecological approach. The following section further describes this social-ecological approach in terms of four modes of thinking from the Baltimore Ecosystem Study: spatial, temporal, scalar, and systems thinking. We propose that these four ways of thinking provide a structure and generalizable complement to the practical and particular aspects we have described for linking communities and forests in urban areas. These modes of thinking are necessary for a truly social-ecological approach to urban community forestry because they are the foundation for integrating the physical, biological, and social dimensions in which urban communities and forests exist.

Spatial Thinking

Understanding communities and forests in urban areas requires many forms of spatial thinking. We intuitively know that all human behavior occurs in space and is spatially dependent at many scales. For instance, the path an individual walks down a street may depend upon and respond to the path of an approaching person. Changes in one community may depend upon changes in a neighboring community, or the competitive advantage of one port versus another may depend upon their differential access to maritime and land routes for transporting goods.

While behaviors occur in space and are spatially dependent, it is also important to appreciate that the spatial characteristics of cities are strikingly heterogeneous (Pickett et al. 2001). For instance, sharp contrasts between neighborhoods are a familiar characteristic of cities (Clay 1973). Within the span of a city block, which is on the order of two hundred or fewer meters, an observer may cross several obvious boundaries. Different kinds of commercial use, shifts between owner-occupied and rental properties, and shifts in socioeconomic resources available to residents are but some of the many contrasts. Such

Figure 2.
A three-
dimensional
view of the
Gwynns
Falls
watershed.

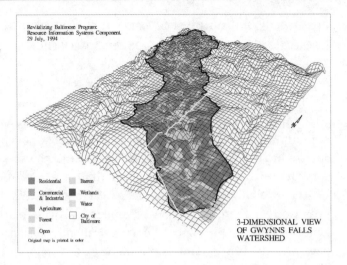

heterogeneity is not unique to dense, central urban districts (Gottdiener and Hutchinson 2000). In fact, the contemporary suburb is frequently zoned for even more discrete transitions than the traditional mixed use of older cities: residential streets, feeder streets, commercial streets, strip malls, regional malls, and industrial parks are notable patches in the suburban landscape. Of course, the scale of transition in post-World War II suburbs tends to be coarser than that of older neighborhoods and districts due to the shift in dependence on the automobile. However, spatial patchiness in the social, economic, and infrastructural fabric of metropolitan areas remains one of their most obvious features.

Understanding the significance of spatial heterogeneity to the allocation of critical natural, socioeconomic, and cultural resources is crucial for understanding communities and forests in urban areas (Grove and Burch 1997; Pickett et al. 1997). For instance, the spatial characteristics of the Gwynns Falls watershed in Baltimore (Figure 2)—the adjacency, connectivity, and configuration of land uses—can have important implications for the economic structure, interactions among neighborhoods, and hydrology of the watershed. Different communities within an urban watershed, due to their level of organization, access to civic decision making, and perceived desirability, are able to attract varying levels of public and private green investments. Some of these green investments are parks, trees, stormwater systems and their maintenance. However, the character of adjacent communities can also affect whether or not investments are made in a community.

For instance, communities whose desirability might be characterized as "medium" and bordered by "low" communities are less likely to receive green investments than "medium" communities bordered by "high" communities. Therefore, the spatial "neighborhood" of communities can affect the investment of public and private resources. The presence of green infrastructure, in turn, affects the hydrologic quantity, quality, timing, and rate that each community makes to the streams in the watershed, which represent each community's hydrologic profile. Further, the hydrologic adjacency, connectivity, and configuration of the community mosaic can affect the overall hydrologic dynamics of the watershed (Band et al. 2002; Figure 3). Thus, spatial characteristics can be critical for understanding complex physical, biological, and social interactions in urban watersheds.

Temporal Thinking

Temporal thinking is crucial to understanding urban communities and forests, particularly because the temporal dynamics of urban areas are probably more elusive a reality than spatial heterogeneity. We often have to reconcile remembrances of the "good old days" with our determined belief in perpetual progress and growth. And to explain many changes over time, we search for linear, cause-and-effect relationships. However, urban communities and forests are frequently characterized by social and ecological legacies. For instance, the historical relationships among soils, floodplains, and waterborne diseases (Hinman 2002) might be the best explanation for the location of low-income housing today. Relationships might be nonlinear, sudden rather than gradual switches in state. A neighborhood might

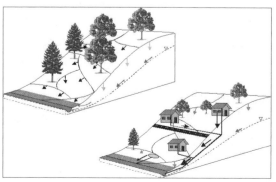

Figure 3. Changes in watershed connectivity: before and after urbanization.

progressively change until a critical threshold is reached, and then a neighborhood with predominantly elderly residents might shift to one with a majority of parents with young children (Johnson 2001). There might also be time lags between changes in neighborhood status and changes in environmental conditions (Grove 1996). Related processes might also be in effect at different time scales. For instance, stream measurements of nitrogen along one stream in the Gwynns Falls watershed are inordinately high. The areas adjacent to the stream are residential land uses and some individuals have claimed that the high levels of nitrogen are associated with the residential urbanization of the stream. Because of the amounts and timing of the nitrogen, however, the Baltimore Ecosystem Study (BES) scientists have determined that the source of the nitrogen is groundwater from agricultural application of fertilizers thirty years ago. This legacy is the result of the fact that groundwater transport in this area is approximately thirty years. Thus, the causal explanation of an urban watershed's dynamics can be quite different with knowledge of different rates of ecological processes—surface runoff versus groundwater transport— and knowledge of the social history of an area. It is important, therefore, to recognize that various social and ecological processes operate over different time spans, can be nonlinear, and have persistent legacies (Lee et al. 1990; Allen and Hoekstra 1992; Grove and Burch 1997).

Scalar Thinking

The preceding sections help to appreciate the fact that different social and ecological processes associated with urban communities and forests occur at different spatial and temporal scales. Scalar thinking, hierarchy theory, and panarchy theory (Berkes and Folke 1998; Holling 2001) extend this appreciation by compelling us to think about how strong and weak linkages within and between scales are related to one another; in particular, how lower levels of organization interact to generate higher-level behaviors and how higher-level units control those at lower levels (Johnson 2001; Figure 4).

The BES has worked to articulate and understand the dynamics of urban communities and forests at different social scales (Pickett et al. 1999; Grimm et al. 2000). Some examples of issues studied include: (1) regional variations: urban-rural dynamics (Morrill 1974; Cronon 1991; Rusk 1993); (2) municipal variations: distribution and dynamics

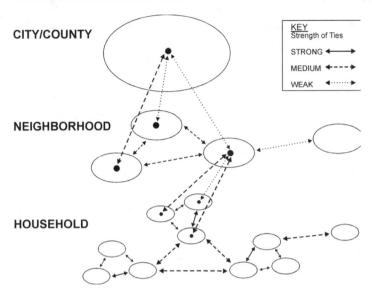

CITY/COUNTY

NEIGHBORHOOD

HOUSEHOLD

KEY
Strength of Ties
STRONG ←——→
MEDIUM ←---→
WEAK ←·····→

Figure 4. Example of an urban hierarchical system (adapted from Urban et al. 1987)

of land use change (Burgess 1925; Hoyt 1939; Harris and Ullman 1945; Guest 1977); (3) neighborhood variations: power relationships between neighborhoods (Shevky and Bell 1955; Timms 1971; Johnston 1976; Agnew 1987; Logan and Molotch 1987; Harvey 1989); and (4) household variations: household behavior within communities (Fortmann and Bruce 1988; Fox 1992; Grove and Hohmann 1992; Burch and Grove 1993; Grove 1995).

The following summary of a study of social stratification and vegetation in Baltimore's Gwynns Falls watershed illustrates how spatial, temporal, and scalar thinking can converge in our understanding of urban communities and forests. This study focused on how the social stratification of groups (i.e., power structures) affects green investments made by private firms and public agencies in neighborhoods within the watershed (Grove 1996). The theoretical foundation for this question comes from Logan and Molotch's (1987) political economy of place theory. Logan and Molotch argued that patterns and processes of social stratification between people and place have significant environmental implications. According to their theoretical framework, the key social variables affecting access to power, the allocation of private and public resources, and subsequently the biophysical characteristics of wealthy residential areas include: (1) the presence of homeowners and the absence of renters or absentee landowners; (2)

residents who are able to migrate to more desirable and healthy areas, effective at community organizing, or willing to become involved in local politics; (3) elites who have differential access to government control over public investment, pollution control, and land use decision making. Conversely, low-income and heavily populated minority areas are disproportionately in or next to polluted areas and their residents are unable to migrate to more desirable and healthy areas and have fewer human resources in terms of leadership, knowledge, tactical and legal skills, and communication networks to manipulate existing power structures.

Logan and Molotch (1987) and Choldin (1984) described these socio-cultural and biophysical interactions as a dynamic process. In this process, residents act individually and collectively to control and maximize the exchange and use values of their neighborhood by restoring, maintaining, or improving their current place or migrating to a more desirable place. Some of these acts of restoring, maintaining, or improving include changing the biophysical characteristics of residential areas (e.g., planting trees, parks, lawns, and community gardens, and clean streets). These restoration activities produce an environment that is both socially and biophysically heterogeneous.

Logan and Molotch's theory was applied to one of the watersheds of the BES study area. The selection of variables and indices of social stratification for the classification of social areas or neighborhoods used the theoretical parameters identified by Logan and Molotch (1987), Choldin (1984) and Bullard (1990). These variables and indices were also further adjusted to incorporate recent adjustments recommended by Johnston (1976), Murdie (1976) and Hamm (1982). These indices of residential social stratification included a socioeconomic index (income and education), a household index (homeownership), and an ethnicity index (race and ethnicity).

A classification of vegetation structure was developed using Bormann and Likens' (1979) theory of vegetation regulation of watershed hydrology and the data requirements of various hydrologic ecosystem models. At the ground surface, areas were classified as impervious or pervious. At the canopy level, areas were classified as having or not having a vegetation canopy layer. Statistical analyses of data were conducted for residential land uses only. In addition, the research included a temporal component (1970 to 1990) to explore possible time lag or nonlinear relationships.

The results indicated a significant relationship between two of the three indices of social stratification—socioeconomic and ethnicity—and vegetation structure. Further, a time lag was found between independent variables and dependent variables (1970 social data and 1990 biological data). In retrospect, the temporal results indicating a time lag were realistic considering that the primary response variable being measured—tree canopies—takes time to grow and die. This highlighted the importance of considering the rate at which response variables may change and the time frames necessary to measure that change, thus demonstrating the significance of temporal thinking.

The absence of a relationship between indices of homeownership and vegetation structure was puzzling since the literature suggested such a relationship should exist. Extensive literature from rural forestry has indicated the importance of ownership and property regimes to land cover (Coase 1960; Hardin 1968; Ciriacy-Wantrup and Bishop 1975; Fortmann and Bruce 1988; MacPherson 1989; Raintree 1987; Ostrom 1990; Bromley 1991). Further, community foresters and community organizers in Baltimore City reported the significance of ownership to their activities. Thus, alternative explanations needed to be explored.

The spatial structure of the three social-stratification indices was re-examined to try to tease apart the lack of a relationship between ownership and land cover on a watershed or city/county scale (Figure 4: neighborhood variations), which suggested the need to examine these data at a different scale. Perhaps the relationship between home ownership and vegetation structure was effective at an alternative scale. Based on an initial exploratory data collection, scale dependence for this relationship was verified (McManus and Steer 1998); the relationship between ownership and vegetation structure occurred at a neighborhood level (Figure 4: household variations).

Systems Thinking: A Human Ecosystem Approach

Systems thinking using a human ecosystem approach (Machlis et al. 1997) provides the means for linking space, time, and scale in our understanding of urban communities and forests. The explicit incorporation of an ecosystem approach within the social sciences dates to Duncan (1961; 1964). Recently, the social sciences have focused increasingly on the ecosystem concept because it has been proposed and used as an organizing approach for natural resource policy and management (Machlis et al. 1997; Cortner and Moote 1998.

The ecosystem concept and its application to *Homo sapiens* is particularly important because of its utility as an analytical framework for integrating the physical, biological, and social sciences. The concept owes its origin to Tansley (1935), in one of modern ecology's clearest yet most subtle founding documents. Tansley noted that ecosystems could be of any size, as long as one's concern was with the interaction of organisms and their environment in a specified area. He noted further that the boundaries of an ecosystem are drawn to answer a particular question. Thus, there is no set scale or way to bound an ecosystem. Rather, the choice of scale and boundary for defining any ecosystem depends upon the question asked and is the choice of the investigator. Further, each investigator may place more or less emphasis on the chemical transformations and pools of materials drawn on or created by organisms; or on the flow, assimilation, and dissipation of biologically metabolizable energy; or on the role of individual species or groups of species on flows and stocks of energy and matter. The fact that there is so much choice in the scales and boundaries of ecosystems, and how to study and relate the processes within them, indicates the profound degree to which the ecosystem represents a research approach rather than a fixed scale or type of analysis.

The application of an ecosystem approach to urban communities and forests requires an analytical framework. The analytical framework or parts diagram (Figure 5) shown here and presented elsewhere (Machlis et al. 1997; Pickett et al. 1997) is not a theory in and of itself. As Machlis et al. (1997) noted: "This human ecosystem model is neither an oversimplification nor caricature of the complexity underlying all types of human ecosystems in the world. Parts of the model are orthodox to specific disciplines and not new. Other portions of the model are less commonplace—myths as a cultural resource, justice as a critical institution. Yet we believe that this model is a reasonably coherent whole and a useful organizing concept for the study of human ecosystems as a life science."

Several elements are critical to the successful application of this framework to urban community forestry. First, it is important to recognize that the primary drivers of urban communities and forests are both biophysical and social—there is no single, determining driver—and the relative significance of drivers may vary over time (Burch and

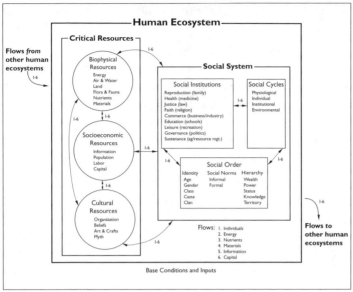

Figure 5. A framework for human ecological systems (from Machlis, Force, and Burch 1997)

DeLuca 1984). Second, components of this framework need to be examined in the context of each other simultaneously (Machlis 1997) with particular concern for how ecological components influence social patterns and processes; how social patterns and process influence the use and management of urban forests; and how these interactions are changing over time. Finally, it is necessary to examine how dynamic biological and social allocation mechanisms—ecological, exchange, authority, tradition, and knowledge—affect the distribution of critical resources—energy, materials, nutrients, population, genetic and non-genetic information, population, labor, capital, organizations, beliefs, and myths—in the context of urban communities and forests (Parker and Burch 1992).

A patch dynamics approach represents both a theoretical and practical means for unifying an awareness of spatial heterogeneity, temporal dynamics, hierarchical nesting, and an ecosystem approach in urban community forestry (Burch and Grove 1997; Pickett et al. 1997; Grimm et al., 2000; Pickett et al. 2001). For instance, a patch dynamics approach focuses explicitly, not only on the spatial pattern of heterogeneity at a given time, but also on how and why the pattern changes through time, and how that pattern affects ecological and social processes. Because cities are both expanding and changing within their boundaries, the dynamic aspect of this approach is crucial to a complete understanding of urban communities and forests. Change occurs over time in the resources available for the management of urban forests and in the requirements and interests of specific communities. In Baltimore, patch dynamics are conspicuous both at the suburban fringe and in the large collection of vacant buildings and empty lots within the dense older urban areas. In both the fringe and core patches, ecological processing of water and nutrients, and the provision of goods and services are not constant in time. The dynamics of patches in and around the city have implications for the ecological processes and status of areas well beyond the city, and even beyond the present suburban and exurban areas. The search for open land, development opportunities, and changes in the economics of farming and production forestry all influence and are influenced by urban patch dynamics.

Conclusion

Like farmers clearing the land in order to see the fields they plan to furrow, we have purposefully painted a broad perspective in this chapter because urban community forestry as a whole is still an emerging area of activity. We believe these fields are fertile for exploring a sociological understanding of communities and forests in urban areas, particularly by weaving theories and approaches from both rural and urban sociology. Already, theories of social stratification, property regimes, collective action, and adoption of innovation from rural sociology have appeared in our work.

What is clear already from our work in Baltimore, both from research and practice, is that there is no single type of urban community forestry approach, theory, or way of thinking. There are multiple types of community forestry in urban areas, requiring crosscutting strategies, theories, and modes of thinking. A patch dynamics approach is both a theoretical and practical means for addressing such complexity. Our efforts in Baltimore illustrate that any approach to community forestry in urban areas will need to draw upon and synthesize knowledge from the social and ecological sciences; both people and forests need to be embraced. The need for such knowledge has never been more pressing, as the constituency, geography, and influence of urban areas come to dominate this century.

Acknowledgments

We would like to gratefully thank the U.S. Forest Service's Northeastern Research Station and the Baltimore Ecosystem Study (NSF Grant DEB-9714835 and EPA Grant R-825792-01-0). This paper has benefited from insights gained through interactions with generous collaborators, students, and community partners from Baltimore since 1989.

References

Agnew, J. A. 1987. *Place and Politics: The Geographical Mediation of State and Society.* Boston, MA: Allen & Unwin.

Allen, T. F. H., and T. W. Hoekstra. 1992. *Toward a Unified Ecology.* New York: Columbia University Press.

Band, L. E., C. L. Tague, P. Groffman, and K. Belt, 2001. "Forest Ecosystem Processes at the Watershed scale: Hydrological and Ecological Controls of Nitrogen Export." *Hydrological Processes*, v.15, 2013-28.

Band, L. E, C. Tague, S. Kenworthy, and N. Law. 2002. Coupling water, carbon and nitrogen cycling with variable source area dynamics in forested and urban catchments. Paper given at the Spring Meetings of the American Geophysical Union, Washington, May 2002.

Berkes, F., and C. Folke. 1998 *Linking Social and Ecological Systems: Management Practices and Social Mechanisms for Building Resilience.* New York: Cambridge University Press (paperback edition 2000).

Bromley, D. W. 1991. *Environment and Economy: Property Rights and Public Policy.* Cambridge, MA: Basil Blackwell, Inc.

Bormann, F. H., and G.E. Likens. 1979. *Pattern and Process in a Forested Ecosystem. Disturbance, Development and the Steady State Based on the Hubbard Brook Ecosystem Study.* New York: Springer-Verlag.

Brun, S. E., and L. E. Band 2000. "Simulating Runoff Behavior in an Urbanizing Watershed." *Computers, Environment and Urban Systems,* v.24, 5-22.

Bullard, R.D. 1990. *Dumping in Dixie: Race, Class and Environmental Quality.* Boulder, Colorado: Westview Press.

Burch, W. R., Jr., and D. R. DeLuca. 1984. *Measuring the Social Impact of Natural Resource Policies.* Albuquerque: New Mexico University Press.

Burch, W. R., Jr., and J. M. Grove. 1993. "People, Trees and Participation on the Urban Frontier." *Unasylva* 44(173):19-27.

Burgess, E. W. 1925. "The Growth of the City: An Introduction to a Research Project." Pp. 47-62 in *The City,* R. E. Park, E. W. Burgess, and R. D. McKenzie (eds.). Chicago, IL: University of Chicago Press.

Cernea, M. 1991. "The Social Actors of Participatory Afforestation Strategies." Pp. 340-93 in *Putting People First: Sociological Variables in Rural Development* (2nd ed.), M. Cernea (ed.).New York: Oxford University Press.

Chambers, R. 1985. *Rural Development: Putting the Last First.* Essex, England: Longman Publishing Group.

Choldin, H. M. 1984. "Subcommunities: Neighborhoods and Suburbs in Ecological Perspective." Pp. 237-76 in *Sociological Human Ecology: Contemporary Issues and Applications*, M. Micklin and H. M. Choldin (eds.). Boulder, CO: Westview Press.

Ciriacy-Wantrup, S. V., and R. C. Bishop. 1975. "Common Property as a Concept in Natural Resource Policy." *Natural Resources Journal*, 15: 713-27.

Clay, G. 1973. *Close-Up: How to Read the American City*. Chicago, IL: University of Chicago Press (paperback 1980).

Coase, R. H. 1960. "The Problem of Social Cost." *Journal of Law and Economics*, 3: 1-44.

Cortner, H. J., and M. A. Moote. 1998. *The Politics of Ecosystem Management*. Washington, DC: Island Press.

Costanza, R., A. Voinov, R. Boumans, T. Maxwell, F. Villa, L. Wainger, and H. Voinov. 2002. "Integrated Ecological Economic Modeling of the Patuxent River Watershed, Maryland." *Ecological Monographs* 72(2):203-31.

Cronon, W. 1991. *Nature's Metropolis: Chicago and the Great West*. New York: W. W. Norton & Co.

Dalton, S. E. 2001. The Gwynns Falls watershed: a case study of public and non-profit sector behavior in natural resource management. Published Doctoral dissertation, Johns Hopkins University, Baltimore MD.

Duncan, O. D. 1961. "From Social System to Ecosystem." *Sociological Inquiry* 31:140-49.

Duncan, O. D. 1964. "Social Organization and the Ecosystem." Pp. 37-82 in Handbook of Modern Sociology, R. E. L. Faris (ed.). Chicago, IL: Rand McNally & Co.

Fortmann, L., and J. W. Bruce, editors. 1988. *Whose Trees?: Proprietary Dimensions of Forestry*. Boulder, CO: Westview Press.

Fox, J. 1992. "The Problem of Scale in Community Resource Management." *Environmental Management* 16(3):289-97.

Garreau, J. 1991. *Edge City: Life on the New Frontier*. New York: Doubleday.

Gottdiener, M., and R. Hutchinson. 2000. *The New Urban Sociology* (2nd Edition). New York: McGraw Higher Education.

Grimm, N. B., J. M. Grove, C. L. Redman, and S. T. A. Pickett. 2000. "Integrated Approaches to Long-term Studies of Urban Ecological Systems. *BioScience* 70:571-84.

Grove, J. M. 1995. "Excuse Me, Could I Speak to the Property Owner, Please?" *The Common Property Resources Digest* 35(September): 7-8.

Grove, J. M. 1996. The relationship between processes of social stratification and vegetation of an urban-rural watershed. Published dissertation. School of Forestry & Environmental Studies. Yale University, New Haven, CT.

Grove, J.M. and W.R. Burch 1997. "A Social Ecology Approach to Urban Ecosystems and Landscape Analysis." *Urban Ecosystems* 1(4):185-199.

Grove, J. M., and M. Hohmann. 1992. "GIS and Social Forestry." *Journal of Forestry* 90(12):10-15.

Grove, J. M., K. Vachta, M. McDonough, and W. R. Burch, Jr. 1994. "The Urban Resources Initiative: Community Benefits from Forestry." Pp. 24-30 in *Urban and High Recreation Settings*, P. H. Gobster (ed.). USDA Forest Service, St. Paul, MN. Gen. Tech. Rep. NC-163.

Guest, A. M. 1977. "Residential Segregation in Urban Areas." Pp. 269-336 in *Contemporary Topics in Urban Sociology*, K. P. Schwirian (ed.). Morristown, NJ: General Learning Press.

Hamm, B. 1982. "Social Area Analysis and Factorial Ecology: A Review of Substantive Findings." Pp. 316-37 in *Urban Patterns: Studies in Human Ecology*. A. Theodorson (ed.). University Park, Pennsylvania: The Pennsylvania State University Press.

Hardin, G. 1968. "The Tragedy of the Commons." *Science* 162: 1243-48.

Harris, C. D., and E. L. Ullman. 1945. "The Nature of Cities." *Annals of the American Academy of Political and Social Science* 242:7-17.

Harvey, D. 1989. *The Urban Experience*. Baltimore, MD: Johns Hopkins University Press.

Hinman, Sarah E. 2002. Urbanization and Public Health: A Study of the Spatial Distribution of Infant Mortality in Baltimore, Maryland, 1880. Unpublished M.A. thesis, Department of Geography, Ohio University.

Holling, C. S. 2001. "Understanding the Complexity of Economic, Ecological, and Social Systems." *Ecosystems* 4:390-405.

Hoyt, H. 1939. The Structure and Growth of Residential Neighborhoods in American Cities. Washington: Federal Housing Administration.

Jenkins, J. C., and R. Riemann. 2001. "What Does Nonforest Land Contribute to the Global C Balance?" In Proceedings, Third Annual FIA Science Symposium, Ron McRoberts and John Moser (eds.). Traverse City, MI, Oct. 18-20, 2001. St. Paul MN: USDA Forest Service General Technical Report NC-GTR-NE-297.

Johnson. S. 2001. *Emergence: The Connected Lives of Ants, Brains, Cities, and Software*. New York: Scribner.

Johnston, R. J. 1976. "Residential Area Characteristics: Research Methods for Identifying Urban Sub-areas—Social Area Analysis and Factorial Ecology." Pp. 193-235 in *Spatial Perspectives on Problems and Policies*. Volume 2, D.T. Herbert and R.J. Johnston (eds.). New York: John Wiley & Sons.

Katz, B., and J. Bradley. 1999. "Divided We Sprawl." *Atlantic Monthly* 284:26-42.

Law, N. L., and L.E. Band 2002. Lawns: One piece of the nutrient puzzle in urban watersheds. Paper given at the Spring Meetings of the American Geophysical Union, Washington, May 2002.

Lee, R. G., W. R. Burch, Jr., and D. R. Field. 1990. "Conclusions: Past Accomplishments and Future Directions." Pp. 277-89 in Community & Forestry: Continuities in the Sociology of Natural Resources, R. G. Lee, D. R. Field, and W. R. Burch, Jr. (eds.). Boulder, CO: Westview Press.

Logan, J. R., and H L. Molotch. 1987. Urban Fortunes: The Political Economy of Place. :os Angeles: University of California Press.

Machlis. G. E., J. E. Force, and W. R Burch, Jr. 1997. "The Human Ecosystem as an Organizing Concept in Ecosystem Management." *Society and Natural Resources* 10:347-67.

MacPherson, C. B., editor. 1989. *Property: Mainstream and Critical Positions.* Toronto, Canada: University of Toronto Press.

Makse, H. A., S. Havlin, and H. E. Stanley. 1995. "Modelling Urban Growth Patterns." *Nature* 377:608-12.

McManus, C. R., and K. N. Stee. 1998. Towards a Unified Strategy for Open Space Management in Baltimore: Community-Managed Open Spaces. A Report to the Parks and People Foundation, Baltimore, Maryland.

Morrill, R. L. 1974. *The Spatial Organization of Society.* 2nd edition. Duxbury, MA: Duxbury Press.

Murdie, R.A. 1976. "Spatial Form in the Residential Mosaic." Pp. 237-72 in *Spatial Perspectives on Problems and Policies,* D. T. Herbert and R. J. Johnson (eds.). New York: John Wiley and Sons. [possibly 2nd Edition]

Ostrom, E. 1990. *Governing the Commons: The Evolution of Institutions for Collective Action.* New York: Cambridge University Press.

Parker, J. K. 1994. Improving the Contribution of Forests to Food Security: A Proposed Conceptual Framework for Designing Research Studies and Practical Field Interventions. U.N. Food and Agriculture Organization, Forestry Department/FOND, Rome.

Parker, J. K., and W. R. Burch, Jr. 1992. "Toward a Social Ecology for Agroforestry in Asia." Pp. 60-84 in *Social Science Applications in Asian Agroforestry,* W. R. Burch, Jr., and J. K. Parker (eds.). New Delhi, India: IBH Publishing Co.

Parker, J. K., V. Sturtevant, M. Shannon, J. M. Grove, and W. R. Burch, Jr. 1999. "Partnerships for Adaptive Management, Communication and Adoption of Innovation, Property Regimes, and Community Deliberation: the contributions of mid-range social science theory to forest ecosystem management." Pp. 245-77 in Ecological Stewardship: A Common Reference for Ecosystem Management, Volume 3, N. C. Johnson, A. J. Malk, W. T. Sexton, and R. Szaro (eds.). 3 Volumes. Oxford, England: Elsevier Science Ltd.

Pickett, S. T. A., W. R. Burch, Jr., S. Dalton,T. Foresman, J. M. Grove, and R. Rowntree. 1997. "A Conceptual Framework for the Study of Human Ecosystems in Urban Areas." *Urban Ecosystems* 1(4):185-99.

Pickett, S.T.A., J. William R. Burch and J.M. Grove. 1999. "Interdisciplinary Research: Maintaining the Constructive Impulse in a Culture of Criticism." *Ecosystems* (2):302-307.

Pickett, S. T. A., M. L. Cadenasso, J. M. Grove, C. H. Nilon, R. V. Pouyat, W. C. Zipperer, and R. Costanza. 2001. "Urban Ecological Systems: Linking Terrestrial Ecology, Physical, and Socioeconomic Components of Metropolitan Areas." *Annual Review of Ecology and Systematics* 32:127-57.

Raintree, J. B. (editor)1987. *Land, Trees and Tenure.* Proceedings of an International Workshop on Tenure Issues in Agroforestry, Nairobi, May 27-31. Land Tenure Center, University of Wisconsin, Madison.

Rusk, D. 1993. *Cities without Suburbs.* Washington, DC: Woodrow Wilson Center Press.

Shevky, E., and W. Bell. 1955. *Social Area Analysis: Theory, Illustrative Application and Computational Procedure.* Stanford, CA: Stanford University Press.

Smith, D. M. 1984. "Silviculture at the Urban/Forest Interface." Pp.101-8 in *Land Use and Forest Resources in a Changing Environment: The Urban/Forest Interface*, G. A. Bradley (ed.). Seattle: University of Washington Press.

Tansley, A. G. 1935. "The Use and Abuse of Vegetational Concepts and Terms." *Ecology* 16:284-307.

Timms, D. 1971. *The Urban Mosaic: Towards a Theory of Residential Differentiation*. Volume 2. Cambridge, England: Cambridge University Press.

Urban, D. L., R. V. O'Neill, and H. H. Shugart, Jr. 1987. "Landscape Ecology: A Hierarchical Perspective Can Help Scientists Understand Spatial Patterns." *Bioscience* 37:119-27.

Whyte, W. F. 1991. *Social Theory for Action: How Individuals and Organizations Learn to Change*. Newbury Park, CA: Sage Press.

CHAPTER 15
Exurban Migration: Implications for Forest Communities, Policies, and Practices

Andrew F. Egan and A.E. Luloff

"There are more people with more money, buying more space . . ." (DeCoster 2000)

Forested rural areas in the northeastern U.S. are experiencing problems due to increases in population. Migration of exurbanites, many seeking an improved quality of life, has occurred in rural areas proximate and/or easily accessible to many urban centers (cf. Brown and Wardell 1980; Johnson and Beale 1994; Doak and Kusel 1996; Kusel 1996). Areas experiencing such changes are often characterized by their high resource amenity values; that is, they are rich in scenic and/or recreational qualities valued by urban residents (cf. Howe, McMahon and Probst 1997; McGranahan 1999; Rudzitis 1999; Smith and Krannich 2000). These urban migrants have needs and values that often differ from those of long-term residents. When translated into policy, they have the potential to impact the uses of rural lands (Danbom 1996; Gottfried 1996; Howarth 1996; Logan 1996) and functions of rural communities. Such shifts are of particular interest in growing rural counties and communities where historically the economy depends on resource extraction, including timber harvesting. Further, the potential for land use conflict among newcomers and long-term residents is heightened in regions where metropolitan centers dominate the political agendas of those with decision-making authority over the disposition of natural resources located in less-populated rural areas.

The exurbanization of the nation's rural countryside has been manifested in attitude changes about the use and management of forests, shifting rural forest economies and social structures, and development of forestry policies and practices that reflect changing forest values. This paper synthesizes both the social science and forest science literatures pertaining to this important phenomenon, and offers suggestions for future research.

There is often confusion about the myriad meanings and uses of terminologies in the forestry and social science literature related to exurbanization. We define exurbanization as the migration of urban residents to rural environments. Further (and in marked contrast) we define forest parcelization as the reduction process that leads to smaller and potentially nonsustainable forest land bases, and forest fragmentation as an interruption in the continuity of forest cover by distinct vegetational, land management, or land use changes (Luloff, Finley and Melbye 2000). Although our primary focus is on exurbanization and its effects on forested landscapes, forest practices, and rural communities, its association with forest parcelization and landscape fragmentation cannot be ignored.

What Do We Know?

America's forested landscape is changing. A quarter-century ago, a general trend reported by Patrick and Ritchey (1974) indicated a decentralization of industry throughout the country. Often, this meant growth in regions that offered employees the quality of life generally associated with rural environs. For example, in Graber's (1974, 52) study of a small rural Colorado town, it was suggested that a large number of Americans would pursue such a quality of life by ". . . moving to and fashioning new exurbs." Others have supported this general concept (e.g., Herbers 1986). The effects of this migration of people, and different or new attitudes toward forest resources, forestry practices, and rural residents and communities, have been the subject of some discourse among land use planners, natural resource planners, and academics.

Changing Forestry Attitudes

Several researchers have attempted to explain the attitudinal differences between traditional and new residents of forested rural areas. Van Es and Brown (1974), for example, suggested that such studies should investigate rural-urban differences in terms of single dimension variables rather than by combining several variables (e.g., occupational and sociocultural) into a vague construct. They found that the character of rural residents was not due to rurality per se, but rather to a variety of socioeconomic traits. Fortmann and Kusel (1990) viewed the issue differently. They explored the hypothesis that rather than importing new attitudes about the environment, rural migrants provided a new voice for attitudes already held by traditional rural residents. However, this appears to be the minority view among social science researchers.

According to Shands (1991), exurban rural residents brought new expectations that were often at odds with traditional residents' more utilitarian forest values and practices. As described by DeCoster (1997, 26), "Modern lifestyles favor living in and around the woods and owning pieces of them but earning most income from urban-oriented work unrelated to forests . . . (F)orests tend to be perceived primarily as decorations, a view that diminishes the value of traditional forestry." Sampson and DeCoster (2000, 4-5) described the phenomenon this way: "With increasing urban backgrounds and lifestyles, these new owners are less likely than their predecessors to participate in standard public forestry programs, largely because they see forestry as irrelevant to their landowning objectives and immediate concerns."

Moreover, these social segments viewed forests differently, with locals demonstrating a more utilitarian view of forest resources and values than exurbanites. Lee (1991), in a finding later echoed by DeCoster (1997), reported that exurban newcomers tended to place higher value on aesthetics. Shannon (1991) appeared to agree, suggesting that rural migrants sought improved environmental quality in rural forest areas, while traditional rural residents viewed the forest as a working asset that needed to be managed to produce a resource-derived commodity. Symptomatic of the differences in the ways long-term and exurban rural residents view and rely on forests, Lee (1991) observed that rural-urban interface zones did not represent cohesive social units. Instead, discrete social networks evolved in these areas with little interaction between traditional locals and recent migrants.

These differences in the ways in which forests are valued and used appear to reflect significant attitudinal differences that result in rather predictable and contrasting behaviors. Green et al. (1996), for example, found that seasonal-recreation residents in northern Wisconsin were more likely to support land use controls than were long-term residents, while Blahna (1990) found that newcomers in Michigan were more likely to support preservation-oriented land use policies than were long-term residents. Studying rural-urban differences in support of environmental protection, Lowe and Pinhey (1982) indicated that rural residents showed lower levels of support for environmental protection than their urban counterparts, but could not strongly support any of the prevailing explanations for this difference.

The existence of a rural-urban continuum, described by Bell (1992) as the notion that community is more characteristic of country places than cities, has long been debated in the sociological literature, but firm conclusions about its utility remain unattained (e.g., Dewey 1960; Friedland 1982; Miller and Luloff 1981; Stinner et al. 1990; Willits et al. 1990; Willits and Luloff 1995). However, studies of the boomtown phenomenon lend insight into changes in rural community life that result from rapid population growth. Gold (1985), for example, suggested that local rural residents needed to adapt to the values and interests of new residents, occupy the role of outsider, or leave. According to Krannich and Greider (1990), rapid and extensive inmigration of new rural residents holding values different from those of traditional residents could result in the emergence of new subcultural groups.

Disconnects in attitudes toward forestry practices among the general public, forest landowners, and forest workers also have been well documented and may shed some light on the differences in attitudes about forests held by long-term and exurban residents. Unfortunately, little has been done to elucidate the direct effects, if any, of exurban migration on these disconnects. For example, Egan et al. (1997), found that 96 percent of West Virginia consulting foresters were opposed to banning the practice of clearcutting. This is in sharp contrast with results reported by Bourke and Luloff (1994), where 59 percent of Pennsylvania's public and 56.7 percent of its non-industrial private forest (NIPF) owners agreed that clearcutting should be banned. At the same time, the Bourke and Luloff results for NIPF owners agreed closely with those from the study by Egan et al. (1997), who found that 54.8 percent of certified tree farmers in West Virginia thought the practice should be banned. That is, on the issue of banning clearcutting, NIPF owners and citizens in Pennsylvania, and certified tree farmers in West Virginia held very similar views that contrasted sharply with those of professional foresters in the region. The effect of exurban attitudes on the results of these studies remains unknown.

Kline and Armstrong (2001), however, found support for an initiative in Oregon to ban clearcutting in more urban counties; opposition to the initiative was strongest in counties containing higher proportions of forest industry employees and native Oregonians. The authors posited that pro-environmental orientations of both new residents seeking the perceived amenities offered by residence in Oregon and urban dwellers not directly connected with or dependent upon the forest industry may well have translated into increased support for initiatives that restricted forest practices, especially clearcutting. In addition, they suggested that exurbanization in Oregon was at least in part responsible for the introduction of the anti-clearcutting initiative on the ballot, and that public attitudes and political activism that restricted forest practices would likely continue to expand in the state. Moreover, while avoiding suggestions of a direct relationship between forest management practices and exurbanization, Barlow et al. (1998) found that timber harvesting rates decreased with proximity to areas characterized by development and higher population densities.

Changing Economic and Social Structures

Some recent studies have investigated attributes of communities dependent on timber (Machlis and Force 1988; Overdevest and Green 1994), mining (Nord and Luloff 1993; Freudenburg and Frickel 1994), and agriculture (Doeksen 1987; Leistritz et al. 1989). Yet few have focused on the reasons for and outcomes of transitions from resource extraction-dependent communities to those dependent on manufacturing, service, or diversified economies. Little work has been done on whether exurbanization has contributed to either a more pervasive attitude opposing resource extraction or land use policies that constrained such activities.

Transitions from extraction-based industries, such as the timber industry, to, first, manufacturing and then to service economies have transformed rural social and economic structures (Kreahling 1994; Kreahling and Smith 1995). Important issues related to the nature and outcomes of these transitions remain unanswered, however, including the identification of factors that explain these shifts, what impacts these transitions have had on those communities experiencing them, and what differences exist among the transitions experienced by communities historically dependent on different extractive resources. Also important is the fact that exurbanization of rural areas has received relatively little attention. In the northeastern U.S., in particular, where many rural communities have been transformed from reliance on extractive industries to other, more diversified economies, little is understood of the effects of such change on the economic and social fabrics of the community, including those that may be related to exurbanization.

Some attention has focused on the transition from natural resource extraction dependency. For example, Kreahling and Smith (1995) and Kreahling et al. (1996), focusing on rural northeastern counties, studied shifts in employment base at the county level from agriculture and natural resources related economies to service, manufacturing, or diversified economies. They found that shifts associated with service or diversified economies had the greatest success in increasing employment. Economies associated with less employment success were those that were initially extractive based or that had remained in manufacturing. Proximity to a large urban area and higher levels of education were other key influences on increasing employment. However, the authors concluded that more detailed data were necessary to obtain policy-relevant conclusions (Kreahling and Smith 1995). In particular, attention should be placed on whether the transitioning phenomenon studied by Kreahling and Smith (1995) and Kreahling et al. (1996) was, in some cases, the ultimate result or logical extension of a pattern of exurban migration to a rural setting.

Drielsma (1984) demonstrated that, in 1970, forestry-dependent communities in the northeast U.S. possessed some similarities in social and economic characteristics that set them apart from other rural communities specializing in agriculture, mining, and tourism. In particular, they had the lowest median family incomes, highest levels of poverty, and lowest housing values of all resource-dependent counties. They also had the lowest levels of community services. Further, he compared and contrasted the social and economic characteristics of three types of forestry communities and concluded that those with either a secondary wood processing sector or a tourism sector displayed greater population stability, prosperity, and community well-being than forestry communities with only a primary wood processing sector. Similarly, results of the Great Lakes Forest Resources Assessment showed that areas with no forest products or tourism development had higher unemployment rates than areas with either one or both forms of economic activity (Chappelle 1994). The Northwest Regional Planning Commission (1995) concurred, suggesting that while forest products manufacturing had greater potential to increase earnings and create year-round employment, recreation development could help capture the income generated by forest products jobs lost in the local area. Perhaps not coincidentally, the favoring of forest amenity values and non-extractive forest uses tends to characterize the attitudes of exurban forest residents.

Finally, according to Krannich and Luloff (1990, 13), resource-dependent rural communities "face a staggering array of obstacles to effective rural development," including outside control of resources. In Maine, for example, recent transfers of ownership of large industrial forest tracts to companies from Canada and the northwestern U.S. have raised concerns among timber-dependent individuals, families, and communities, as well as the environmental community and other Maine residents, about the future disposition of these lands. There is some speculation that these land transfers, recent referenda targeting forest practices regulations in the state, a drive to convert the White Mountain National Forest and other forested areas in Maine into national and state parks may have combined to heighten uncertainties about employment in sectors of state's forest products industry. As boundaries between urban and rural landscapes and communities continue to blur, future conflicts over the use of forest resources will occur, ultimately impacting the future of forest-dependent communities and families.

Changing Forest Policies and Practices

The regulation of forest practices has been posited as one symptom of exurban migration. A spate of activity has been associated with the implementation of local forest practices ordinances, many attributable to the proliferation of forestry-related municipal and county regulations (Ellefson and Cheng 1994). Martus et al. (1995) agreed that local ordinances were a relatively recent occurrence, and that they were often driven by (a) the differences in social and economic ties to forests between exurbanites who had moved to rural settings and traditional rural residents; and (b) the exurban migrants' lack of familiarity with agricultural and forestry management practices. The assertion that local forest practice ordinances were attributable to social conflicts between urban and rural residents in forested urban fringes and exurbanized rural areas has been supported (e.g., Wolfgram 1984; Cubbage and Raney 1987). While Salazar (1990) did not address conflict between urban and rural residents directly, she suggested that forest practice regulations reflected local economic development priorities. Such regulations were more prevalent in communities attempting to promote tourism than in those promoting traditional wood processing industries. In addition, in a survey of professional foresters in the northeastern U.S., Egan (2001) found that most respondents agreed that forestry was entering a period of increasing regulation, and that environmental groups would play a greater role in defining forest policy. Perhaps most telling was that nearly one-third of the foresters surveyed thought that, in the future, fewer professional foresters would be involved in the management of forests.

Several authors have provided insight into the relationship between government regulation pertaining to resource management and community stability. For example, Schallau (1974) suggested that forest regulators began to consider the stability of timber-dependent communities superfluous due to a preoccupation with other, more pressing forest resource issues (e.g., controversies surrounding logging practices, log exports, and wilderness preservation). He articulated a need for forest-regulation guidelines that balanced the promotion of economic stability with environmental concerns. Many scholars of sustained-yield policy have concluded that the U.S. Forest Service (USFS) has used the community stability argument to justify stabilization of the forest products industry (Clary 1987; Fortmann et al. 1989; Lee 1991; Schallau 1989). Waggener (1977) defined a forest-dependent community broadly as one with a functional relationship between the community and the forest, but suggested that community stability, as a forest policy objective, was merely inferred. Agreeing with Schallau, Waggener stressed a need for renewed interest in community stability as an economic concept. But what does this say about the effects of exurbanization on rural community stability, especially that of communities that depend on the extraction and processing of natural resources?

Cramer et al. (1993) studied the changing values of USFS personnel and the implications of those changes for policies that affected forest-dependent communities. They suggested that future USFS policies might be more advantageous for communities pursuing recreation and tourism than for those dependent upon traditional processing industries. Further, these authors suggested that communities not influenced by exurban migration could well have fewer development alternatives because of their spatial isolation and the existence of economic monocultures that offered little opportunity for diversification. They indicated that shifts in management emphasis that led, for example, to reduced levels of timber harvests or mineral extraction could result in local initiatives to increase tourism. However, the latter communities were likely to experience serious economic and social dislocations. This conclusion paralleled that of Humphrey (1990), who said that residents of timber-dependent communities in the U.S. faced an increasingly uncertain existence. He concluded that continued instabilities within the timber industry in the western U.S. could lead to the impoverished character found in older eastern timber-dependent communities. Further, Humphrey and Lin (1989) suggested that, with the depletion of mature timber on private lands of the Pacific Northwest, future locations of timber-dependent communities would be created in the southern and northeastern states as production shifted to these other regions. The role of non-industrial (for some, the phrase "private forest landowners" may more accurately characterize these people; cf., Finley et al. 2001) private forest owners in the eastern U.S. would define the nature of this dependency and the future of timber-dependent communities in the region. The increasing rate of forest exurbanization in the region would clearly be a significant factor in shaping this future. The non-commodity emphasis of exurbanites and landscape gentrification that appears to accompany such migration will likely result in further conflict over the disposition of timber resources and impact forest-dependent communities and workers.

Timber extraction practices other than clearcutting are receiving additional, relatively recent scrutiny. For example, some researchers have begun to investigate the proliferation of terminal harvests—harvests made prior to land development that render the parcel too small or too unproductive to be managed for timber in the future (DeCoster 2000), and their effects on forestland bases and timber supply (Thorne 2000). However, although relationships between terminal harvesting and exurbanization have been suggested (Thorne 2000), direct, empirically described associations remain vague or nonexistent.

In Maine, a related phenomenon currently referred to as liquidation harvesting is receiving attention from bureaucrats, foresters, landowners, and many of the state's citizens. The term, as currently conceived, describes two distinct phenomena: a commercial clearcut (or nearly so) and a subsequent sale of the land (or at least the intent to sell the land within five years). Although somewhat unclear as to what is driving concern about the practice (e.g., timber supply, sustainability of the state's forests, public perception, parcelization, sprawl, fragmentation, misuse/abuse of current use assessment and/ or cost share funding), the state is moving ahead to both study and curb the practice.

When the relatively recent exurbanites' orientation toward amenity forest values is coupled with both conventional forest management and more exploitative terminal and liquidation harvesting, perplexing questions emerge. This is particularly the case for the management of forested landscapes and broad forest policy initiatives. For example, so-called forest ecosystem management emphasizes the consideration of forests at the landscape level. However, when disparate forest value systems are overlain across forested landscapes composed of both a mosaic of private forest ownership and exurban and long-term rural residents, prospects for ecosystem management remain murky, particularly in the eastern U.S. (Egan 2000).

Finally, suggestions have been made about ways to address both the objectives of new forest owners and the attitudes of new rural residents. For example, forestry practices compatible with exurban forest ownership have prompted recommendations for a professional specialty in exurban forestry (Larsen 2000). Others have suggested a form of woodscaping (Tyson et al. 1998) that might better fit the ownership objectives of the new generation of forest owners than traditional multiple use forest management.

Where Should We Go From Here?

The exurbanization of America will continue to shape our forested landscapes and the environment within which forestry is practiced. Yet there is still much about this phenomenon that we do not understand. Will urban migrants, unaccustomed to the sights and sounds of forest practices, move closer to supporting working forests, as they have supported working farms and mines? Or will forests touched by exurbanization be a source of conflict between exurbanites and long-term rural residents, those supporting resource preservation and those in favor of extraction efforts, and those concerned about economic change and forest dependency?

The arguments are not simple, nor are they restricted to amenity vs. commodity forestry. Exurbanization's influence has transcended the more traditional debates of forests as decorations vs. forests as working assets, or single use vs. multiple use forestry. For example, the 2001-2004 fire experiences have clearly heightened the public's concerns over how forests are managed, including the placement of exurban residences among fire-prone wildlands. The attitudes of long-time rural and exurban residents toward wildfire will help define wildfire management and wildland-settlement strategies, particularly at the residential interface (Rodriguez Mendez et al. 2003). At the same time, new wood-shingled trophy homes will continue to be built in areas not serviced by local water systems, even in places like Missoula, Montana, one of the nation's prime fire-training sites.

Formerly isolated forest workers and logging workplaces will likely experience further dislocations and constraints on their activity, either through regulation or voluntarily as a way to placate exurban forest owners and neighbors. The possible implications of exurban migration on the organization of formally isolated rural residents and forest workers (Egan 2002) have yet to be explored in detail. In addition, much exploration is needed of the relationships among exurbanization, parcelization, urban sprawl, terminal and liquidation harvesting, and related phenomena.

Addressing questions about the effects of exurban migration on forests, forestry, and rural communities will be of value to policy makers and program administrators attempting to work with resource-based economies. In order to understand the effects of exurbanization and the expanding urban fringe on forest-based economies and land use policies, further research on the social dimensions of forestry is critical. Indeed, in a study identifying emerging issues in forest resource management, problems associated with the wildland residential urban interface were ranked high by national forest supervisors and district leaders (Jakes et al. 1990). Furthermore, Cortner (1991) referred to interface challenges as the future direction for forest management in this country, and cited the need to better understand attitudes of new residents.

Longitudinal studies, broader case studies (Freudenburg 1992), and historical case studies (Fruedenburg and Frickel 1994) have been suggested as ways of avoiding the tenuousness of long-term predictions of community transitions from extractive economies often characterized by either cross-sectional or short-term data. Humphrey et al. (1993) called for more comparative research on impoverished forest communities that were more or less successful in local economic development. Similar recommendations may be made for research on the exurban migration phenomenon and its effects on forest management practices and forest-dependent communities. In addition, studies employing multiple methods (Denzin 1970) have been shown to provide information on rural residents' attitudes toward natural resources that carries more depth and insight than similar information derived from the use of a single method (Egan et al. 1995; Luloff et al. 1995; Bourke et al. 1996; Luloff 1999; Elmendorf and Luloff 2001). Such an approach may be particularly important in studies where survey responses are used to describe or predict forest management practices, attitudes, and/or behaviors (Egan and Jones 1993).

As America's population distribution changes, so too will the social, economic, and political influences that shape the use and management of its forests. If urban dwellers continue to pursue a perceived quality of life in the country's forested rural areas, they will bring changes in attitudes about both the disposition of and values assigned to open spaces, including forests. A better understanding of the effects of this transition on long-term rural residents, local forest-dependent economies, the regulation of forest practices, and the nature of forested landscapes will enable both land use planners and natural resource managers to better anticipate, influence, and adapt to the changes associated with this migration. Social science research that explores the exurbanization phenomenon will continue to provide insights into the implications of these changes to the forestry community.

Demographic and forest ownership data confirm that there are more people with more money buying more space, creating new forested exurbs. The values ascribed to this space—by long-term and exurban residents, as well as the rest of society—will ultimately determine their disposition and the future directions of forest policy, forestry practices, and rural community stability.

References

Barlow, S. A., I. A. Munn, D. A. Cleaves, and D. L. Evans. 1998. "The Effect of Urban Sprawl on Timber Harvesting: A Look at Two Southern States." *Journal of Forestry* 96(12):10-14.

Bell, M. 1992. "The Fruit of Difference: The Rural-Urban Continuum as a System of Identity." *Rural Sociology* 57(1):65-82.

Blahna, D. J. 1990. "Social Bases for Resource Conflicts in Areas of Reverse Migration." Pp. 159-79 in *Community and Forestry: Continuities in the Sociology of Natural Resources*, R. G. Lee, D. R. Field, and W. R. Burch, Jr. (eds.). Boulder, CO: Westview Press.

Bourke, L., and A. E. Luloff. 1994. "Attitudes Toward the Management of Nonindustrial Private Forest Land." *Society and Natural Resources* 7:445-57.

Bourke, L., S. Jacob, and A. E. Luloff. 1996. "Response to Pennsylvania's Agricultural Preservation Programs." *Rural Sociology* 61(4):606-29.

Brown, D. L., and J. M. Wardwell. 1980. *New Directions in Urban-Rural Migration: The Population Turnaround in Rural America*. New York: Academic Press.

Chappelle, D. E. 1994. Interaction of Tourism and Forest Products Sectors on Community Employment/Unemployment in the Lake States Region. Final Project Report for Lake States Forest Resources Assessment.

Clary, D. A. 1987. "What Price Sustained Yield? The Forest Service, Community Stability, and Timber Monopoly under the 1944 Sustained Yield Act." *Journal of Forest History* 31(1):4-18.

Cortner, H. J. 1991. "Interface Policy Offers Opportunities and Challenges." *Journal of Forestry* 89(6):31-34.

Cramer, L. A., J. J. Kennedy, R. S. Krannich, and T. M. Quigley. 1993. "Changing Forest Service Values and Their Implications for Land Management Decisions Affecting Resource-dependent Communities." *Rural Sociology* 58(3):475-91.

Cubbage, F., and K. Raney. 1987. "County Logging and Tree Protection Ordinances in Georgia." *Southern Journal of Applied Forestry* 11(2):76-82.

Danbom, D. 1996. "Why Americans Value Rural Life." *Rural Development Perspectives* 12:19-23.

DeCoster, L. 1998. "The Boom in Forest Owners – A Bust for Forestry?" *Journal of Forestry* 96(5):25-28.

DeCoster, L. 2000. "How Forests Are Being Nibbled to Death by DUCS, and What to Do about It." Pp. 2-12 in Proceedings of the Forest Fragmentation 2000 Conference, L. DeCoster and N. Sampson (eds.). Alexandria, VA: Sampson Group, Inc.

Denzin, N. K. 1970. *The Research Act*. Chicago, IL: Aldine Publishing Company.

Dewey, R. 1960. "The Rural-Urban Continuum: Real but Relatively Unimportant." *American Journal of Sociology* 66(1):60-66.

Doak, S., and J. Kusel. 1996. "Well-being in Forest-dependent Communities, Part II: A Social Assessment Focus." Pp. 375-400 in Sierra Nevada Ecosystem Project, Final Report to Congress, Status of the Sierra Nevada. Vol. II: Assessments and Scientific Basis for Management Options. Davis, CA: Wildland Resource Center, Report No. 37.

Doeksen, G. A. 1987. "The Agricultural Crisis as It Affects Rural Communities." *Journal of the Community Development Society* 18(1):78-88.

Drielsma, J. H. 1984. The Influence of Forest-Based Industries on Rural Communities. Unpublished dissertation. New Haven, CT: Yale School of Forestry.

Egan, A. 2000. "Timber Harvesting on Private Forests: Some Observations from the Northeastern U.S." Pp. 298-306 in Proceedings of the Forest Fragmentation 2000 Conference, L. DeCoster and N. Sampson (eds.). Alexandria, VA: Sampson Group, Inc.

Egan, A. 2001. "Clearcutting and Forest Regulation in the 'New' Forestry: Views from Professional Foresters in the Northeastern U.S." *International Journal of Forest Engineering* 12(2):19-25.

Egan, A. 2002. "Uniting an Independent and Isolated Workforce: The Logger Association Phenomenon in the United States." *Society and Natural Resources* 15(6):541-52.

Egan, A., and S. Jones. 1993. "Do Landowner Practices Reflect Beliefs? Implications of an Extension-Research Partnership." *Journal of Forestry* 91(10):39-45.

Egan, A., S. Jones, A. Luloff, and J. Finley. 1995. "The Value of Using Multiple Methods: An Illustration Using Surveys, Focus Groups, and Delphi Techniques." *Society and Natural Resources* 8(5):457-66.

Egan, A., J. Rowe, D. Peterson, and G. Philippi. 1997. "West Virginia Tree Farmers and Consulting Foresters: Views on Timber Harvesting." *Northern Journal of Applied Forestry* 14(1):16-19.

Ellefson, P. V., and A. S. Cheng. 1994. "State Forest Practice Programs— Regulation of Private Forestry Comes of Age." *Journal of Forestry* 92(5):34-37.

Elmendorf, W. F., and A. E. Luloff. 2001. "Using Qualitative Data Collection Methods when Planning for Community Forests." *Journal of Arboriculture* 27(3):139-51.

Finley, J. C., S. B. Jones, A. S. Reed, M. G. Jacobson, and G. R. Glover. 2001. "Finding a Name to Fit The Owner." *Journal of Forestry* 99(3):48.

Fortmann, L., and J. Kusel. 1990. "New Voices, Old Beliefs: Forest Environmentalism and Long-standing Rural Residents." *Rural Sociology* 55(2):214-32.

Freudenburg, W. R. 1992. "Addictive Economies: Extractive Industries and Vulnerable Localities in a Changing World Economy." *Rural Sociology* 57(3):305-32.

Freudenburg, W. R., and S. Frickel. 1994. "Digging Deeper: Mining Dependent Regions in Historical Perspective." *Rural Sociology* 59(2):266-88.

Friedland, W. H. 1982. "The End of Rural Society and the Future of Rural Sociology." *Rural Sociology* 47(4):589-608.

Gottfried, H. 1996. "Corridors of Value: Rural Land in Rural Life." *Rural Development Perspectives* 12:13-18.

Graber, E. 1974. "Newcomers and Oldtimers: Growth and Change in a Mountain Town." *Rural Sociology* 39(4):504-13.

Green, G. P., D. Marcouiller, S. Deller, D. Erkkila, and N. R. Sumathi. 1996. "Local Dependency, Land Use Attitude, and Economic Development: Comparisons between Seasonal and Permanent Residents." *Rural Sociology* 61(3):427-45.

Herbers, J. 1986. *The New Heartland: America's Flight Beyond the Suburbs and How It Is Changing Our Future.* New York: Times Books.

Howarth, W. 1996. "The Value of Rural Life in America's Culture." *Rural Development Perspectives* 12:6-12.

Howe, J., E. McMahon, and L. Probst. 1997. *Balancing Nature and Economy in Gateway Communities.* Washington, DC: Island Press.

Humphrey, C. R. 1990. "Timber-dependent Communities." Pp. 34-60 in *American Rural Communities*, A. E. Luloff and L. E. Swanson (eds.). Boulder, CO: Westview Press.

Humphrey, C. R., and H. Lin. 1989. "High and Low Technology Development for American Timber Dependent Communities." Paper presented at the annual meeting of the Society for the Study of Social Problems. Berkeley, CA; August, 1989.

Humphrey, C. R., G. Beradi, M. S. Carroll, S. Fairfax, L. Fortmann, C. Geisler, T. G. Johnson, J. Kusel, R. G. Lee, S. Macinko, N. L. Peluso, M. D. Schulman, and P. C. West. 1993. "Theories in the Study of Natural Resource-Dependent Communities and Persistent Rural Poverty in the United States." Pp. 136-172 in Persistent Poverty in Rural America, G.F. Summers, (ed.). Boulder, CO: Westview Press.

Jakes, P. 1990. "Emerging Issues in Forest Management and Use: What Do Forest Supervisors and District Rangers Think?" *Journal of Forestry* 88(4):25-28.

Johnson, K. M., and C. L. Beale. 1994. "The Recent Revival of Widespread Population Growth in Nonmetropolitan Areas of the United States." *Rural Sociology* 65(1):27-49.

Kline, J. D., and C. Armstrong. 2001. "Autopsy of a Forestry Ballot Initiative." *Journal of Forestry* 99(5):20-27.

Krannich, R. C., and T. R. Greider. 1990. "Rapid Growth Effects on Rural Community Relations." Pp. 61-73 in *American Rural Communities*, A. E. Luloff and L. E. Swanson (eds.). Boulder, CO: Westview Press.

Krannich , R. S., and A. E. Luloff. 1990. "Problems of Resource Dependency in U.S. Rural Communities." Pp. 5-18 in *Progress in Rural Policy and Planning*, Gilg (ed.). London, UK: Belhaven Press.

Kreahling, K. S. 1994. Economic Restructuring in the Northeast: Nonmetro Counties in a Changing Economy. Unpublished Masters Thesis. University Park: The Pennsylvania State University, Department of Agricultural Economics and Rural Sociology.

Kreahling, K. S., and S. M. Smith. 1995. Economic Restructuring in the Northeast: Nonmetro Counties in a Changing Economy. Staff Paper 284. University Park: The Pennsylvania State University, Department of Agricultural Economics and Rural Sociology.

Kreahling K., S. Smith, and A. E. Luloff. 1996. Economic Restructuring in the Nonmetropolitan Northeast: Adaptations to Transitions. Penn State Research Report No. AERS 253. University Park: The Pennsylvania State University, Department of Agricultural Economics and Rural Sociology.

Kusel, J. 1996. "Well-being in Forest Dependent Communities, Part 1: A New Approach." Pp. 361-73 in Sierra Nevada Ecosystem Project, Final Report to Congress, Status of the Sierra Nevada. Vol. II: Assessments and Scientific Basis for Management Options. Davis, CA: Wildland Resource Center, Report No. 37.

Larsen, K. 2000. "Taxation, Regulation, and Fragmentation of Forestland." Pp. 271-75 in Proceedings of the Forest Fragmentation 2000 Conference, L. DeCoster and N. Sampson (eds). Alexandria, VA: Sampson Group, Inc.

Lee, R. G. 1991. "Four Myths of Interface Communities." *Journal of Forestry* 89(6):35-38.

Leistritz, F. L., R. W. Rathge, and B. L. Elstrom. 1989. "Farm Families in Transition: Implications for Rural Communities." *Journal of the Community Development Society* 20(2):31-48.

Logan, J. 1996. "Rural America as a Symbol of American Values." *Rural Development Perspectives* 12:24-28.

Lowe, G. D., and T. K. Pinhey. 1982. "Rural-urban Differences in Support for Environmental Protection." *Rural Sociology* 47(1):114-28.

Luloff, A. E. 1999. "The Doing of Rural Community Development Research." *Rural Society* 9(1):313-27.

Luloff, A. E., L. Bourke, S. Jacob, and S. Seshan. 1995. Farm and Non-farm Interdependence at the Rural-Urban Interface. Final Project Report for the Pennsylvania Department of Agriculture. University Park: The Pennsylvania State University, Department of Agricultural Economics and Rural Sociology.

Luloff, A. E., J. C. Finley, and J. Melbye. 2000. "Social Issues and Impacts Associated with Land Parcelization." Pp. 183-90 in Proceedings of the Forest Fragmentation Conference, L. DeCoster and N. Sampson (eds.). Alexandria, VA: Sampson Group, Inc.

Machlis, G. E., and J. E. Force. 1988. "Community Stability and Timber Dependent Communities." *Rural Sociology* 53(2):220-34.

Martus, C. E., H. L. Haney, and W .C. Siegel. 1995. "Local Forestry Regulatory Ordinances." *Journal of Forestry* 93(6):27-31.

McGranahan, D. A. 1999. Natural Amenities Drive Rural Population Change. Washington, D.C: US Department of Agriculture, Economic Report No. 781.

Miller, M. K., and A. E. Luloff. 1981. "Who Is Rural? A Typological Approach to the Examination of Rurality." *Rural Sociology* 46(4):608-25.

Nord, M., and A. E. Luloff. 1993. "Socioeconomic Heterogeneity of Mining-dependent Counties." *Rural Sociology* 58(3):492-500.

Northwest Regional Planning Commission. 1995. Community and Social Effects of Future Forest-Based Economic Development in the Lake States. Final Draft for the Lake States Forest Resources Assessment.

Overdevest, C., and G. P. Green. 1994. "Forest dependence and Community Well-being: A Segmented Market Approach." *Society and Natural Resources* 8(2):111-31.

Patrick, C. H., and P. N. Ritchey. 1974. "Changes in Population and Employment as Processes in Regional Development." *Rural Sociology* 39(6):224-37.

Rodriguez Mendez, S. R., M. S. Carroll, K. A. Blatner, A. J. Findley, G. B. Walker, and S. E. Daniels. 2003. "Smoke on the Hill: A Comparative Study of Wildfire and Two Communities." *Western Journal of Applied Forestry* 18(1):60-70.

Rudzitis, G. 1999. "Amenities Increasingly Draw People to the Rural West." *Rural Development Perspectives* 14(2):9-13.

Salazar, D. H. 1990. "Counties, States, and Regulation of Forest Practices on Private Lands." Pp. 241-55 in *Community and Forestry: Continuities in the Sociology of Natural Resources*, R. G. Lee, D. R. Field, and W. R. Burch, Jr. (eds.). Boulder, CO: Westview Press.

Sampson, N., and L. DeCoster. 2000. "Forest Fragmentation: Implications for Sustainable Private Forests." *Journal of Forestry* 98(3):4-8.

Schallau, C. H. 1974. "Evolution of Community Stability as a Forestry Issue: Time for the Dry Dock." Pp. 5-11 in *Community Stability in Forest-Based Economies*, D. E. LeMaster and J. H. Beuter (eds.). Portland, OR: Timber Press.

Schallau, C. H. 1974. "Can Regulation Contribute to Economic Stability?" *Journal of Forestry* 72(4)214-16.

Shands, W. E. 1991. "Problems and Prospects at the Urban-Rural Interface." *Journal of Forestry* 89(6):23-26.

Shannon, M. A. 1991. "Resource Managers as Policy Entrepreneurs." *Journal of Forestry* 89(6):27-30.

Smith, M. D., and R .S. Krannich. 2000. " 'Culture Clash' Revisited: Newcomer and Longer-term Residents' Attitudes toward Land Use, Development, and Environmental Issues in Rural Communities in the Rocky Mountain West." *Rural Sociology* 65(3):396-421.

Smith, S. M. 1993. "Service Industries in the Rural Economy: Their Role and Potential Contributions." Pp. 105-126 in *Economic Adaptation: Alternatives for Nonmetropolitan Areas*, D.L. Barkley (ed.). Boulder, CO: Westview Press.

Stinner, W. F., M. Van Loon, S. Chung, and Y. Byun. 1990. "Community Size, Individual Social Position, and Community Attachment." *Rural Sociology* 55:494-521.

Thorne, S. 2000. "New Hampshire Forest Land Base Study." Pp. 276-90 in Proceedings of the Forest Fragmentation 2000 Conference, L. DeCoster and N. Sampson (eds). Alexandria, VA: Sampson Group, Inc.

Tyson, C. B., S. M. Campbell, and E. S. Grady. 1998. "Woodscaping for Small Landowners in Southern New England." *Journal of Forestry* 96(12):4-9.

van Es, J. C., and J. E. Brown. 1974. "The Rural-urban Variable Once More: Some Individual Level Observations." *Rural Sociology* 39(3):373-91.

Waggener, T. R. 1977. "Community Stability as a Forest Management Objective." *Journal of Forestry* 79(11):710-14.

Willits, F. K., R. C. Bealer, and V. L. Timbers. 1990. "Popular Images of Rurality: Data from a Pennsylvania Study." *Rural Sociology* 55(4):559-78.

Willits, F. K., and A. E. Luloff. 1995. "Urban Residents' Views of Rurality and Contacts with Rural Places." *Rural Sociology* 60(3):454-66.

Wolfgram, S. 1984. "Regulations Grown in New York." *The American Tree Farmer* 3(3):13-14.

*Community Complexity: Postmodern Challenges to
Forest and Natural Resources Management*

Robert G. Lee and Donald R. Field

Complexity in the Postmodern World

The forestry profession is a product of modernity. Its foundations were laid during an era in which Enlightenment rationality and the application of science were presumed to be sufficient for directing practical action (Hays 1969). The "messiness" of politics, passions, and human emotion were to be replaced by the rule of reason. The focus on rationality has persisted. Even today, policies are legitimated by chartering scientific studies and policy and management decisions by developing "science-based plans." Communities, especially territorial communities, are the recipients of "rational" decisions made by experts—what we today often refer to as the many "ologists": biologists, ecologists, sociologists, ornithologists, etc. Professional decision makers may solicit community "input," and make decisions in the interests of interested publics, including communities. Community participation is often avoided because it is replete with the sorts of "messiness" that was to be supplanted by rationality and science-based decisions.

Sociologists have questioned the assumption that decisions are based on rationality and scientific facts by discussing "postmodernity," or the "postmodern" world. Zygmunt Bauman (1993, 32), a British sociologist, talks about postmodernity as "modernity without illusions. . . . The illusions in question boil down to the belief that the 'messiness' of the human world is but a temporary and repairable state, sooner or later to be replaced by the orderly and systematic rule of reason." He also says that modernity refuses to accept its own truth—that the "messiness" is part of the human condition, and will stay whatever we do or learn. No orderly system can make people less conflict prone or emotional.

Postmodernity poses a daunting challenge to professional forestry. Massive public investments have been made in research and development activities to construct rational and orderly procedures for making decisions. Linear programming models, ecosystem management models, wildlife habitat simulation models, conservation planning, and social and environment impact assessment are all based on the belief in the sufficiency of "the orderly and systematic rule of reason." Yet postmodern sociologists would point out that all these rational schemes are based on the illusion—the faith—that rationality can and will bring order to human conduct.

Nowhere is the truth underlying this illusion revealed more clearly than in the "re-enchantment" of the natural world and the people who live and work in it. Bauman (1993, 33) points out how modernity unsuccessfully sought to "dis-enchant" the world:

> The mistrust of human spontaneity, of drives, impulses, and inclinations resistant to prediction and rational justification, has been all but replaced by the mistrust of unemotional, calculating reason. Dignity has returned to emotions; legitimacy to the inexplicable, nay irrational, sympathies and loyalties that cannot explain themselves in terms of their usefulness and purpose. . . . The postmodern world is one in which *mystery* is no more a barely tolerated alien awaiting a deportation order. (emphasis in original)

Communities of interest, especially those that share concerns with protecting the integrity of the natural world, have found political legitimacy by naming the "mysteries of nature" and their "intrinsic value." Expressions of passionate concern have become politically efficacious. Re-enchantment of the natural world has been confusing to rationally trained foresters, and caused great consternation.

Equally passionate are occupants of rural resource-producing communities who struggle to protect and perpetuate their way of life. Their pride in and attachment to work, love of place and land, embeddedness in local social relationships, and appreciation for the natural world are just as emotional as the concerns of those who fight to remove resource-producing practices. The clinical view of the modern rational decision maker who adjusts incentives and training programs to stimulate the migration of workers from rural locations fails to appreciate the enchanted world in which many rural people actually live.

Some leading natural resource scientists have at least implicitly acknowledged the breakdown of modernity's illusions when speaking about nature. Jack Ward Thomas (1999, p. xxiv, emphasis in original) a leading wildlife biologist and former chief of the U.S. Forest Service, wrote an introduction to an edited volume focused on the topic of "spirit and nature," in which he said, "ecosystems are not only more complex than we think—they are more complex than we humans can think. . . . This means that resource management decisions will have both subjective and objective components." In these comments, Thomas implicitly embraced a postmodern view of nature by calling up its mystery. He views ecosystems not simply as rational scientific constructs (the modernist scientific definition); they also function as symbols for the mysterious workings of nature, or reified as respected, even sacred, things.

Postmodernity acknowledges personal morality as the basis of social morality by rejecting modernity's artificially constructed moral codes or attempts to eliminate moral impulses and emotions. The forestry community is uncomfortable with the pluralistic forms of morality associated with a postmodern world. The profession has long advocated universal and abstract forms of morality typical of modernity. Economic rationality, with its rules of efficiency, has been advanced as a common denominator for moral disputes. Economic efficiency served as the moral code for national forest planning during the 1970s and 1980s, and was only later replaced by "biocentric ethics," pushed by advocates for environmental preservation. Centralized federal land management policies adopted these "biocentric ethics" and have attempted to impose a universal moral consensus that largely ignores place-based agreements on what is right and wrong in particular circumstances. Hence, even where morality has been officially acknowledged, it has taken a distinctly modern form of a universal rule or principle. The forestry profession is generally not prepared for postmodern moral contingency and ambiguity arising from clashes of diverse communities. We will review and interpret the contributions assembled in this volume to highlight ways of understanding and appreciating a postmodern view of communities associated with forests and forest policy issues.

Three themes are evident in the essays contained in this volume: (1) formalization of theory that can be used to replace sole reliance on rationality; (2) dilemmas of modernity's attempt to rationalize resource use and community stability; and (3) acknowledgement of the role of community processes in the postmodern world through initiation of community forestry programs. None of these essays explicitly refer to postmodern themes, but all anticipate or observe these social changes.

Formal Theory of Resource Conservation and Development

Many of the essays in this volume contain implicit postmodern themes, acknowledging the breakdown of modernist illusions that have occupied the attention of forest and natural resources scholars for over one hundred years. The work of Walter Firey, partially represented in Chapter 2, was by far the most systematic attempt at building a formal theory of resource conservation and development. The primary contribution of Firey's sociological career was the emphasis he placed on nonrational decisions. This work began with his dissertation at Harvard, where he studied how sentiments attached to places influenced economic value of real estate. However, it was in his later development of a theory of how conservation is possible that nonrationality was fully formalized as a foundational principle for social action.

According to Firey (1960, and 1963 reprinted as Chapter 2 in this volume), a stable relationship between human resource use and the environment requires that resource practices meet three independent conditions. They must be: (1) biologically possible (nature must be capable of producing resources and/or accommodating management actions without losing its productive capacity and ecological resilience); (2) individually gainful (providing an acceptable return on investment of capital and labor); and (3) socially acceptable or culturally adoptable (conforming to the cultural norms of a group or community). This formulation is familiar to us as the image of the three intersecting circles often used to define sustainability—what some refer to as the "triple bottom line."

However, Firey recognized that joint considerations of social, economic, and ecological conditions were necessary but insufficient for conservation of natural resources. Conservation requires that current consumption be reduced so that options are preserved for the future. Hence, individuals must be motivated to undertake resource practices that are not maximally gainful. Firey realized that conservation was not possible unless people adopted practices that were both sufficiently gainful but also nongainful. Therefore, he asked a pivotal question: why would people engage in nongainful behavior, or what modern economists would term nonrational behavior?

People adopt nongainful practices, such as soil conservation or stream protection, along with gainful practices, such as growing corn or timber crops, in part because they are expected to do so as members of a community. When other resource producers also conform to these expectations, it becomes highly likely that voluntary conformity will be elicited from all resource producers. Interpersonal judgments that others are likely to conform ensure that all will abide by the nongainful practices (Firey 1960).

When such social expectations are widely shared, they are internalized and take the form of moral obligations to the community. Under these conditions, social control over individuals is governed by what Firey called a "conservation conscience" that acknowledges the needs of others or the integrity of the natural world, both in the current and future generations. To a sociologist such as Firey, social obligations are never universal or abstract, as supposed by the assumptions of modernity. They are instead contingent on relationships with particular people and places. This is why all of his work examined human behavior at the scale of communities of place.

Firey (1960, 233) clearly anticipated a basic tenant of postmodernity when he emphasizes that conservation requires nonrational behavior:

> . . . it involves prolonging into the future the availability of certain physical resource processes by the device of reducing a population's present consumption standards. As such, conservation represents diseconomic behavior. It is a form of investment in which the marginal revenues that a resource will yield fall short of the marginal costs, over whatever periods of time resource users are able to realistically plan. Conservation achieves this end, quite literally, by obstructing the individual's capacity to completely order alternative resource processes on a single scale of evaluation. In place of such a unidimensional ordering of resource processes it endows the individual with two distinct and heterogeneous

> standards for judging value—one, moral and altruistic,
> the other private and egoistic. It thereby confounds him
> and renders him less rational—indeed, a nonrational—
> decision maker.

The tension between rational (involving the calculation of private gainfulness) and nonrational (nongainful conformity to group expectations) resource practices is the fulcrum upon which Firey's theory rests (Firey 1993). Resource practices are dynamic (subject to change) because there are historical shifts in the relative emphasis placed on private gainfulness and social obligation. Historical periods of loosened expectations give rise to personal insecurity. Individuals can no longer predict the future based on what had been likely in past situations. Under these conditions, willing conformity to group expectations is replaced by the "calculating opportunism" of rational individuals.

Loss of predictability leads to the breakdown of social sanctions that support nongainful practices, creating the necessary condition for the development of new natural resources through individual gain seeking. Firey (1960, 36) defines resource development as the "conversion of inert natural processes into potential capital" capable of "decreasing the magnitude of scarcity attaching to people's activities." According to Firey, resource development involves the adoption of practices that are privately gainful and unlikely to meet the moral expectations of others. For this reason, adoption of new resource practices calls for the development of a new social order that will permit implementation of the new practices without the constraints of conscience and social pressure. In this sense, resource development is inherently a revolutionary activity that undermines the old social order and makes way for new social forms.

Natural resources conservation, by contrast, requires emphasis be placed on the perpetuation of old social forms. Conservation involves maintenance of social obligations rooted in moral necessity. Firey (1960, 203) stated, "Conservation of natural resources becomes conservation of the social order." Conservation is possible when people acquiesce to constraints that require them to lower their consumption standards. They voluntarily conform to these constraints when stable social and political conditions enable them to predict how others will behave.

Such predictability will be manifest in maintenance of a wide variety of rights and social conditions: rights to private property, rights to use public or community lands, rights to participate in decisions affecting one's welfare, social relationships in residential communities, access to investment capital, orderly change in government regulation of private economic activity, and supportive family, friendship, and helping networks. Threats to these sources of predictability tend to privatize security, leading people to begin calculating the gainfulness of their activities. Hence, natural resources conservation is contingent on the conservation of the social relationships in which people live their daily lives—their communities.

Extensions of Firey's theory to a wide variety of contemporary problems have been summarized by Field, Luloff, and Krannich (Chapter 2). Formal theory has provided a foundation for over forty years of work in the sociology of natural resources, examining problems as diverse as outdoor recreation, community stability, and social impact analysis. The community-empowerment project described by McDonough and Vachta (Chapter 13) is a particularly clear illustration of how Firey's principles work in practice. When given authority to manage local resources, urban residents discovered that their lives were more predictable and enriched by successful community projects and shared pride in their accomplishments. Shared sentiments and an ecological conscience replaced the alienation that had accompanied opportunistic individual attempts at survival in a world that demanded compliance with abstract rational rules.

Modernity and the Struggle for Community Development and Stability

Several studies illustrate how the illusion of modernity had limited success in natural resource management and community development. Nancy Langston's (Chapter 4) discussion revealed the futility with which federal land managers struggled to secure desired future conditions in eastern Oregon forests and wetlands. The managers she described were burdened by all the assumptions associated with modernity—land management agencies insistent on centralized control, abstract rules, universal operating procedures, and an engineering mentality directed toward the stabilization of both human and natural communities. As she describes their struggle, one is struck with how their failures can be traced to the ways in which they were trapped in modernist illusions of control over both people and nature.

Similar responses are evident in comments of the assistant regional forester who commented on the Kaufmans' study of Libby, Montana (Chapter 6). When provided with a rich description of how community stability could be enhanced by actions we would today refer to as means for building "social capital," the Forest Service responded with a defense of how its regulation of timber supply contributed to community stability. Such modernist illusions are not limited to federal agencies, as illustrated by Bliss and Bailey's (Chapter 8) analysis of a state's attempt at community development in rural Alabama. A focus on industrial investments in a rural community placed gainful economic considerations above social needs. Pulp mill work was not culturally adoptable without commensurate investments in education and human capital development.

The lack of appreciation for the role of occupational communities discussed by Carroll, Lee, and McLain (Chapter 9) also illustrates the hegemony of modernist institutions. Emphasis on the substitution of individual rights for messy and unpredictable community affiliations is a key characteristic of Enlightenment rationality. To modernists, occupational communities are archaic forms of organization that disappear with economic rationalization.

Professional foresters' struggle to understand private forest landowners has long been limited by normative, modernist assumptions about how these small landowners should behave. Findley, Luloff, and Jones (Chapter 12) point out the diversity of economic lifestyles and attitudes of private landowners, and reveal mythical thinking (illusions) shared by the professional forestry community. Landowner sentiments have been dismissed as irrelevant emotional feelings when they were in fact the basis for enormous diversity in the valuation and use of land and trees.

A historical view of rural communities can reveal ways in which social change fails to conform to modernist assumptions. London, Starrs, and Fortmann's (Chapter 7) longitudinal study of Quincy, California, describes how community affiliations formed and reformed around a succession of issues, beginning with a wood-fired power plant and culminating in attempts to implement co-management strategies for federal lands. A rational, reified view of Quincy as a rural community is succeeded by far more fluid associations formed and re-formed around issues over which people shared passionate positions and viewpoints. Expression of emotion was central to these dynamics, and a recent historical record of Quincy would not be possible without noting competing sentiments and ambitions.

Similar fluidity in social affiliation was observed in the reformation of communities on what is often termed the "urban forest interface." Hays and Glendenning (Chapter 5) describe a succession of communities occupying forests in the Great Lake states. Natural resource extraction was replaced by farming, and farming was in turn replaced by rural residential settlement. The social meaning of land and trees—definition of what constitutes a natural resource—changed with its community transition. The most recent stage of rural settlement is also explored by Egan and Luloff (Chapter 15). They describe how new residents have brought new attitudes and practices to previously isolated rural locales. Cultural conflicts and competition for resources such as land and water accompany these recent demographic shifts. Romantic views of land and rural living, expressive of the re-enchantment of nature, replace pragmatic and materialistic motivations. The scenic and amenity values of nature affect choice of location on lands where choices were once dictated by rational considerations of soil productivity, resource quality, and profitability.

Community Forestry Initiatives

Community forestry initiatives have attempted to institutionalize a more postmodern approach to forest policy. Noneconomic sentiments and motivations are given a place in forest policy making and management. Bull and Schwab (Chapter 10) describe how Canada is attempting to involve diverse communities in decisions about the use of forests administered by large administrative agencies. These programs are largely attempts to broaden the stakeholder groups involved in decision-making processes.

A far less formal attempt to assist, coordinate, and facilitate community forestry initiatives is discussed by Krishnaswamy (Chapter 11). These attempts at building community capacity for self-governance and information gathering are far more of a bottom-up strategy than the Canadian programs for community involvement, and are inspired by the successes of community forestry initiatives in other parts of the world, especially in less-industrialized countries.

Emphasis on enhancing the ecological functions of forests in urban settings is described by Grove, Burch, and Pickett (Chapter 14). They describe an urban forestry project in Baltimore, Maryland, in which community-scale initiatives have focused on the protection or creation of tree-covered spaces. Like the work of McDonough and Vachta (Chapter 13), these projects go well beyond immediate utilitarian concerns to urban livability and amenity concerns that build social capital and strengthen the human spirit. Both essays explore the terms for cultural adoptability.

Community and Forestry in the U.S. Forest Service

The U.S. Forest Service, until the 1990s, epitomized the rational order of modernity. Economic efficiency was the principal criterion guiding the development of forest plans, producing a simplified landscape well ordered for the production of timber and other goods and services. The implicit paradigm guiding federal forest management was the German forest (see discussion and reference to James C. Scott in Chapter 1, above). Although the forests were generally well managed for timber production, the Forest Service came under devastating criticism for failing to protect the natural biological order of the forest, as well as failing to provide opportunities for citizens who did not find well-managed timber stands a suitable habitat for human recreation, aesthetic appreciation, fisheries production, or protection of endangered species. Ubiquitous use of clearcutting was a central issue. Legal challenges culminating in the adoption of a policy of ecosystem-based management forced the Forest Service to abandon its emphasis on timber management and commit to serving a broader range of objectives.

Rural communities that had grown dependent on an assured supply of federal timber were adversely impacted by the sudden withdrawal of over 90 percent of Forest Service timber. This adjustment was most traumatic in the Pacific Northwest, where President Clinton initiated a new planning process to resolve conflicts over harvesting in the national forests. FEMAT (Forest Ecosystem Management Assessment Team) established an ecosystem-based approach to planning in place of forest plans that had been founded on the rational criteria of efficiency and a commitment to maintaining the viability of rural industries and communities. Along with FEMAT came a new approach to the rural communities that had long benefited from U.S. Forest Service management activities.

The Forest Service sought collaboration with pluralistic groups of local stakeholders. The Quincy Library Group described by London, Starrs, and Fortmann (Chapter 7) involved local Forest Service officials. The Applegate Partnership in southern Oregon was a similar experiment in redefining community by facilitating collaboration among local stakeholders. These efforts inspired other initiatives, some of which are described by Krishnaswamy (Chapter 11). The Forest Service has sponsored other community forestry initiatives to involve local residents in the ecological restoration of damaged landscapes, stewardship contracting for projects designed to meet a variety of ecological objectives, and community efforts in hazardous-fuel reduction. All these initiatives represented an emerging postmodern theme in which people's feelings and sentiments were taken as seriously as facts about local economic welfare.

Conclusion

As stated in Chapter 1, the forestry profession is challenged by the rapid pace of social change. The modernist assumptions of its dominant institutions are a poor fit for a pluralistic culture in which emotion takes its place beside reason, nature is re-enchanted with spiritual meanings, and broad moral consensus collapses in the face of localism and particularistic values and beliefs. Most research, educational, and land management institutions maintain a manifest commitment to the modernist paradigm, while individual members of these institutions explore the emerging postmodern world with discrete political agendas stemming from external loyalties. The Society of American Foresters, the only professional association representing the field of forestry, struggles to maintain harmony among its members, with some clinging to reason, science, and tradition, and others seeking to incorporate a more holistic, emotional, and spiritual commitment to forest conservation and management. The internal dialogue is not always well informed by an understanding of the larger social changes that are disturbing the profession.

Communities, including their territorial, interest-based, or occupational variations, provide forums for easing the transitions from a modern to a postmodern society, and promise to take their place as an integral part of postmodern society. People who interact in the context of a community embrace the mixture of reason and emotion and accept nonrational expressions and ambiguity as part of everyday social life. Face-to-face interaction, together with shared norms assuring interpersonal predictability, enable people to accept their messy humanness while living or working together. However, most importantly, this shared way of life also motivates individuals to forego opportunistic gain seeking and to work for the welfare of the group as well as themselves. Sustainability, if expressed as a commitment to the future welfare of others and the environment, grows naturally from well-functioning communities.

The essays assembled in this volume explore how communities function in the context of a changing society. Some have focused on the rigidities of modernist institutions, and sought viable alternatives in community building. Others anticipate emerging paradigms in which community will play a more central role in the use and management of forests across diverse geographic landscapes. However, all are united by a common message: the future welfare of both people and forests is contingent on the protection and enhancement of community life.

The future of forestry will depend on how it deals with a crucial paradox arising from Walter Firey's theory of conservation: promoting sustainability by favoring opportunistic scientific and technological innovations weakens the social bonds that limit excessive individual gain seeking. Although purporting to promote sustainability, modernist institutions actually erode it by rewarding individual gain-seeking behaviors. Community building is at least a partial resolution to this paradox, since it promises to embed creativity and innovation in social contexts governed by a social/ecological conscience. Perhaps the most important response forestry can make to the postmodern challenge is to accept the decline of modernist institutions and encourage the sort of community-centered initiatives in technical innovation and conflict management represented in this volume.

References

Bauman, Zygmunt. 1993. *Postmodern Ethics.* Oxford, UK and Malden, MA: Blackwell Publishers, Ltd.

Firey, Walter. 1960. *Man, Mind, and Land: A Theory of Resource Use.* Glencoe, IL: The Free Press.

Firey, Walter. 1963. "Conditions for the Realization of Values Remote in Time." Pp. 147-159 in *Sociological Theory, Values, and Sociocultural Change: Essays in Honor of Pitirim A. Sorokin,* Edward A. Tiryakian, (ed.). New York and Evanston, IL: Harper and Row, Publishers.

Hays, Samuel P. 1969. *Conservation and the Gospel of Efficiency: The Progressive Movement, 1890-1920.* New York: Atheneum.

Thomas, Jack Ward. 1999. "Forward." Pp. xxii-xxv in *Nature and the Human Spirit: Toward an Expanded Land Management Ethic,* B. L. Driver, Daniel Dustin, Tony Baltic, Gary Elsner, and George Peterson (eds.). State College, PA: Venture Publishing, Inc.

Contributors

Bailey, Conner. Alumni Professor of Rural Sociology, Department of Agricultural Economics and Rural Sociology, Auburn University.

Bliss, John C. Professor, Starker Chair in Private and Family Forestry, and Associate Department Head, Oregon State University.

Carroll, Matthew S. Professor, Department of Natural Resource Sciences, Washington State University.

Bull, Gary Q. Professor, Department of Forest Resources Management, University of British Columbia.

Burch, William R., Jr. Frederick C. Hixon Professor of Natural Resource Management and Professor at the Institution for Social and Policy Studies, Yale University.

Clendenning, Greg. Ph.D. Candidate, Forest Ecology and Management, University of Wisconsin-Madison.

Egan, Andrew F. Professor. Laval University, Department des Sciences du Bois et de Foret, Universite Laval, Sainte-Foy, Quebec G1K 7P4.

Finley, James C. Professor of Forest Resources, School of Forest Resources. The Pennsylvania State University.

Firey, Walter. Professor Emeritus, Sociology, University of Texas.

Fortmann, Louise. Rudy Grah Professor of Environmental Science, Policy, and Management at UC-Berkeley. Specializes in forestry and agriforestry, land tenure, and gender issues.

Grove, J. Morgan. Research Forester, Social Ecology, Northeastern Research Station, Burlington, VT.

Hays, Samuel P. Professor Emeritus of History, University of Pittsburgh.

Jones, Stephen B. Chancellor, University of Alaska, Fairbanks.

Kaufman, Harold F. Emeritus, Sociology, Mississippi State University (Deceased).

Kaufman, Lois C. Emeritus, Sociology, Mississippi State University (Deceased)

Krannich, Richard S. Professor of Sociology and Forest Resources, Utah State University. Department head, Sociology, Social Work, and Anthropology.

Krishnaswamy, Ajit. Director, National Community Forestry Center, National Network of Forest Practitioners.

Langston, Nancy. Associate Professor, Nelson Institute of Environmental Studies and Department of Forest Ecology and Management, University of Wisconsin-Madison.

London, Jonathan. Executive Director, Youth in Focus, Davis, California.

Luloff, A. E. Professor of Rural Sociology, Department of Agricultural Economics and Rural Sociology. The Pennsylvania State University.

Mclain, Rebecca. Institute for Culture and Ecology, Portland, Oregon.

McDonough, Maureen. Professor, Forest Sociology and Social Forestry, Michigan State.

Pickett, Steward T. A., Ph.D. Scientist, Institute of Ecosystem Studies. Baltimore Ecosystem Study Long-Term Ecological Research Program.

Schwab, Olaf. Ph.D. candidate at Department of Forest Resources Management, University of British Columbia.

Starrs, Paul F. Professor, Department of Geography, University of Nevada, Reno.

Vachta, Kerry. Assistant Professor, Environment, Community and Social Change. The Pennsylvania State University, Harrisburg.

Index